Umbrellas Make Poor Parachutes

and

Other Life Lessons

by
LaVelle Pitts

Cover design by: Kim Koceja, Digital Design class, Haney
Technical Center, Panama City, Florida

Dedication

This book is dedicated to
my family.

*Arnell
LaVelle Dix*

Acknowledgments

I am grateful to the many friends and colleagues in local, state and federal law enforcement I have been privileged to work with over the years, as well as good citizens who furnished information to help in our endeavors.

I am indebted to Dr. Craig Conner, Sheriff Frank McKeithen, Judge David Taunton, Author Marlene Womack, and Dr. Larry Bruce who previewed this manuscript and made comments and suggestions. To Sherry Anderson, Desiree Anderson, and others in the Writer's Aglow community, I appreciate your help, critique, and technical expertise with this project.

A special thanks to my wife, Sally Jo, who encouraged me and did what was necessary to get this book in print. Each time I became discouraged, she prodded me to continue, and pushed when necessary.

Foreword

Comments about *Umbrellas Make Poor Parachutes*

It is a great honor for me to write a foreword for the book *Umbrellas Make Poor Parachutes* written by LaVelle Pitts. As you read the life lessons of LaVelle, these lessons will keep you on the edge of your seat. My initial reaction to this book was, how could it be possible for so many experiences to be wrapped up in the life of one man?

The story of the author's life will stir up an array of emotions in the reader. As a reader you will be gripped with laughter at one moment and moved to tears the next. One of the things that makes this book such a refreshing read is the absolute honesty of the author in speaking of his shortcomings and failures. His life story is a true inspiration for those who are honest enough to admit their own failures.

Umbrellas Make Poor Parachutes is a true "rags to riches" story as it chronicles the life of a man with such meager beginnings who rose to great success. LaVelle's success was the result of one thing that is constantly referred to in the book, the blessing of his spiritual heritage. This heritage was the foundation that shaped his life; a heritage he would not leave behind.

I commend this life story of my dear friend to you. His story will be a blessing and encouragement to all who find this book in their hands.

– Dr. Craig Conner
Senior Pastor, First Baptist Church
Panama City, Florida

The life stories shared in this book, especially in the law enforcement section, humbly showcase LaVelle Pitts' true courage and crime-solving ability. Reading this book will show the reader why I believe he is the best law enforcement officer and leader I have ever known.

– Sheriff Frank McKeithen
Bay County, Florida

Umbrellas Make Poor Parachutes, a childhood lesson learned by two country boys, is a compilation of an assortment of intriguing experiences in the life of retired Bay County Sheriff, LaVelle Pitts. Raised on a farm in rural Holmes County, Florida, the son of a hard working preacher man, LaVelle learned early on that there were no excuses, just tackle any challenge head-on and trust in the "Good Lord" that everything will turn out all right.

Considering all the dangerous (and sometimes hilarious) predicaments this one individual faced during his colorful lifetime, the fact that he lived to tell about it is a testimony within itself that God was always with him. How else could he have survived!

A story of faith, courage and perseverance, this book will be an inspiration to all who are fortunate enough to read it, young and old alike. In addition to shedding light on his own uniquely interesting life, LaVelle also shares memories and experiences involving legendary area personalities such as Sheriff "Doc" Daffin, Deputy Marvin Freeman, Attorney-Judge Fred Turner and many others.

Thanks LaVelle for preserving a very special era that otherwise might have largely been forgotten. And thanks for setting such a powerful example for generations to come.

– David L. Taunton
Retired Judge, Gulf County,
Florida

This is an excellent book–one that should be required for all criminology students and those interested in learning more about Bay County history.

In his book, *Umbrellas Make Poor Parachutes*, Lavelle Pitts details the experiences in his life–from childhood years in Holmes County on the family's farm to his days spent in the U.S. Marine Corps followed by junior college. He writes with a style that's easy and enjoyable to read.

In April 1957, Pitts pinned on a badge and began his lifetime career of 32 years in law enforcement that started under Sheriff M. J. "Doc" Daffin, the master politician who ruled with an iron fist.

Daffin required him to be a citizen of Bay County, a graduate of Bay High, a Democrat and a jailer until he reached the age of 25 because no one under that age "had enough sense or was mature enough to be a patrol deputy."

It didn't take long for Pitts to learn the ways and whim of the legendary sheriff. Pitts went on to work in a number of different offices and organizations. He served as Bay County Sheriff from 1981-1989.

– Marlene Womack
Florida Historical Author

Contents

Introduction

Life is a journey each of us travels. During our lifetime, God works in our lives and missteps to teach us lessons. Like the time my buddy, Jake, and I decided to parachute out of the barn using an umbrella. I convinced him to go first. When he finished making the leap I learned that umbrellas make poor parachutes.

Umbrellas might have the basic structure needed for a parachute, but without vent holes it won't hold you in the air. And so it is with us, we are born with the basics to live our life, but need to be "vented" with nurture and guidance to make it along life's journey.

1

I used to trail suspects with Twigs, the Bay County Sheriff's Office bloodhound. So, in this book I've set out to track down and share some of my life stories and what I have learned from them.

Twigs, BCSO bloodhound, 1958

It is my prayer that these snapshot remembrances will help my children, my grandchildren and any others who might read them, to find meaning in their own life's journey. Deuteronomy 4:9 presents the challenge *"...do not forget the things your eyes have seen or let them slip from your heart as long as you live. Teach them to your children and to their children after them."*

CHILDHOOD
(Mid-1930s-1940s)

On October 9, 1934, a new 9 ½ lb. baby boy was born on a 40-acre farm in a small frame house that sat on the edge of a corn field. The house was located half way between Bonifay and Bethlehem, Florida. A midwife from Black, Alabama, assisted in the delivery. The baby's name was to be Eugene LaVelle, but the midwife's handwriting and spelling was so poor, the name was officially recorded as Enger

LaVelle, age two.

Lenull. The mother's name was listed as Annie Mae Saulk and father, D. C. Pitts.

My name as well as my mother's and father's were corrected to read Eugene LaVelle Pitts, Annie Mae Sauls Pitts and Dallas Eugene Pitts, and a new birth certificate was reissued when I filed for retirement. (Although my sister, Ruth, says the correct spelling of my father's name is Dallis.)

I was the fifth child born to the Pitts family. The oldest child, Ruby Lee, died at age 12, then came Ruthie Mae. After Ruth came a baby girl Juanita and later a baby boy, unnamed. Both died at birth. Another boy, Larry, was born 12 years after me and died at age 12. Only two children made it through childhood, Ruthie Mae and me.

I remember several things about the third and fourth years of my life. My mom, dad, sister and I lived on a small farm about five miles north of Bonifay, Florida. My sister was four years older than me and often found me to be quite irritating. Looking

3

back I really can't blame her. I guess one reason was that I was the baby, and people made extra allowances for the baby in the family. Second, I think I really was a pain in the rear.

Following are some of my early remembrances:

Dad the Preacher

My father pastored New Smyrna Assembly of God. The church was about six miles north of Bonifay, Florida, between the Wrights and Ten Mile Creeks. He worked our 40-acre farm, about three miles from the church, during the week and preached every Wednesday night and twice on Sundays. Once each year, he brought in an evangelist who ran a two or three week revival, preaching every night.

Dad attended a small school near Burnt Mill Creek in north Bay County. He was one of nine children and grew up on a small farm. School was only in session until it was time for the kids to help with the farming. Dad and his brother, Henry, had to drop out of school in the 8th grade when their father died. They were needed to help run the farm for the family.

Mama, one of five children, had to drop out of school in the 4th grade. Even with only a 4th grade education, Mama was an avid reader. Since Dad was a poor reader, he asked Mama to read the Bible verses when he preached. She sat next to the pulpit and read the scripture for Dad and he preached the word. After he preached, I saw many people go to the altar and pray to receive Christ. At each service, after altar call, there was a prayer time and a lot of people went forward for prayer.

There were times late at night someone knocked on our door and asked Dad to come to their home and pray for a family member who was sick or hurt. Mama stayed home with Ruth and me while Dad left and was sometimes gone for hours.

At other times a knock on the door might be a request for Dad to perform a marriage. Dad counseled the two on what marriage really meant and the commitment each were about to make.

There were times when one or two members of his church met at our barn to build a casket for someone who passed away. Sometimes the casket was small, for a little child. The casket was hauled to the person's house and for one or two days the dead person laid in the casket in the front room while family and friends brought food and drink. Folks sat for hours around the house talking about the life of the person in the casket.

The children laid down on blankets on the floor to sleep. After a couple of days the family slid the casket in the back of a wagon and transported the body to the church where Dad preached the funeral. Then the casket was taken to the graveyard behind the church. A grave had been dug by church members and Dad spoke final graveside rites. Plow lines were placed under both ends of the casket and four men gently lowered the casket into the ground. As soon as the family went back to the church, the men shoveled dirt on the casket, covering the grave.

I have always had a lot of respect for a preacher and his family. If you've ever heard the saying that the preacher's son is the meanest kid around, I can tell you why. Everyone knows the preacher's kid and watches wherever he or she goes. If the child does anything wrong or doesn't mind his elders, his mother and dad will hear about it. That usually meant a "butt whippin'." I know from personal experience.

My parents believed in that scripture about not withholding correction from a child. (Prov. 23:13)

Dad the Handyman

In my eyes, my dad could fix anything, knew everything, and everyone loved him. He was the greatest shooter in the world, best fisherman, farmer, mechanic, preacher, and fighter. If he didn't know how to do something or have the proper tools, he improvised. I grew up with my dad as my hero.

One afternoon a woman walked up to our house with a little girl and boy. The girl was crying uncontrollably. The woman explained that her two children were fishing on the creek and the boy snatched a hook into the lip of his sister. She wanted my dad to get it out.

5

Dad had no doctor training, but he got a razor blade and enlarged the hole in her lip a little and pulled the hook through. This came with many screams and tears from the little girl.

This incident left a lasting impression and I learned that many skills are discovered out of necessity.

Sam the Ox

We had a big ox named Sam. Dad used him to plow the crops and pull logs from the woods when he cut timber. A short distance out in the field, we had a board well. It was a deep hole going down to the water with boards around the opening, about 4x4 feet square. Thus the name, "board well." We drew water from the well for our livestock.

One day the ox walked up to the well and apparently saw himself reflected in the water. He got close to the edge of the well and the ground gave way and he slid backward down into the well. My dad heard the mournful bellowing and found him. This ox was a valuable animal. We couldn't afford to lose him.

Dad got into his old truck and went out and gathered up some of the church folks and returned with several men and their shovels. After several hours of digging that lasted into the night, they made a long trench at an angle down to the ox and were able to lead him to safety.

Mama cooked and kept the men fed while they were working. Back then neighbors did not charge you to do things like this–just a thank you was all that was necessary.

When a man in the community got sick and couldn't work, the other men in the community gathered their plows, wives and children, put them on their wagon, hooked their mule to the wagon and all met at the sick neighbor's house for a work day. The men plowed the crop and took care of his stock while the wives helped with the house cleaning, cooking, washing clothes and whatever else the season called for. We kids had a great time playing, climbing trees and shooting at birds with our sling shots on these work days.

LaVelle, age 3

 I saw the reality of loving your neighbor at an early age.

Watermelons

During summer season, Dad placed three or four watermelons under his bed. This kept them kind of cool, because it was so hot in the field. When I was little, I begged for watermelon when they were in season. But the melons were only cut at certain times or occasions. I noticed that if a melon looked like it had a crack or was leaking, Dad cut it immediately. So I came up with a great idea.

If I could somehow make all the watermelons leak, we could have a big cutting and I could eat all I wanted. I took a butcher knife out of the kitchen and crawled under the bed. Beds back then were high enough off the floor for a full-grown person to crawl under. After I got under the bed, I made one or two incisions into the melons with the knife. That night when Mama went into the bedroom she had no problem noticing the melons had a "crack" in them. Watermelon juice was covering the entire bedroom floor. As I recall, I didn't get any melon because they took them out to the hogs. What I did get was a "reward" which caused me great discomfort each time I sat down for two or three days.

I learned there is a penalty for greed.

Our Old House

Growing up, we lived in several different old wood frame houses. For the first years of my life, we had no electric lights, newspapers or paved roads. We used kerosene lamps for light and a fireplace for heat. On hot summer days and nights we opened the wood shutters. We had no screens or glass in the window. The shutters were about four feet square, hinged to swing open and with a latch and hook to hold it open or closed. During the day even the doors were left open for air circulation, but at night we usually closed the doors so animals wouldn't wander into the house.

Across the dirt road in front of our house was a huge forest of large pines. There were many cracks in the walls of the house and you could hear everything happening outside. When the wind blew, the sorrowful moan of the wind could be heard through the pines. That was a lonely sound that made good sleeping weather unless it brought up a storm.

I heard a country song on the Grand Ole Opry called *In the Pines*. It went something like this; "In the pines, in the pines where the sun never shines and you shiver when the cold wind blows..." I used to think of the pine forest across from our home each time I heard that lonesome song.

We always had cats and dogs around the house, and the cracks in the walls made it easy to hear what they were doing. The cats sometimes fought under the house and woke everyone. If a varmint of some sort got too close to the house at night you could hear old Joe and Fanny, our dogs, come unglued and take off after whatever it might be.

The greatest cat we ever owned was a big female cat, also known as an alley cat. We called her Kitty Cat. She was smart.

When I was growing up, cats were graded by their ability to catch rats. Kitty Cat was the best. She hung around the big crib where we stored the corn. That's where most of the rats hung out. They built nests under the piles of corn and as we used the corn the rats moved deeper into the larger piles. Any time we were shucking corn or feeding the mule, horse or cows, Kitty Cat hung around waiting for us to uncover a rat.

When the corn was getting low, Dad and I moved all that was left out into the center of the floor to shuck it. As we moved the corn, the rats started to move. We'd move the corn slowly, so Kitty Cat had time to catch as many rats as possible. One time she caught a rat and held it in her mouth. Another rat ran out and she jumped across the floor and nailed that one. She somehow got the second one into her mouth with the other one. A third ran out and she grabbed it with her front paw. She sat there growling when another rat emerged. She popped another foot on top of it. She now had two in her mouth and one under each of her front paws.

Dad was in awe. "I've never seen anything like that before."

That cat had a special place in my dad's heart. He never let any of the other animals bother her. With pride, he spoke of her often, especially when he and some of the other farmers were bragging about animals on their farm.

The house leaked when it rained. We had no ceiling, only a roof. If a rainstorm came up during the night, Dad knocked on the wall of my room and said, "Get up and put out the pots." We knew where all the leaks were and started putting buckets and pans all around on the floor. The rest of the night you could hear the "plink-plink-plink" of the drops of water falling into the metal containers. It was wonderful because I knew it would be too wet to plow the following day or two, so I was a happy young boy.

I learned that in an old house, if you want to stay dry when it rains, you need to learn where to put the pots.

Farm Travel

We didn't have a lot of vehicles on our dirt roads. Most of the traffic was by horse back or mule-drawn wagons. When a vehicle did come by, it moved slowly because cows and hogs loved to sleep on the road and in the ditches near the road. They served as our speed bumps.

Riding my horse at night could be tricky. I had no saddle and had to hold on real tight, because if a hog sprang up from the ditch it scared the daylights out of my horse. He jumped sideways instantly, and if I didn't have a good hold on his mane, then the horse and I parted ways.

I recall going to Uncle Bob's store after dark. I was passing a neighbor's farm about a mile from our house. I grabbed hold of the horse's mane and held on until we passed the farm. I relaxed and just as I did, a dog leaped from the ditch where he was hiding. He barked like crazy in front of my horse. The horse reared straight up and I immediately slid off the horse's butt into the dirt road. The horse came down, almost stepping on me, and left in a cloud of dust headed back home. There I sat, flat on my bottom, staring at that stupid dog as he turned proudly and calmly trotted back to his house. I got up, started walking back home and met my dad riding my horse. He was running wide open, fearing I was hurt.

Very few families had vehicles. Much of the local travel was by mule and wagon unless you were going to church or town.

Our family did have an old 1940 Ford car, but many times we used the mule and wagon. There were no springs on our wagon and when the wagon wheel hit a bump or hole you felt it from your butt to the top of your head. Most of the roads were three trail roads. Two of the trails were where the wheels of the wagons rolled and the third trail was where the mule or horse walked while pulling the wagon.

In the winter hay rides were fun. We loved to pack the wagon with several kids with blankets and cuddle up to keep warm. This was one of the few times we could snuggle up to the girls and get away with it.

Our Ford car was old and had a flat tire almost every time we went on a long trip. We had to jack the car up, and take the wheel off. Using tire tools, we'd pry the tire loose from the rim, pull the tube out and find the hole that caused it to go flat. Dad scraped the tube to rough it up and put on a hot patch which sealed the hole in the tube. The tube was then put back in the tire and an old hand pump was used to air the tire up. This was a major project. If the hole in the tire was large then Dad put in a boot, a thick piece of rubber inside the tire between the patched hole and the tire. Dad did most of the work, but let me pump some, so he could rest. There were no tubeless tires back then. The tubes were red and real heavy rubber. I loved it when Dad bought a new tube. He gave me the old one and I used the rubber for my sling shots.

With all the drawbacks of our old means of travel, one thing we didn't have to worry about was the price of gas.

Hoover's Grist Mill

When we needed meal for bread, Dad and I shucked several hundred ears of our choice corn. Then we ran them through the corn sheller, grinding all the corn off the cobs. This corn was put in a large burlap sack. I got on the old plow horse, Maude, and Dad put the 100, or so, pound sack across the back of the horse or in front of me. Then he sent me off to Hoover's Grist Mill on Wrights Creek. This was about two or three miles from our farm.

If the bag ever fell off, I'd have to go back and get Dad, because I couldn't lift it. When I got to the mill, the mill operator,

11

Mr.Gilley, took take the sack of corn off my horse and carried it inside the mill. The mill was built all the way across the creek. There was a large paddle wheel in the middle of the creek. The current turned the wheel and ground the corn into meal.

After grinding the meal he put the sack back on my horse, less the amount he kept as the mill's share for payment for grinding the corn to meal.

In the early 1940s, many times payment was made by exchange rather than money.

This detail took most of the day, according to the number of people who got there before I did.

I always looked forward to the trip and having to wait all afternoon. That's because the mill man, Mr. Gilley, had a pretty daughter, Norma. She was a year or two older than me, but that didn't matter. I was 12 years old and in love. (Of course I never told her or anyone else that.) Just seeing her made the trip worthwhile.

I recall spending most of the afternoon visiting with her while waiting for the meal to be ground. We walked around through the mill watching her dad work and back to her home where my horse was tied. It was about first dark and she walked to the edge of her yard where I had tied my horse. As I was about to mount up for the trip home, she gave me a light kiss on my lips.

I thought I had died and gone to heaven. I could have flown home without my horse. I ran my horse all the way home and I don't remember sleeping much all night, because I was in love. That was my very first kiss. It was also the first and last from Norma. That's why I remember it so well.

It's a good thing that was the only kiss I got from her, 'cause my heart might not have withstood it.

Entertainment

Looking back it is hard to believe that we could have had so much fun without the modern conveniences of today. Boat motors, TV, computer games, store-bought fishing poles, weather reports, four-wheel drive vehicles and daily newspapers–we had none of these. We didn't have the luxury of having the world and local news every day and hour.

I got with other boys sometimes and compared sling shot staffs and spent hours whittling and making new ones. During the early years of my life, all young boys wouldn't dare be caught without a sling shot in their back pocket and a pocket knife in the front. The big exception was when we went to church. Mama never allowed me to take weapons. (We could only take our sword–the Bible).

One "luxury" we did have was a tube radio. It was tuned in to WSM Nashville, Tennessee, every Saturday night for the Grand Ole Opry. For years, this was the highlight of our week.

My dad really loved the Opry. We listened to Hank Williams, Hank Snow, Eddie Arnold, Bill Monroe and his Blue Grass Boys, Little Jimmy Dickins, Roy Acuff and his Smokey Mountain Boys, Mother Maybelle and the Carter Sisters, Amos and Andy along with many, many others.

My friends all lived within a few miles of each other and most of us attended the same schools and church. All our parents were friends and many were relatives. I got together with the other kids and played games occasionally, but nothing like they have these days. Our parties were usually at someone's house for a birthday dinner and games after supper. We played drop the handkerchief, spin the bottle, tug of war, red rover, hide and go seek, hop scotch and mumblety-peg. If it was day time, and we had enough kids, we chose up sides and played softball, football or shot marbles.

We never played games that prevented both boys and girls from participating together. Sometimes we brought a group of boys and girls together to go coon or possum hunting. We never caught one, but we had fun racing through the woods following our dogs tracking some animal. I never knew what the dogs were chasing, because nothing was ever caught.

The greatest get-together was about one or two times a year when we had a cookout, usually on Wrights Creek. Boys and girls gathered, usually late in the afternoon at the creek to have a chicken fry. The girls fried the chickens after the boys cleaned and cut them up. Those country girls could really cook.

None of our get-togethers was like ones heard about in this day and time. There were no drugs, no alcoholic beverages, no cigarette or pot smoking, no dirty jokes, no profane language or sexual misconduct.

However when I was around the older boys, I'm sorry to say, we did have more than our share of dirty jokes and cigarette smoking. This usually happened before and after church when parents were inside socializing. That's where I received my sex education. Sex was never spoken of in our home–ever.

The first time I ever heard sex talked about at my home, was when Sally Jo explained sex and answered questions that our young son and daughter had during grade school. I questioned her about this since it was a "no-no" when I was growing up. She, being much smarter than I, said she would rather the children hear truthful answers to their questions than those on the school ground by their friends. I recalled my childhood and had to agree with her.

Some of the best entertainment was when two or three families got together and sat around the fireplace in the living room and told stories. One after another told stories, each trying to tell a bigger yarn than the last person. I looked forward to these story times. But many nights I couldn't sleep much (or else slept with my head under the covers) when the stories were scary.

The story-teller, back then, swore they were telling the truth and that these things really happened or the people who witnessed them told them and they believed them.

My dad was a master story teller and so was Grandma, my dad's mother. She told of her experiences growing up, especially the ones about her kin, the Cherokee.

There is an old saying that the only difference between Grandma and George Washington was he wouldn't tell a lie and Grandma couldn't tell one. So, following are some of Grandma's stories as I remember them.

Martha Jane Ellerbee Pitts
(Grandma)

Grandma's Father, a Confederate Soldier

Grandma was part Cherokee Indian. I'm not certain if her Cherokee blood came from just her father or mother or both. She was proud of her Cherokee heritage but not so proud of some of the outlaw tribes that stole livestock and killed farmers and their families. She said this happened to a small community near her family's farm.

The Indians took all the livestock and killed several men, women and children. The farmers called a meeting and got all the men to join forces to hunt the Indians who had done this. Grandma's father, an expert tracker, led the farmers. She thinks there were about twenty men, most of whom were former Confederate soldiers. They returned in about two weeks and her father told the family the following story:

15

The farmers were very bitter and tracked the group of outlaw Indians to their village. All the braves were gone and only the older adults, mothers and children were alone in the camp. They surmised the braves were gone on another raid.

The group of farmers stayed concealed in the woods for about three days and nights hoping the braves would return, but after three days they decided to attack the village. They killed the men and women. Then they climbed some of the young pine trees, bent them to the ground, chopped the tops off with an ax and sharpened the end of the tree to a sharp point. Two held a tree down while one took a child and impaled him on the sharp point of the tree. The tree was let loose so it straightened back up with the child left on the top of the pine.

I thought this was extremely cruel, but Grandma explained this was the only thing the renegade Indians understood, because it was the sort of thing they did.

Grandma said on another occasion their small settlement was awakened at daybreak to the sound of a turkey gobbling from a big swamp near the settlement. Everyone thought it would be nice to have a big turkey dinner. The following morning one of the men took his rifle and went to the swamp.

After awhile, gun fire was heard and everyone thought about the turkey dinner. But when the farmer didn't return, some of the men went to check on him. They found him just inside the swamp with a bullet hole in his head.

Grandma's father recognized the killing was the work of an Indian, and said he'd take care of it. The following morning he went to the woods a few hours before daybreak, and concealed himself. He sat quietly until the crack of dawn when he heard the turkey gobble. After the turkey gobbled two or three more times, he spotted a large clump of moss in a large oak tree and saw a little movement when the turkey gobbled. He raised his rifle, aimed at the moss and fired one shot. An Indian brave fell from the tree with a bullet in his head. That ended the turkey gobbling around their settlement.

Grandma's father fought for the Confederacy in the Civil War and was with General Robert E. Lee when he surrendered at

Appomattox, Virginia, on April 9, 1865. Grandma's father told this story of the experience:

When General Lee surrendered to General Grant the Confederate soldiers had to give up all their weapons and were told to go home. Her father began the walk of over 700 miles from Virginia to Burnt Mill Creek settlement in north Florida with a friend.

The only items they carried were pocket knives and a roll of fishing line with a hook on one end wrapped around a little stick. He and his friend walked through old farms General Sherman had burned. Sometimes they found an ear of corn or some vegetables to eat. They caught fish in creeks and rivers along the way using their fish line, hook, and a grasshopper or other bug they might catch for bait.

One day they found some geese wandering around near a farmhouse that was occupied. They put a grain of corn on one of their hooks, dropped it on the ground and one of the geese swallowed it. They walked slowly and led the goose into the woods where they found an old burned out cabin that had a cast iron pot left behind. They built a fire, filled the pot with water from a nearby stream and prepared to cook the goose. They boiled that goose several hours to get it tender enough to chew. Even though it was the toughest piece of meat he had ever eaten, it was also the best since he and his friend were near starvation.

With her father's trapping and other survival skills they were able to eat rabbits and other small animals on their long journey home.

Her father stood a towering six feet eight inches. When he left for the war he weighed about 250 pounds, but when he returned he looked like a walking skeleton, weighing less than 100 pounds.

Jesse James

When Grandma was a small girl, they lived on different farms as share croppers. They moved around a lot, never making enough money to buy their own farm.

In one of the places they farmed, an old widow woman lived alone down the two trail dirt road a short distance away. She had a rail fence around her house to keep the cows and hogs out of her yard. She sat on her front porch most of the time and rocked in an old rocking chair.

Jesse Woodson James,
American outlaw

One afternoon, Grandma and some of her brothers and sisters were playing not far from the old widow's home and heard a horse galloping up. They recognized the rider as the famous Jesse James. He was riding his white horse. He rode straight to the widow's home and the horse jumped over the rail fence and stopped at the edge of the porch.

The old woman just sat there and Jesse tossed a canvas bag on the porch. He tipped his hat to the old lady, turned his horse, jumped back over the fence and galloped away.

They heard later the bag was filled with gold coins. Grandma said this was not unusual. Jesse James was known to do things like this quite often. She said her dad told her that even Jesse's horse was well-trained. When Jesse hid in the woods and slept, his horse watched over him. If he smelled or heard someone coming, he nudged Jesse with his nose, waking him up. She remembered him as being friendly and wearing two pearl handled pistols.

The Mysterious Ghost Light

Grandma's family moved into a new area to share crop with a wealthy farmer who lived in town. They moved into an old frame house that sat in the middle of a 60-acre farm. They had plowed and planted most of the farm when late one night they spotted a light coming from a big swamp joining the back of their farm.

The light seemed to be someone walking with a lantern. The light stopped about two hundred yards from their house and stayed there for several minutes. It then turned and retraced itself back to the woods and disappeared into the swamp.

This went on for several nights and finally her dad took his rifle and started walking toward the light as it moved from the wooded area. Her dad also had a lantern and the family watched as the two lanterns met about the middle of the field.

The two stayed together for quite some time and then both lights moved away from each other. The one returned to the woods and her dad returned to the house where all the kids and her mother waited. He came in and put his rifle away and went over to the fireplace and sat down.

Grandma's mother and all the kids were real excited and asked what happened and what was said. He was very reluctant to talk about what happened. Her mother asked if he was able to communicate with the other light. He said he was and that was all they needed to know about it. From that day on the light never returned and her dad refused to talk about it again.

The KKK (Ku Klux Klan)

After my grandma was married and had a family, she told of a farmer who lived a short distance away. According to Grandma this was a very mean white man who had a bad reputation in the community. When he went on a drunk, it usually resulted in him beating his little wife. On Sunday morning, her battered condition was noticeable when she hobbled into church.

The following night someone knocked on Grandma's door. Grandpa (Bill) opened the door and said, "Be out in a minute." He went to his room and returned with his rifle and a sheet and hood over his head. Grandma looked out the window and watched him

19

join several others sitting on their horses dressed like Grandpa in white sheets and hoods.

William Henry "Billy" & Martha Jane Elleree Pitts, (Grandpa and Grandma). Grandma was part Cherokee and it is believed that Grandpa was part Cherokee also. Whatever the combination, their children were said to be ¼ Cherokee, making me 1/16.

They rode off and returned home a couple hours later. He told her they went to the home of this drunk, pulled him out and tied him to his wagon wheel. They ripped his shirt off and used a buggy whip to severely beat him. They told him if he ever laid hands on his wife in anger again, they would return. Grandma said she never heard of this man ever beating his wife again.

Grandma explained that because the law wasn't readily available in those days, the KKK members were a hidden force in the community. They considered themselves protectors of the people and righted wrongs they believed had been done—such as thievery, and mistreatment of women, children, animals, or even klansmen they believed had gone astray.

 The KKK has the reputation of a hate group that I have dealt with in law enforcement because many of them believe they are justified in operating outside the law, but these members in Grandma's day saw

themselves as a brotherhood who protected the people in their community.

Turkey Hunting

Grandpa went out one afternoon hunting turkey. He told Grandma he thought he had spotted where they were roosting in a big swamp about a mile or so from the farm. Holidays were approaching and they needed some turkeys for expected company.

Grandpa located the roosting tree, concealed himself in the bushes and waited. About dark, several turkeys flew in and started landing in the big tree. Grandpa fired three times and killed three turkeys before they flew away.

He picked up the three turkeys and started walking home. By this time it was dark and he was walking in an old wagon trail that led back to the farm. In the distance he heard the scream of a panther. He knew there were several of the big cats in the area. Normally, they would not attack a person unless they were backed into a situation where they felt threatened or were hurt.

The panther screamed again. When a panther screams it sounds like a woman screaming. The sound will cause the hair to rise on the back of your neck, especially when it's getting dark and you're holding three bleeding turkeys.

Grandpa picked up his pace. The panther, getting closer by the sound of the screams, may have been hungry and attracted to the smell of the turkeys. The cat got closer and closer. Grandpa checked his rifle and noted he had only two bullets left. Walking as fast as he could he suddenly heard the patting of feet directly behind him. (According to Grandpa, a panther will pat his two front feet on the ground before he attacks.) He yelled and charged toward the sound. The cat apparently ran off, but a few minutes later he heard the patting feet again. Again he yelled and screamed and charged toward the sound. Silence. He couldn't see anything in the darkness.

This cat and mouse game continued and it was obvious the cat was not running very far any longer. Grandpa feared the panther was about to attack. The next time he heard the patting and yelled, he caught a glimpse of the cat. Grandpa fired one of his last two bullets toward it.

21

The panther took off this time and Grandpa was able to get much closer home before the cat returned. He could see the lamp light in the window at home and knew if he fired his last bullet and missed, the panther would have a mixed plate of turkey and farmer for dinner.

When the patting of feet started again he ran toward the sound and fired his last shot. He heard the cat race through the bushes and thought he must have come close to hitting him or nicked him. He raced the last few yards to his house and safety.

Grandma, after hearing the story, asked why he didn't give the panther the turkeys. He said that thought never crossed his mind. He had worked hard to get those birds and "no overgrown cat was going to take them without a fight."

Bear Hunt

A bear loves pork as much as most farmers. One big bear kept hanging around Grandpa and Grandma's farm and stealing a hog about every week. Grandpa swore payback, gathered his six hounds and his 30-30 Winchester rifle and found where the remains of the last pig lay after the bear ate his fill. He put the dogs on the track and away they went. Deep in the swamp the dogs caught up with the bear and started baying. (That means they surround the bear and stay just out of reach of his claws and teeth.)

If the bear tries to run, they nip him on the back leg and he stops and turns to fight. This went on until Grandpa arrived at a little stream at the edge of the woods. Grandpa started walking a log that formed a bridge over a stream. About half way over the water, the log broke and suddenly he was in a muddy stream up to his knees. At about the same time the bear decided to change locations and ran out of the bushes directly toward Grandpa. Grandpa quickly raised his 30-30 and fired five rounds into the chest of the bear.

This was good and bad. The good thing was he killed the bear; the bad thing was the bear's momentum carried his 350 pounds into the stream and right on top of Grandpa. To make things worse the pack of hounds, seeing the bear on Grandpa, attacked the bear. Grandpa was having trouble breathing and was only able to keep part of his head above water. He kept yelling at the dogs until they finally got off and he was able to work out from under the huge black bear.

Ethel the Ghost

(My dad tells this story, and Grandma supports it as the truth.) When my dad was probably six or seven years old the family moved to another share cropper house on a large farm. The land owner advised my Grandpa that because the old house was haunted, he couldn't keep a farm family for long. No family lasted more than two or three weeks.

He went on to say that an old lady, named Ethel, was the last occupant and died several years earlier. People who moved into the house told stories of hearing strange noises upstairs like someone was walking from room to room. The sound of footsteps could be heard, but no one was ever seen. The owner asked if my Grandpa was willing to stay for the entire year and farm the land. Grandpa advised the owner he was desperate for a home for his family and would not be leaving because of a so-called ghost.

The house was a large frame two story home—a grand fit for a family with nine children. On the ground floor was a large living area with a big fireplace and rocking chairs all around. A large kitchen, with a long eating table, adjoined the living room. The stairs ran from the living room to the second floor where all the bedrooms were. There was an old rocker near the foot of the stairs facing the fireplace. The land owner said this was the rocker where Ethel always sat.

About a week after moving in, the family finished supper and suddenly heard a high-pitched humming coming from upstairs. Everyone looked at my Grandpa and he said, "Everyone just sit tight and keep quiet." Dad said they could hear a bedroom door open and then close and someone walking down the hall to the next bedroom. They heard that door open and close. This continued until all the upstairs doors sounded like they were opened and closed. Naturally every eye was on the stairs.

They heard the steps squeak like someone was coming down. The humming had stopped and the footsteps continued to the bottom step and then the old rocker started rocking back and forth slowly. There was not a sound in the room other than the rocking chair slowly rocking back and forth, back and forth.

This went on for several minutes and then my Grandpa called out, "Ethel that's enough, go to bed." The rocking stopped and the footsteps again started back up the stairs. They heard a door open and close from one of the bedrooms. Everything was quiet for the rest of the night. Grandpa told everyone to go to bed and not worry about it. My dad said he didn't think anyone slept that night because they didn't know what bedroom she'd gone into.

Dad said this same scenario took place at least one time a week and sometimes two or three times. If the humming got very loud, Grandpa called out, "Ethel, quiet down," and she did. After supper each night it was no problem getting all the kids to gather around the fireplace until bedtime. No one was about to go up and go to bed until all of them went together. They didn't want to be alone in their room when Ethel made her rounds.

General Andrew Jackson

Grandma told me about her grandfather and the farm they lived on near Burnt Mill Creek. It was in Washington County at that time, which later became a part of north Bay County.

According to her, in the early 1800s General Jackson was marching to New Orleans to fight the British. He set up camp and sent out runners all over the area asking for volunteers to join up with his army and many men from area families joined up.

Grandma also told a story about Andrew Jackson being in Florida to fight the Spanish in Pensacola. One of his men was caught for desertion, court marshaled, and hanged from a big oak tree. The area where this happened is still known today as Court Marshal Lake which is near Highway 77 and Highway 20. (Historian, Marlene Womack, has researched the subject and says Jackson did not personally visit Court Martial Lake, but she did talk to an old-timer about 35 years ago who said a tree once held the names of those who may have been killed or executed there. That tree was destroyed years ago.)

This story-telling entertainment was more enjoyable than most Hollywood movies–and it was free.

The Lost Cows

There was no stock law in Florida when I was growing up. All livestock roamed wherever there was grass and water. Sometimes we lost some cows for two or three weeks before finding them, maybe several miles from where they were supposed to be.

I remember one time we lost four or five cows and we searched everywhere for them. Each day Dad sent me out on my horse to look for the cows. These were beef cows that Dad was going to sell to buy supplies for the family and farm.

Mama and Dad really got anxious and started doing special prayer for God to help them find the cows. One morning Dad got up and said he had a dream and believed God had shown him where the cows were. In the dream he saw the cows grazing several miles east of our farm near Highway 79.

This was miles from where they usually wandered, but we went to this location. Much to my amazement, the cows were in the exact spot Dad said his dream showed him.

I started believing in prayer at a young age.

The Forehand Boys

There were many goats and sheep that were tame and traveled in small herds throughout the unpopulated areas of the county. Most of the sheep belonged to the Forehand family. My father's sister was married to one of the brothers.

The Forehands rode horses all around the county checking on their sheep and cattle. There were times dogs got together and started killing sheep. The Forehand boys were believed to carry poison biscuits in their saddle bags and drop them off near a house that had dogs they suspected of killing sheep.

25

Farmers didn't take kindly to this practice. (However, on occasion dogs were killed caught in the act of killing sheep and that wasn't questioned much.)

One day my dad told us about a neighbor farmer who had lost a dog to a poison biscuit a few months earlier, and had been on the lookout for the Forehand boys since then. He feared they might pay another visit and try to poison his other catch dog.

The farmer saw one of the Forehands ride by and discretely drop a biscuit beside the dirt road in front of the farmer's house. Concealed in some bushes, the farmer stood up with his shotgun and said, "Get off your horse and pick up that biscuit."

The Forehand boy said, "I just ate lunch, there's nothin' wrong with the biscuit. I had one left and decided to throw it away."

The farmer cocked his shotgun, pointed it at the boy and said, "If there's nothing wrong with it then eat it, or I am going to blow you off that horse."

The boy started begging and tried to say it was dirty and he didn't want to eat a dirty biscuit. The farmer raised his gun and said, "Eat it."

He quickly ate it, and word was, he nearly ran his horse to death to get to Bonifay and the doctor's office. I understand he had a close call, but the doctor pulled him through.

We didn't hear of any other dogs dying from poison.

Daily Farm Chores

My daily chores on the farm changed often, but there was always plenty of work to do each day. Dad had a built-in alarm clock and woke up about an hour before daylight every morning. Mom and Dad's bedroom was next to mine and when Dad woke up, he bumped on the wall and said, "Son, time to get up."

One of my winter chores was to start a fire in the fireplace. I lit some fat-lightered splinters, which I prepared each evening for starting a fire the next morning. Next was the placing of oak wood over the splinters. When the oak caught fire, we had a big hot fire that warmed the entire room.

After the wood started burning, I raced back to my bedroom to dress. I put on Duckbill overalls over my long handles (long underwear), pulled on high-top brogans (heavy work shoes) and a denim jacket. I didn't have gloves. (My first pair of gloves came with my Marine dress blues at age eighteen.)

After dressing, I went into the kitchen where Mama had fired up the stove. She always got up when I did to start cooking breakfast. She heated water for coffee and some for the milking detail. She poured warm water in a bucket for me to use to wash the cows tits before milking.

I headed for the barn, hung my milk bucket on a peg, and put food in the trough for the cows, horse and mule. I milked the cow and took the milk to Mama in the kitchen. (See details on cow milking under "Things Mama Taught Me.")

I returned to the barn and turned the calf out of another pen where he had been kept away from the mother cow all night. If you left the calf with the cow, the calf nursed all during the night. When morning came there would be no milk and the calf would be sick from drinking too much. We always left one tit for the calf to nurse on after we finished milking for the household.

Next I went around the barnyard and hen house picking up eggs (details under "Things Mama Taught Me") from nests scattered around. After egg gathering, Mama usually had breakfast ready and on the table. This was one of my favorite meals. Mama loved to prepare a variety of different items every time she cooked.

Breakfast included things like big cathead biscuits, smoked sausage, country ham, thick slices of smoked bacon, fresh yard eggs, rice and/or grits, homemade fig and strawberry preserves. Sometimes she fixed sawmill or tomato gravy for our biscuits. Of course there was coffee, and in the winter months, hot sassafras tea–good for colds and flu. We almost always had a big dish of homemade butter and a jug of fresh milk and a quart jar of honey.

The milk was kept cool by attaching a rope to a gallon glass jug or syrup bucket and lowering it deep into the well in the cool spring water. We used a glass jug because we had no plastic jugs back then.

We thought we had made it to the big time when Dad brought home a used ice box to keep things cool. Mama insisted we drink plenty of milk. I usually drank a quart each day after I arrived home from school.

Fresh milk had a lot of thick cream that rose to the top of the container. We had to shake it to mix it up before drinking it. (You can't buy that kind of milk in stores anymore. Whole milk is homogenized to keep the fat from separating.)

After the crops were harvested in the fall, Dad and I plowed all the weeds, grass and old plants under with a steel beam plow. The rotted plants fertilized the ground. Breaking up all this land with a mule and horse was a major job. Sometimes we burned the weeds and dead grass before plowing it under.

My summer chores also started just before daylight. I had most of the same chores I did in the winter except for building a fire in the fireplace. Sometimes the milking chores were really rough when there were two cows to be milked each morning. That was double trouble and time-consuming.

If it was during school days I had to rush in after the chores, eat breakfast and take off for the long walk to school. If it was Saturday, a holiday or during summer vacation, I had to eat and rush to the barn and put the gear on the mule and horse for a day of plowing the fields with my dad. We arrived at the field, hooked each animal to their plow, and waited for enough daylight to start plowing.

We plowed until Mama came outside the house and placed a white sheet on the clothes line pole and raised it high. That was our signal that dinner was ready. We unhooked the animals and headed for the barn. At the barn, I took the harnesses off the animals and fed them.

Dad plowed the mule and I had the big horse, Maude. She was a good horse even though she almost killed me on several occasions by falling down, throwing me off and running over me. This usually happened when my friend Jake and I were racing, or occasionally Maude would just be walking along and stumble and fall. She was clumsy.

After Dad, Mama, Ruth, and I finished dinner (it's called lunch now at midday), I headed for the barn, placed the harnesses back on the horse and mule and went back to the field with Dad. We continued to plow until dark.

28

Many times after we fed the mule and horse, we ate supper and then went down to the creek and took a bath. I loved this because it beat having to sit in a #2 washtub and have Mama scrub me with lye soap and dig the dust and dirt out of my ears.

I learned the responsibility of doing jobs that needed to be done, even if I didn't want to do them.

Some Things Mama Taught Me

Among other things, Mama taught me how to milk a cow, gather eggs, ring a chicken's neck, clean a chicken, pick cotton, dig potatoes, know when a watermelon was ripe, know when to cut the okra, pick and shell peas and butterbeans.

**Annie Mae Pitts
(Mama)**

Cow Milking

Mama always sent me to milk the cow with some warm water in the milk bucket. When the cow had a young calf, it bit the mother cow's tits and cut little nicks in them that became very sore. If you grabbed a tit too hard to milk the cow, especially on a cold morning, she kicked the fatal daylights out of you. More times than I can remember, I got knocked off the milk stool and flat on my back with the bucket turned over and milk spilled.

Mama taught me to gently wash the cow's tits with the warm water. If you squeezed really gently, there was a good chance the cow let you get away with it.

The cows loved to wade around in a pond in the back of the field. This helped to keep them cool and get the flies off their bodies. We had cock spurs, sandspurs and cockle burrs around our field and the cows, horse and mule got them in the bushy end of their tails.

Burrs on the cow's tail could be a dangerous weapon, especially when damp after lying in the barnyard that was often wet with urine. While I was milking, sometimes a horse fly or dog fly bit the cow and she swiped at it with her tail. When that happened, the bushy part of her urine-soaked tail, full of sharp burrs, wrapped around my head and neck. This caused much pain, discomfort and scratches all over my neck and face when she connected.

Mama taught me to catch the tail and sit on part of it while milking. That wet, prickly tail was uncomfortable, so I usually tried to ease through the milking process without sitting on the tail and sometimes paid dearly.

Another rule of Mama's was to always milk from the right side of the cow. If you tried the left side, look out for a swift kick. I don't know why it had to be the right side, no one ever told me, it must have been a mutual agreement between Noah and his cow and just handed down to the present day. (Another unexplained rule is that a horse should be mounted on the left side. I don't know who made these rules but if you try the wrong side, you will know immediately that you have made a mistake.)

Gathering Eggs

Hens laid their daily eggs in various nests along with the other hens. When it came to sitting time to hatch out baby chicks, one hen would not sit on another hen's nest. She had to have her own personal nest to sit on each day and night, and picked the one where she had laid most of her eggs.

When one hen began her nesting period, the other chickens did not go near her or her nest. In picking up the eggs from the entire flock, I always left one nest egg. This enticed the chicken to lay again the following day. Thus the name "nest egg." If you took all the eggs, the hen probably would not use that nest again.

Every so often the time came for a hen to sit on her eggs and raise little ones. Mama could tell that time by the way the hen started clucking and not wanting to leave her nest. Mama gave me a basket full of eggs and had me place 18 to 21 eggs in the hen's nest.

It depended on the size of the hen as to how many eggs she could cover in her nest. Most of our chickens were Rhode Islands, a large breed that could accommodate 21 eggs and totally cover them. She had to be able to cover all the eggs and keep them warm or they rotted.

The hen stayed on the nest 24-hours a day and only left when she had to eat. She rushed to the trough where Mama put the chicken laying mash, ate her fill and then raced back to her nest. She had to get back before the eggs got cold. If she didn't, the baby chicks inside would die.

When the baby chicks started hatching, they usually all came out within two or three hours. Once they broke through the shell and started moving around, the hen climbed off the nest and started clucking. Those little chicks immediately fell in line and followed her across the yard. She started the feeding process by finding bugs, chicken feed and worms, then clucking to call the chicks. The baby chicks ran to their mother and pecked on what she had found.

It was always exciting to see a new batch of chicks hatch out. Everyone came outside and watched the little ones trying to stay up with their mom. We had 40 or 50 hens that looked alike in the barnyard. Those little chicks could walk through and around them and go straight to the hen that was their mom.

Wringing a Chicken's Neck

Mama taught me how to wring a chicken's neck and skin the chicken out for her to fix a quick meal if we had unexpected company. Put the chicken's head between your right thumb and right index finger and squeeze tight. Then flip the chicken around a couple of times, make a kind of sudden snatch and the neck breaks. The chicken will bounce around on the ground a few seconds and then it is ready to be skinned out.

31

It sounds cruel but as a young kid and seeing this done by adults, it did not bother me at all. My sister was bothered by it and to my knowledge she never killed a chicken, but her tummy as well as mine was a graveyard for many chickens.

Mom wringing a chicken's neck on the farm.

The Wash Pot and Bathing

One of my duties was to help Mama with anything that had to do with the wash pot and boiling water. I had to draw water from the well and build a fire to boil the water. The wash pot, made of cast iron, held about 20 to 25 gallons of water. This pot was used for a number of different jobs. Mama heated the water to wash our dirty clothes, during the winter time for baths, at hog killing time to take the hair off the hogs, to cook the grease out of the hog fat to make lard, and to make lye soap.

We never had any of that sweet-smelling, store-bought soap. Lye soap smelled terrible, but it removed stains, cleaned your body, and was subject to take off hide with it. The first store-bought soap I ever used was when I went out for football and took a shower after practice. (The football locker room is also where I took my first shower.) We had nothing like that on the farm. We bathed in the creek or a #2 wash tub filled with well water that sat on the back porch.

Tub baths were rough in the winter time. Even when the water was heated, it was just a small amount that was added to the cold water. Mama always inspected me after my bath, checking for clean ears, washed hair and any dirt I might have missed. When she spotted dirt she grabbed a rag with a little lye soap and went after it with a vengeance.

I learned it was much better for me to do a good wash job than to let Mama do it.

Other Things Mama Taught Me

Mama showed me how to hoe peanuts, cotton and other plants that a plow could not reach.

She taught me table manners. If she called us to eat and I said I was not hungry, she said, "Son, that's why you eat, so you won't get hungry." If I didn't like what she had prepared for dinner, she said, "That's okay son, just sit there long enough and you'll get hungry enough to eat it." It always worked. My mama was a smart lady.

Besides teaching us to say "mama" and "daddy" some of the first words we learned to say were "yes ma'am, no ma'am" and "yes sir, no sir." A one word "yes" or "no" to an adult could get you a swift backhand or in a lot of trouble.

Looking back now, I think my mother and dad would have made good drill instructors in the Marine Corps, because the drill instructors told us that the first words out of our mouth would be "sir," and the last word out of our mouth would be "sir."

33

There were very few times I turned my nose up to the food at the kitchen table. Mama was the world's greatest cook. We could have unexpected company, especially a visiting preacher, and she'd always encourage them to stay and eat. She went to the smokehouse with a pan and butcher knife, sliced off some ham, pork chops, ribs or sausage and headed back into the kitchen. She told me to run out and catch a young fryer (chicken), dress it and bring it back inside. I never saw anyone who could prepare a meal as good and quick as she did. Within what seemed a few minutes, she had iced tea, hot biscuits, fried chicken, country ham, ribs, peas, cornbread, okra, corn on the cob and usually a blackberry cobbler ready to eat.

I really looked forward to a preacher coming for a visit. Now that I think about it, these visitors always seemed to time their visits near eating time.

I found out, later in life, that we were real poor folks and dirt farmers. Funny I didn't know this while I was growing up. We were happy, had plenty to eat and hardly ever got sick.

If you did get sick, or acted like you had a little cold or sore throat, Mama got out a home remedy–Black Draft, SSS tonic, or castor oil. When you went to bed, she'd press a big poultice, soaked in gobs of Vick's salve, tight on your chest. After one of her medical treatments, you had to have a serious sickness and be at death's door before you told Mama you were sick again.

Much of our clothing was made by Mama with her old Singer foot peddle sewing machine. When she bought laying mash for her laying hens she let my sister and me pick out the pattern on the feed sack. She made my shirts and Ruth's skirts from those sacks. It was funny how many kids you ran into wearing the same pattern shirts and skirts.

Remembering Things My Dad Taught Me

When my father died, my family and I were driving from Tallahassee to Live Oak, Florida, for his funeral. I started thinking of all the things my dad taught me—many I had taken for granted. Reflecting made me wish I had been as good a father to my children as my father was to me. Some of the things he taught me will be of little interest to others, but they meant a lot to me. Maybe my children and their children and grandchildren can take some lessons from my father as well.

Dallas Eugene Pitts–Dad
(Correct spelling is Dallis, according to my sister Ruth.)

Learning to Plow at Age Four

I used to follow my dad to the field and watch him plow the crops. I recall following him down the furrows when I was around four years of age. Even though he was walking rather slow, I had to run every now and then to stay up.

I begged him to let me plow. He'd stop the mule and let me hold the Joe Harrow. This was a plow for working the peanuts and had iron spikes on two sides of the plow that fit over and on each side of the peanut rows. It loosened the dirt and turned over the young grass that was growing around the peanut plant. I could barely reach the plow handles and the mule walked too fast for me.

I ran to the house and got a quart jar of water from the well for my dad every now and then. Another big thrill was when we stopped for lunch and unhooked the mule. Dad lifted me and sat me behind the harness on the mule's neck and led the mule to the barn. I hung on to the gear around the mule's neck and loved the ride to the barn and back to the field after lunch.

I helped dad do everything. He taught me how to take the harness off the mule and put it on when headed back to the field. I really did very little because of my size, but he let me think I did.

Reminiscent of learning to plow with Dad. (Photo from Blackleg Acres website.)

One afternoon, we returned to the barn earlier than usual. Dad put the mule up and drug out an old Joe Harrow and got out his tools. He was a fine carpenter and even built several homes in the community. He sawed and trimmed the Joe Harrow until I could stand behind the handles and walk without having to reach up and stand on my toes.

The next morning when we went to the field he hooked up Sam, the ox, and along with the mule we went out to the peanut field. The ox is a fine working animal but is known for walking very slow. That is why most farmers stopped using an ox and started using mules and horses for their farming.

Dad hooked Sam up to my little Joe Harrow and put the plow lines in my small hands and said "go on son you can plow the row next to mine.

We started off. Dad let me go first and helped me plow the first row. I finally got the hang of it and made it down most of the row without toppling the plow over. Dad let me go ahead and waited for me to get a big lead and then started the mule. He caught up and then stopped and waited for me to get another big lead before catching up again.

I had made it to the big boy world. I felt six feet tall. When I was with my dad, I copied everything he did. I walked like him, spit like him, talked to the mule and the ox like him and even peed in the bushes at the end of a row, just like him.

Fishing

One of the first things Dad taught me was to improvise. We had very little money, so I never owned a store-bought fishing pole as a youngster. Dad taught me how to cut a fishing pole from bushes in the woods near the creek and to rig it with line about six inches longer than the pole. He explained that the size hook, type of bait and way to hook the bait depended mostly on the kind of fish you were trying to catch.

For bream, we usually "snored up" earthworms (more on this later under "My First Fish"). We found wigglers beneath the kitchen window where Mama threw the dish water out the window. These worms loved dish water with scraps of food in it and made excellent bait for bream and warmouth. For catfish, we looked under logs, limbs and driftwood near the creek in wet or damp places. Here we found puppy dogs (dark colored lizards) that catfish loved. We also used chicken guts for catfish. They were tough, making it hard for the fish to get off the hook.

When we walked down the creek bank and fished off the bank, Dad caught most of the fish. I complained and asked Dad what I was doing wrong. He laughed and said, "Son you are fishing where all the other fishermen have fished–in beautiful spots where the water is calm and there are no bushes to hang up on. You have to fish where no one else fishes because of vines, bushes, swift water, and steep banks."

Sometimes he rolled his line up on the end of his pole all the way to the hook and bait. He crawled into heavy bushes on the creek bank and gently unrolled his line, letting his hook and bait down into the water. Almost immediately he got a bite and ended up fighting a large fish until he tired the fish out. Then he rolled the line back up until he brought the fish up to the end of his pole and backed out of the bushes. He'd still be on his hands and knees and carrying a huge bream. He said most people don't know how to do this or don't want to pay the price of crawling through the bushes, but that's how you catch the big ones.

Dad taught me how to go striking for fish at night. He took metal straps from old barrels and hammered them out straight with the end bent back making a handle of about six inches. We went to a branch off the creek. That is a small stream that usually runs off the main stream and is shallow enough to wade in about knee deep.

For light, we bound up fat lightered splinters, lit the end, and held it in our left hand. The striking iron we held in the right hand. We started wading and made as little noise as possible. When Dad saw a fish lying real still near some bushes or logs, he'd move the metal striker over the fish and come down quickly on the fish's back just behind the gills. The fish died instantly. We put the fish in a bag with a strap hanging around our necks and wade on up stream. We got some really nice size fish this way.

He taught me to make lead sinkers. He first made forms by rolling a page from the Sears catalog around a pencil. He stuck it into soft dirt and then pulled the pencil out and rolled another. We fired up a blow torch and melted lead weights used to balance car tires in an iron dipper and poured it into the paper sticking in the ground. After it cooled we peeled the paper off and with a knife cut off the size lead we wanted for our fishing line.

Dad taught me how to put bush hooks out along the river or creek bank. We cut a short pole, put a line on one end and sharpened the other end to stick in the bank. Sometimes we just tied the line and hook onto a bush hanging over the water.

To set out a trotline for catfish we used a boat and placed this line across the creek or out from the bank in deep water. A trotline is thirty to forty feet long with several short lines with hooks and bait attached along the line. One end is attached to the creek bank or a bush and the other end is attached to a floating object, such as an empty milk jug. Another line was attached to the floating object with a weight on the end that reached the bottom of the creek to keep the line in place.

Rules

Dad taught me some rules. 1. Never mistreat a woman. He really emphasized this and said that regardless of what a woman might do or say to you, never retaliate by striking her. 2. Try to never borrow anything. But if you have to, take real good care of it and return it in the same or better condition than when you got it. 3. When working for another person, do a good job. Always strive to work in such a way that when you leave a job, you would be welcomed back anytime you wanted your old job back. 4. Never make fun of a person because he or she fails. This includes anyone who may have a physical or mental handicap. 5. Always try to help anyone in need. He stressed God's Word, "Do unto others as you would have them do unto you." 6. Never put off until tomorrow what you can do today. 7. Never point a gun at anyone unless you are prepared to use it. Never bluff, they may call you on it. 8. Never catch more fish than you are going to eat or give to a needy person. Always clean the fish you catch. 9. The same rules apply in hunting. Never kill game you are not going to eat, and then only what you need for your personal use. 10. Don't ever waste the food God has given you to eat. 11. Never mistreat a dumb brute, animal.

Dad gave an example of a good reason to never mistreat a dog. If you go hunting or fishing and get lost in the woods, tell your dog, "Let's go home." The dog can lead you back to the place you entered the woods. As a kid I did this many times and my dog never failed me.

Later in life, when I chased escaped prisoners with Twigs, the bloodhound, I might end up so deep in woods in unfamiliar territory that I'd be hopelessly lost. After handcuffing the escapee, I could say, "Twigs, let's go home," and he led us out.

My dad was an expert marksman. He started teaching me to shoot when I was five years of age. He stressed safety and made sure I checked to see if a weapon was loaded when I picked it up or someone handed me a weapon. No matter if the other person tells you it is unloaded, you check it. Dad used to say that most people and especially kids were killed with "unloaded" guns. That is, guns they thought were unloaded but were not.

I learned to shoot the .22 caliber rifle first. He taught me the finer points of breathing, sight alignment, and trigger squeeze. These points stayed with me to this day. Even when I was in the Marine Corps, the pointers he taught me helped me excel in firearms, both rifle and pistol.

I will always remember a pistol match in Georgia when I was a member of a five-man USMC pistol team and competed against Georgia police officers, state troopers, deputies and other law enforcement officers one weekend. This was not a big thing for our team but an effort by the Marine Corps to cooperate and show respect for law enforcement in the State of Georgia. Our team was a group who could handle firearms and some worked on the pistol and rifle range.

The Saturday morning we met, I was surprised to see my dad in the crowd of spectators. I had mentioned to him on a trip home about the match. It was no big deal for me; the main purpose was for public relations. If I had known how much this meant to my dad, I probably would have been very nervous.

The match we were going to shoot involved three types of fire and an overall total of all three matches. A trophy or medal was given to the top three shooters in each of the three matches and another to the overall winner for the least number of points dropped during the entire match.

The pistol range was made up of targets set on rails. The range officer ran the targets out to the yard line to be shot. After that round was shot, he ran the targets back in. Scorers assigned to each target scored and recorded them.

Sgt. — L. PITTS
... Marksman

Local Marine
Match Winner

Marine Sgt. —
son of Mr. and Mrs. — —
Route 2, Panama City — won —
place trophy in the Class A
individual match. As one of a
man team representing the Ma-
Corps Base at Albany, Ga.
captured the second place trop
in the Class AA match.

Each shooter set up on his assigned target and the range master, on a loud speaker, called out for the shooters to load their weapon with five rounds. He explained the upcoming stage such as, "This is slow fire at fifty yards." When the targets turned to face the shooter you had ten minutes to shoot ten rounds.

At the end of ten minutes the targets automatically turned away and the range officer announced, "Cease fire on the line, make your weapons safe and lay them on the shooting stand." The targets were then run up the rail to the shooter where the scorer checked for the number of holes in the target and scored it. Ten points for each bull's-eye, nine points for the next ring, eight for the next, and so on.

After the targets were scored, everyone was ordered to prepare for timed fire from 25 yards. The targets were then moved up to 25 yards. The range officer announced that this round was timed fire or 5 rounds in 25 seconds. The shooters were told to load their weapons. The following orders were given, "Ready on the right? Ready on the left? All ready on the firing line?" When he said "line," in three seconds the target turned to face the shooter and at the end of 25 seconds the target turned away.

The range officer told the shooters to reload with 5 more rounds. The same order was given again and the targets turned again as before. The targets were scored as they were the last time. The range officer announced that the last stage was rapid fire or 5 rounds in ten seconds at fifteen yards. The same commands were given, the targets turned and turned back after 10 seconds. This is where many shooters lose the most points.

A trophy was given to the top three winners of each distance: 50 yards, 25 yards and 15 yards. Three more trophies were given to the three top teams with the highest overall score for the three courses. Then the scores were totaled for each 5-man team and each of the three top team scores.

Each police department entered at least one 5-man team. The top three teams were also awarded a large trophy for the winning team and each team member received a trophy, also.

That day was a good day for me as I won first place in each of the matches and as a member of the winning team. I also received a large trophy award for the highest individual score for the day. I walked over to my dad, who was grinning from ear to ear, and handed the awards to him.

I told him he had taught me well. I will never forget the look he gave me as he received the trophies. I really think that might have been one of the proudest moments of his life.

It's hard to understand the pride of a parent until you become one.

Planting Crops

Farming is a very hard life. I have all the respect in the world for a dirt farmer. We had a mule and horse. Dad plowed the mule and I used the horse. We started breaking the land for planting in the fall. If it had grown up a lot with grass and weeds, we burned it before plowing it under. We used a steel beam plow and it turned over about four inches of ground at a time. We circled the field and the rows were ¼ mile long in one of the fields. After we made several rounds and plowed from daybreak to dark, it didn't look like we had done very much. There was still so much more to do.

After all the 40 acres were broken up and plowed under, we started laying off rows to be planted. Each field had to be prepared differently for the different crops you planned to sow. Dad taught me how and when to plant the seed. He explained how to care for the young plants as they broke through the earth and out into the sunlight. We used, as most farmers still do, the Old Farmer's Almanac for planting times, weather and the moon. Most farmers swear by their almanac.

Butchering Hogs

Many hours, days and years went into the do's and don'ts around the farm. This also applied to butchering a hog. First of all hogs were usually butchered in the winter time. This was for different reasons. First the meat was less likely to spoil and the farmer had more time because the crops have been laid by and harvested.

Hogs are hard to kill unless you hit the right spot. The right spot to aim your weapon is between the eyes and about an inch higher, this will hit the brain and cause instant death. We always used a .22 caliber rifle. Dad used to let me do the honors. If the hog moved his head slightly when I pulled the trigger then we had a wild time. He squealed and ran around charging anything that moved. If this happened, Dad took the rifle, and waited for the hog to either charge him or run in a straight line. He fired one shot and the hog was dead. He was an expert with weapons. Some farmers killed a hog by using an ax. They turned it over and used the blunt edge instead of the sharp cutting edge and struck the hog between the eyes with a swift hard swing. This caused immediate death if done correctly.

Much instruction went into how to clean and process the hog after it was killed. Most farmers used a 55 gallon barrel and placed it at a 45 degree angle into the ground. Water was heated in the wash pot and the barrel was filled as full of hot water as could be without spilling when the hog was put in.

We built a big fire around the barrel to keep the water as hot as possible. A handful of turpentine, collected from the sides of pine trees, was added to the water. This assisted in getting the hair off easily.

When the water was ready we slid the hog down into the boiling water head first, held the back feet and turn it over and over a couple of times. The hog was pulled out, changed ends and the process repeated.

Dad in the hog pen on the farm.

Next, the hog was placed on a platform of boards on the ground in front of the barrel. Two or three people started pulling out the hair by the handfuls. As the next hog was being dragged up, the first one was pulled over and the skin on the back legs was slit exposing a strong white leader. We took a singletree (used to hook a mule to a plow) and hooked the hog by both legs. A rope was attached to the singletree and run through a pulley attached to a large tree limb. The hog was hoisted up about head high. The women usually took over at

43

this point and with large knives they scraped off any remaining hair.

One of the men split the hog from the tail all the way down to the head. All the insides were rolled out into a #2 washtub. This tub was taken into the house and Mama removed the liver, lights and guts. The guts were scraped, cleaned and saved to make link sausages.

Dad cut up the hog outside and as he cut the hams, hocks, ribs, etc., he placed them in tubs along with the head to be carried into the house where Mama trimmed it up saving all small pieces to be ground up for sausage. The head, liver, lights, ears and heart were set aside along with other tidbits to make souse or hog head cheese.

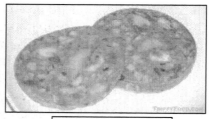

Hogshead Cheese

Very little was lost from the pig. My dad used to joke that when he was a kid his dad said they never threw any of the pig away. "The head, ears and tongue were ground up for hogshead cheese. All the scrap pieces were saved to make sausage, the fat for lard. The hair was used to make toothbrushes and the squeal was used to make whistles for the children."

After all the hams, ham hocks and other parts of the pig were trimmed, Mama ground some of the meat with a little fat and seasonings. She made a small patty and cooked it in a frying pan. She had several people taste it, add more or less seasoning, until everyone agreed on the taste. Sometimes she fried several pieces before everyone agreed the taste was just right.

She seasoned all the ground up meat like everyone had approved and then the meat was fed through a hand-operated machine into the gut casings that had been cleaned out. This link sausage was "born" to be smoked for several days. This was one of the best parts of the hog to me.

My dad explained the smoking process to me when he was visiting our home in Tallahassee just prior to his death in 1978. These are his words that I have on tape:

"Son, after you have butchered the hog and cut it up you do the following: Get a tub and use meat salt or what they call ice cream salt. Pour a large amount in the tub and dump a piece of meat in the salt. Rub the salt in real good on both sides. The large portions, use a butcher knife with a long blade and a narrow blade. Run the blade down by the bone of the ham or the shoulder. Pack salt in the hole next to the bone until completely full. The ribs, rub salt on both sides. Do the same on all the other pieces including the smaller pieces. Stack the salted meat up as close as possible and cover up for 3 days and nights. The salt will draw the blood out of the meat. The blood is what causes the meat to spoil. After three days and nights, the meat will have blood covering it from the salt drawing it out. Pour the blood off and re-salt the meat the same way you did before. Place pine tops in the bottom of a large hole and place a layer of meat on the pine tops, careful not to let one piece touch another. Lay more pine tops over the layer of meat and stack another layer. Do this until you have all the meat covered and not touching each other. After all the meat is covered, put a canvas or some type covering over it to keep animals from digging it up and flies from getting to it. Let the meat sit for seven or eight days. After the seven or eight days, build a fire around a large wash pot full of water. Uncover the meat and take a wire and attach it to the corner of the slabs of meat and make a loop to run a pole through and hang it up in the smoke house. Put a hook in the wire loop and dip the meat in the pot of boiling water. Lift it up and down two or three times and the salt will melt and come off the meat. Take each piece of meat, after dipping, and immediately hang it on one of the poles in the smoke house.

Build a small fire under the meat about four feet below the meat. Usually we used green oak to place on the small fire. The oak will start to burn a little and put off a lot of smoke. If you have a good steady smoke let it continue for 4 or 5 days. You can tell when it has enough because the meat will start to dry out and that means it is done."

The smoke house was about 12'x14' and had a dirt floor with a hole in the center about three or four feet deep. The poles ran parallel to the floor and were spaced where all the meat could be hung up without touching another piece of meat.

At this point, when I was a kid, the entire operation was turned over to me. I became the fire chief. I had to build a small fire in the hole and put green oak wood over the fire. The big problem was I could not let the fire burn high enough to touch the meat. We wanted just smoke and lots of it. I had to continue to crawl in and out of the smoke house and keep the small fire going just enough to keep the oak smoking.

The smoke house was very tight, dog and cat proof, but smoke filtered out through the small cracks and my mother and dad better see smoke coming out continuously or I was in trouble. This went on for several days until the meat was completely smoked and turned a deep brownish red. I shed many a tear during this operation from crawling in and out of the smoke house tending the fire.

From that point on the meat was ready to cook at a moment's notice. If Mama wanted to cook sausage or ham she went to the smoke house, cut the amount and kind of meat she wanted, walked back to the house and threw it into the frying pan. We ate very well year round.

Plowing

Dad taught me how to attach different plow points and blades and how to plow different plants, such as peanuts, corn, and cotton.

For breaking land, the steel beam was used. The scrape and scooter were for siding peanuts. The middle buster was used for laying off rows to plant seed. The 'fertilizer boy' was used to spread fertilizer in the rows to be planted. The planter was used to drop the seed in a uniform pattern. All of these plows were pulled by an ox, mule, or horse.

Dad taught me to tie a ham string on the bottom of a collar under the mule's neck to hold the harness together, to hook a mule or horse to a wagon or plow with trace chains and singletree, and to hook a yoke around the neck of an ox when the ox was needed to pull something.

I was cautioned to never let the mule or horse switch his tail over the plow lines running from the mule's head to the driver's hands sitting on the seat behind the mule. He said this made the animal go kind of crazy and hard to control.

I thought about that a lot and something kept bugging me about wanting to know what would really happen. My imagination ran wild about all the possibilities that could happen. So one slow dull day, I was on the backside of the cornfield driving the wagon. It was heaped up with corn my dad and I had pulled that day. I was sitting in the seat directly behind the mule. Dad told me to drive the mule and wagon back to the barn.

Mule and wagon
Photo courtesy of State Archives of Florida, *Florida Memory* **#9052**

"Park at the crib next to the barn and I'll meet you there to unload the corn after I gather some tools."

It was close to dark and horseflies and bugs were out in force. The mule was steadily switching his tail back and forth to keep the flies off. Finally his tail fell over one of the plow lines. Instead of gently shaking it loose, I kind of lifted it up a little and suddenly he clamped his tail down real hard, trapping the line tight under his tail. It's hard to remember everything that

47

happened after that–things happened fast, yet seemed to be in slow motion.

First, the mule kicked both feet straight back and farted real loud. The fart got me and smelled terrible. The kick almost did, dirt from his back feet hit me in the chest and face. He took off for the barn, about a quarter of a mile away, like the devil himself was right behind him. I started yelling, "Whoa, Whoa, Whoa," and pulled back on the reins to stop him. This was a bad move. When I pulled the rein more snug under his tail, he responded by running faster, kicking up his heels about every third jump and farting each time he kicked. I gave up trying to stop him and decided if I didn't get off that wagon, I'd be killed when we came to the first cross fence post.

I dropped the lines and looked for a place I could jump off. Every time I spotted what looked like a good place to jump off, we'd already passed it. Somehow during the run the line worked out from under his tail since I had dropped the reins. He came to a stop at the barn gate with me shaking like a leaf. Behind us was a quarter mile trail of corn across the field.

I told my dad that it was an accident. The mule was switching flies and caught the line under his tail. Dad didn't comment except to say, "Tomorrow, hook up the mule and pick up the corn you lost coming to the barn."

It took all of the next day to pick up the corn ear by ear that had flown out of the wagon. As I recall dark caught me. I finished gathering the corn the following morning, and was never tempted to test my dad's directive about how to hold the reins again.

 Never allow the reins to get underneath a mule's tail.

Moving 100 lb. Sacks of Fertilizer

Sometimes I listened to my dad's instructions, but many times his advice only aroused my curiosity until I tried what he told me not to do.

One day we loaded the wagon with several 100-pound sacks of fertilizer to put out on our plowed field. Dad knew about how far the fertilizer plow would go before it had to be refilled, so we were dropping off the bags at these locations. I was driving the wagon and my dad dragged a bag to the rear of the wagon, jumped out, backed up to the tail gate and pulled the 100 pound sack onto his back. He then walked to the exact spot he wanted to leave it and dropped it. Naturally, I wanted to try this but Dad smiled and said, "No, it's much too heavy. The sack weighs more than you." I still thought I could handle it.

My opportunity came sooner than I expected. Someone came down the road on an old car, stopped at the fence and started blowing the horn. Dad recognized the man as a member of his church. He told me to sit tight and went to see what the man wanted. I got tired of waiting and decided to prove my dad wrong and unload a bag by myself.

I was twelve years old and thought I could do anything my dad did. I backed up to the wagon and pulled the sack on my back and immediately went to the ground, face down, with the 100 lb. bag on top of me. I barely had enough space to breathe and holler for dad. I lay there until he came and pulled the bag off. The perfect imprint of my body remained on that freshly plowed ground.

My dad just smiled and continued to unload the bags. He asked if I wanted to try another bag and I replied, "No sir." He always gave me good advice, but I didn't always heed it.

 I had a knack for, unintentionally, proving my dad right.

Learning to Swim

Dad taught me to swim when I was about six years old. We were at what was known as the Blue Cod Wash Hole on Wrights Creek. This was where the "in-crowd farm boys" went swimming. This spot on the creek was very deep. A huge oak tree was on the bank with a rope hanging from a limb about 20 feet above the water. There was also a small platform on the limb where the rope was tied. The brave climbed the tree and jumped or dove off the platform. The not so brave swung out on the rope and dropped off in the creek. The cowards, like me, and the others who couldn't swim, splashed around on a sand bar on the edge of the creek. We watched the big boys try to outdo each other and impress the girls with their diving and swinging out far above the creek and dropping into the water.

One day, I started walking down to the shallow spot where kids always played, and Dad said, "No. It's time you learned to swim." I was delighted and thought he was going to get in the water and show me how. He reached down, picked me up and tossed me out in the real deep water where all the grown folks swim.

I had on overalls, and he used them to get a handhold to toss me. I sailed out toward the deep water. It seemed everything was in slow motion. I was in the air a long time and started talking to God.

As I remember, I started flailing away with both arms and legs before I crashed into the water's surface. I was paddling so fast I don't even remember going under the water. I somehow made it back to the bank. Dad smiled and said, "Now that's the way to learn to swim."

 In a pinch, we can do things we never thought possible.

Cleaning a Well

The old well brings back memories. We had a back porch that ran from one corner of the house to the other, north and south. At the south end, we had a well that was about four feet square at the top and fifty or sixty feet deep in clay. There was a curb around the top with a large bar that had a rope for a bucket to be lowered down to the water, and then wound back up to the top filled with water. This was the only water we had for drinking, washing clothes and watering the animals. We did have a pond in the back of the field where the animals that were loose could drink. If we had a planted field around the pond we had to draw all the water for the animals each day. Sometimes we drew fifty to one hundred buckets of water in one day.

There was a large cover that fit on top of the well. This was to protect our water from anything falling in. Covering the well was on my list of things to do each night.

Many times at night the dogs or some varmint got after one of the cats around the house. The chase took them across the porch and over the covered well and if they kept pursuing, the cat finally climbed up a tree.

One night I forgot to cover the well. I heard a chase begin. Something was after one of the cats. I listened as they hit the back porch, ran to the end of the porch and then I heard a long "meeeowww" as the cat went down the uncovered well.

Dad heard it also and went outside and dropped a board into the well for the cat to get on until daylight, so he wouldn't drown. The next morning, needless to say, Dad was very unhappy. After he surveyed the situation, I became very unhappy.

First he instructed me to draw all the water out of the well, bucket by bucket, since it was contaminated by the cat. Now that was a several-hour job. After that he tied the rope around me and let me down into the well with a short-handle shovel to clean out the well and dig the well a little deeper. First I had to catch that blasted cat and bring him up. There was no problem catching the cat. The problem was turning him loose. As soon as I got close enough, the cat latched on to me, wrapped his legs around my arm and the harder I tried to shake him off, the tighter he held on to my arm. I don't know who was more frightened, me or the cat.

The fresh spring water seeped in very slowly so I was able to stand at the bottom of the well, dig the wet clay at the bottom and fill the bucket. Dad drew it up one bucket at a time, dumped it out and let the bucket back down. All I could think of was if that rope broke, the bucket would have a hard time missing me as it fell back down to the bottom of the well. It took most all day to do the job, but I finally got in the bucket and Dad drew me up to the top.

I never knew the world looked so wonderful and I never forgot to cover the well again. There were times when Mother and Dad got their point across to me so I would never forget–this was one of those times.

51

 *Whoever conjured up the saying, "bought experience is the best kind," knew what they were talking about.*

My First Fish

There was a small pond in our field where Dad took me fishing sometimes when it was too wet to plow and we had a short break. I was about four years of age and we were using our home-made poles that Dad cut from bushes in the woods.

Gone Fishing
State Archives of Florida, *Florida Memory*

We went out to a grassy area and "snored up" some earthworms. To do this you needed a wood stake about three feet long and an ax.

You drove the stake down about a foot and half and turned the ax on its side and slid it across the top of the stake. It made a grinding noise and vibrated the ground several feet around the stake. This caused the worms to crawl out of the ground.

I picked them up and put them into a can. You have to let the worm get completely out, because if you grab one before it is totally out it will lock itself into the ground and break in two. Dad sat me on a large cypress stump. He was fishing near me. I saw my cork go down and I pulled it back. I had hooked something really big. I was slowly sliding off the stump and yelled to my dad that my "block" (what I called my cork) had sunk. He dropped his pole and grabbed my pole and me just

52

before I took the plunge. It took a while but he finally got the fish out. It was the biggest fish I had ever seen up to that time. It was a large mouth bass, which weighed about 12 lbs. according to my Dad. I don't know if I was as proud of the catch as my dad was. He told everyone he saw about his boy and the big fish. I think it got a little larger each time he told it. Dad cleaned it and that fish fed our entire family that night.

I learned that the accomplishments of your child somehow far outshine your own.

Ruth, Mama, Dad & LaVelle, 1940

Fishing and Camping with Dad on Rattlesnake Pond

In my early years, what little I knew about camping I learned from my Dad. We tried to go camping one time a year after we laid the crop by. (That means we finished all the plowing and it was just before the harvest.)

We snored up several hundred worms, loaded our old 1940 Ford car, tied an old bateau 12-foot boat on top, and headed for Rattlesnake Pond located in the sand hills of south Washington County. Sometimes Mama went along and sometimes just Dad and I went. Occasionally, Lavohn Price and his dad came along and we had a blast.

The water was crystal clear and we caught lots of fish. At the crack of dawn we were on the lake, and around 10:30 am we came ashore and start cleaning the fish. We had no tent just a tarp spread out between some trees. We made tea from the lake water and cooked piles of fish and hushpuppies.

After eating we went swimming. Lavohn and I decided to sleep late one day and just go swimming. Our dads warned us to get out of the water after an hour or two or we would get sunburned. Well it didn't feel like we were burning, so we stayed out most of the day.

That night we found out how right our dads were. Both of us were beet red. I don't think I have ever hurt so much as I did that night. Our two fathers thought it was real funny, but Lavohn and I didn't see anything funny about it.

To make it worse I was gathering firewood and got stung by a scorpion. That's a little varmint that has a long tail that curls up over its back until he lowers it and starts stinging you. My arm had a line of sting marks where he went up my arm before I could get rid of him. That had to be the worst fishing trip I ever experienced.

On another trip we took a large number of glass jugs and put lines with hooks and bait on them and dropped them off around the lake. We put worms on some and small bream on others. This

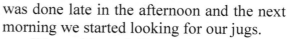
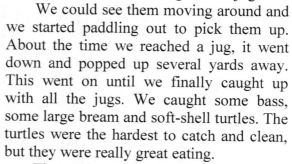

was done late in the afternoon and the next morning we started looking for our jugs.

We could see them moving around and we started paddling out to pick them up. About the time we reached a jug, it went down and popped up several yards away. This went on until we finally caught up with all the jugs. We caught some bass, some large bream and soft-shell turtles. The turtles were the hardest to catch and clean, but they were really great eating.

The real test came when we started home. Dad drove as fast as he could to make it up those sand hill two-trail roads. Most of the time we got stuck three or four times before we got back to the highway. There were no four-wheel drives back then. We used shovels to shovel out the sand and cut small trees to put under the wheels and slowly made it out to Highway 77.

The last year we made the trip to the sand hills, we had a 10-horse Wizard boat motor. Dad had sold some hogs and had enough money to buy this motor from Western Auto in Panama City. On our first trip to Rattlesnake Pond we did little fishing.

We just rode that boat around and around that lake. It sure beat paddling.

Dad only ran it about half speed and finally decided to see how fast it would run, so he dropped me off on the landing and went out alone. Mama and I watched him race across the lake and make a sharp turn and race back.

The last trip back he made the turn too sharp and rolled that boat over. He had to swim and push the boat all the way back to the landing. Naturally the boat motor had gone under the water. He got a blanket out and took that motor apart piece by piece and dried off all the water. It took most of the night but he finally got it back together and it cranked. I noticed he never tested the speed on turns again.

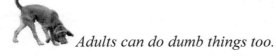
Adults can do dumb things too.

Fishing on My Own

I started camping alone on Wrights Creek at about the age of nine or ten. There were times Dad could not go, so I went alone—just me, my dog Joe, and my .22 rifle. I had to walk about a mile to the creek swamp where I set out my hooks.

Setting out catfish hooks was something most farm boys learned at a very early age. You start out by cutting some poles from bushes that are half-inch in diameter and five or six feet long. A heavy line was attached on the end, four or five feet long, with a hook and heavy sinker on the end about four inches above the hook. When you finished fishing, the line and hooks were rolled up on a stick to take home. The poles were concealed in bushes near the creek where they could be retrieved on the next fishing trip and used again.

Before leaving home for an overnight camping and fishing trip, I got a corn sack and put my necessities in it: a quilt, to cover myself and my dog when we bedded down; an empty gallon syrup can with a bail, for making coffee; two or three pint jars with some corn meal, salt, pepper and onion; another small jar with coffee; a frying pan; a long fork; my pocket knife; a metal cup; a small jar of grease; a hatchet and some kitchen matches in a pint jar closed up to stay dry.

I had to walk about a mile, as the crow flies, to Wrights Creek. As soon as I got to the creek, I tried to find a hole where, during high water, the creek had washed out a stump. This was usually about three or four feet deep. It made an ideal spot to lay my blanket down on leaves and be out of the wind. We never owned a tent. I slept under the stars with a quilt and my dog, hoping it didn't rain.

After finding a suitable place, I started looking under logs, dead limbs and driftwood that floated in during high water for black lizards. These were called "puppy dogs." I'd gather about 20 or 30 puppy dogs and place them in a jar.

Then I set out my lines and hooks. I tried to find my old poles from the last trip or cut new ones, sharpen one end, put my line on the other end and a puppy dog on the hook. I looked for a calm spot in the water near the bank. Sometimes I crawled through the bushes to the edge of the water and stuck my pole into the bank and lowered the hook on or near the bottom of the creek. Usually, I put out about twelve poles. This was enough for a good mess of fish for supper, and plenty to take home for the family.

All this was done in the late afternoon before dark. Then I set up camp with Joe. Joe was a large cur dog with one eye. Joe would catch almost anything and that's how he lost his eye. (Dad and I were wild hog hunting. Dad ordered Joe to catch a big boar. He did, but the boar knocked Joe's eye out with a big tusk. Joe almost lost his life in that battle. We later got the hog but not that day. Joe recovered from his injuries and was my good friend.)

Most of my catfishing was in the wintertime when there was no plowing to be done. It was usually cold, so I always had a hatchet and cut some wood before dark to build a good fire.

After getting the fire going I cut two forked sticks and stuck them into the ground on each side of the fire. I placed a third stick in the forks running parallel across the fire. I filled the gallon syrup bucket about half full of water from the creek and hung it on the parallel stick over the fire. This was my coffee pot. When the water came to a boil, I threw a handful of coffee in, took it off the fire, and set it on some coals. Then I poured a half cup of coffee and tried to sip a little without swallowing too many grounds. I hated to drink that stuff, but all the grownups did, so I had to also.

After dark I made a torch from lightered wood and went to fish my hooks. (We never owned a flashlight while we lived on the farm.) Usually, I could hear water splashing before I got to the pole. My heart started beating fast, knowing I had a big catfish on my little pole. I took the fish off, put him on a string, re-baited my hook, stuck it back into the bank and went on to the next one. I might get four or five catfish the first time I fished my poles.

I knelt at the edge of the creek and, using my pocket knife, I cut around the catfish head and pulled the skin off strip by strip. After cleaning the fish, I sprinkled them with salt and pepper, rolled them in cornmeal, got out my frying pan and a pint jar of grease, and arranged my fire coals for cooking. I mixed up hushpuppies from the meal I mealed the fish in, then added a few chopped up onions and a little water from the creek and started cooking. That was some fine eating consisting of catfish, hushpuppies, creek water and coffee.

After Joe and I ate our fill of catfish and hushpuppies, I built up the fire so it burned a long time. I washed my dishes in the creek, using sand to clean the grease and grime off, rinsed the dishes off and put them back in my sack. I fished my poles one or two more times before I went to bed, and strung up the fish to take home.

Getting ready for bed consisted of: spreading my quilt over some leaves and moss in the washed out hole, pulling off my shoes, laying my rifle close by, laying down on part of the quilt and covering up with the other part. Joe curled up next to me and I was soon sound asleep. Sometimes Joe heard or smelled something, during the night. He started growling and his hair stood up on the back of his neck. I'd wake up and immediately reach for my gun. I felt like every hair on my head was standing up just like Joe's. I'd sit there with my .22-rifle, scared silly.

Sometimes, if Joe continued to growl, I'd yell and shoot my gun in that direction two or three times. That usually did the trick. Finally when Joe settled down I'd build the fire back up and crawl back into my quilt and lay awake thinking about all the old stories my grandmother told me about panthers eating people they caught away from home. On those nights, it would take a while for me to drop off to sleep. I never could have made it were it not for my prayers and old Joe.

At the crack of day, I got up and packed up to go home. I fished my hooks one last time and usually had a catfish on every pole. I put them on a string and marched home like a brave Daniel Boone with no one knowing just how frightened I had been. When my friends asked me if I was ever scared, I would lie and say, "No way, didn't bother me at all."

When I got home, Mama was very proud of me for bringing a big mess of catfish home for dinner. She bragged about her baby staying in that creek swamp all alone and how brave he was. She never knew the truth.

Later in a foxhole under live fire during Marine Corps training, I had no problem praying because I had learned in a washed-out stump hole on a creek bank.

Cousins Doyle and Barnard Pitts

I had two cousins living on a farm about a half mile from our house and every so often they walked across our field toward Wrights Creek. One of them had a corn sack over his shoulder that had a net in it. They strung the net across the creek and put stakes through the bottom of the net to hold it down on the bottom and tied the ends on either side of the creek.

These cousins Doyle and Barnard were three or four years older than me and they always invited me to go fishing with them. They caught big Red Horse Suckers that were really good eating. Dad finally agreed to let me go and my first trip was a memorable one.

We made camp much like I did when I was catfishing, but used no poles or hooks. These Red Horse Suckers were large and usually weighed five or six pounds each.

Red Horse Sucker

They ran up the creeks during the winter, and it was against the law to catch them by net. Doyle and Barnard said there was no worry since there was only one game warden in Holmes County and he was real old. "He can't catch us and besides he never comes out at night."

That first night I watched my cousins set the net. It was really cold and they made a big fire and told me to keep it burning big while they set the net. They took off their clothes and waded across the creek staking out the net. When they finished they raced back to the fire about to freeze. They hovered around the fire and got warm and dry and put their clothes back on.

After about two hours, one of them again undressed and went into the creek. He walked behind the net and let the current push the net into his legs as he waded along. When he felt a fish bump into his legs, he stopped and gently removed the fish from the net and brought it back to the shore. This went on until he had fished the entire net. Then he raced back to big fire. The other brother fished it the next time.

We cleaned one of the fish and fried it. One fish was so big that we only needed one to feed all three of us. The others we took home. The net was fished two or three times that night and usually two or three fish were caught each time. After eating and drinking and listening to their stories, we rolled out our blankets and went to sleep. The next morning another large fire was built and I kept it going while they fished the net and took it up.

About three weeks went by before I saw them again and I asked where they had been.

Doyle explained they almost got caught by the game warden. They were net fishing on another freezing cold night and he was warming by the fire when the game warden walked up and said, "Well, I finally caught you boys. Doyle, you just get in the creek and take up your net up son. We're going to have to go downtown. Both of you are under arrest."

Doyle said he just got in the creek, pulled the net up threw it over his shoulder, and just walked off on the other side of the creek into the woods.

The game warden shouted, "Doyle get back here with that net," and Doyle, naked in the freezing cold, just kept walking. He figured the game warden wouldn't get in that cold water and he was right.

In the meantime, Barnard grabbed Doyle's clothes and took off into the woods. The two waited until they heard the game warden start up his truck and leave. Doyle went back across the creek, dressed and they went home.

They decided to wait awhile before fishing their nets in case he was still trying to catch them. He didn't go get a warrant and then arrest them like they do in law enforcement now. Back then, if the law didn't bring the suspect in, they were out of luck.

The law against net fishing was passed primarily to prevent commercial fishermen from over-harvesting freshwater fish and/or selling them on the black market. So even though it was against the law, local farmers felt it was okay to net fish if it provided food for their families.

The game warden's actions taught me that some things aren't worth pursuing, especially in freezing weather in the middle of the night.

Adventures with Jake

This is the barn of one of my dad's cousins, Bill John Pitts, b.1891, and looks like the one where Jake took a leap.

The Parachute

When I was about nine or ten years old and living on the farm, my best friend was Lavohn Price. (I started calling him Jake when we were real young and he did the same with me.) Jake and I were playing out at the barn. The barn was a typical two-story barn where you pulled a wagon in and handed the bailed hay up to another person who stacked it upstairs in the loft.

When we bailed the peanuts and made up the hay, we filled the top of the barn with hay for the winter. This was used for our livestock during the cold months. The loft of the barn was also a favorite place for us kids to play.

On this day, no one was around but Jake and me. One of us came up with the idea of parachuting out of the loft of the barn with a homemade parachute. After discussing sheets and other possibilities, we agreed that a large umbrella would surely work. I rushed to the house and got Mama's big umbrella and brought it back. I convinced Jake to go first and I would go next. (Later in life I found Jake to be a very intelligent person. But on the farm, sometimes, I had my doubts. Of course, I have tried to forget the dumb things I did.) I don't know how I talked him into bailing out of the top of that barn with Mama's umbrella first, but I did and he did. If he had held out, I'm sure I would have gone first.

Old Jake ran down the floor of the loft and sailed out like a real paratrooper. He was holding the umbrella with both hands and went out in open space about fifteen feet above the ground. Jake probably broke the sound barrier on his way down. The umbrella turned inside out. It did nothing to slow him down. (My mom never did understand why her umbrella never worked after that.)

Jake hit the ground and probably left an impression in the dirt where he hit. He rolled around and cried, groaned and hollered for a while as I was doubled up laughing. After he finally got all his breath back and the dirt out of his mouth, ears and eyes, he picked up the umbrella and turned it right side out. He held it out to me and said, "Your turn."

I said, "No way. You ruined the umbrella now."

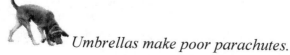 *Umbrellas make poor parachutes.*

(The more I thought about that venture, the more I became convinced Jake was not too smart. However, when we joined the

Marine Corps–another thing I talked him into–he scored higher on the IQ test than anyone else in our platoon. I wondered if somehow he cheated, but that was impossible. He eventually went on to college and earned his doctorate.)

Love Whippin's

Jake's mom and dad, Lovie Mae and H.L. Price, were a lot like my parents. They said they whipped us because they loved us so much. Before I was twelve years old, it sure seemed that my parents loved me much more than Jake's parents loved him.

Lovie & H.L. Price

(I know they loved me more than my sister. I can't remember a time that my sister got a whippin' and it's hard to remember a week when I didn't get at least one.)

I guess Jake was smarter and knew how to hide things better than I did. It's certain that we could never tell on each other without incriminating ourselves. (A pity I didn't know about the Miranda warning back then.)

It wasn't until I had six children of my own that I understood about love and punishment.

The Bull

Jake had a first cousin, Marion, who was a few years older than us. When she came to visit, she wouldn't stay in the house and play with his sisters. She wanted to hang out with the boys. That grieved us a great deal.

Jake's mom, Aunt Lovie Mae (she wasn't really my aunt, but I claimed her), insisted that we take Marion along.

One day, Marion went with Jake and me to a large pasture where cattle were grazing. There was no stock law. The only fencing was around the fields where we farmed to keep the cows out, not in.

In this pasture, there was a large mulberry tree where we went to eat mulberries when they were ripe. Across the pasture were several small trees and the remainder was just grass. We were really hurting for something to do. We couldn't go swimming, because we always went in the nude and we had this old girl with us. We couldn't do anything wrong, because we knew she would tell Jake's mom. So we wandered aimlessly across the pasture heading toward the large mulberry tree located in the center.

Jake decided we should catch a calf and ride it. He got close enough to grab a calf by the tail and the race was on. The calf ran for dear life with Jake holding on to the tail. The calf cried and started running faster and faster. Jake was going so fast he was afraid to turn loose. Marion and I were laughing like crazy until suddenly a big bull came charging out of the herd and headed for 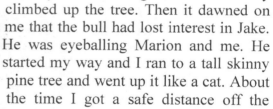 us. Jake hung on to the calf's tail until he got close to the big mulberry tree. He let go and immediately climbed up the tree. Then it dawned on me that the bull had lost interest in Jake. He was eyeballing Marion and me. He started my way and I ran to a tall skinny pine tree and went up it like a cat. About the time I got a safe distance off the ground, I felt the tree bending over. I looked down and that blamed girl was climbing up behind me, causing the tree to bend over.

I knew I was a lost soul. When I was about five or six feet off the ground I jumped off and headed for the mulberry tree. I knew that the bull was getting closer, so I ran like I never ran in my life. I could almost feel the hot breath of the bull on the back of my neck. I never looked back because I was determined to outrun that bull. If I failed, I was dead meat.

Jake was sitting on a limb, screaming, "Run, run, run! He's gaining on you. He's about to catch you!" I made the last few yards, jumped, grabbed hold of a low limb, and scrambled up that

He could see the bull

tree. When I caught my breath and looked back, that bull was nowhere in sight.

Jake almost fell out of the tree laughing. He could see the bull had stopped running after me, but chose not to share that information. He never missed a chance of doing a number on me when he could (but neither did I on him).

I'll always wonder if I could have really outrun that bull if he had kept coming. And Marion? I looked back and saw Marion sitting in the pine tree I had to vacate. The tree had straightened back up after I jumped off. She was perfectly safe with a smile on her face.

I learned that even a best friend can't be trusted completely.

Horse Racing

Jake and I lived about three miles from each other, but after we got horses we spent a lot more time together.

The big problem was Jake's dad bought him a mustang that was really beautiful and weighed about 700 lbs. That horse could run like the wind and was the envy of all the other boys.

Plow Horse

My horse, Maude, was a plow horse and weighed about 2,000 lbs. She had a mind of her own, was clumsy and very hard to handle. She could just be walking along and stumble and fall, throwing me over her head to the ground.

She was subject to do the same thing when I put her into a run. Sometimes if I hit the ground and didn't roll out of the way fast enough, she stepped on me as she was getting up. It was only by God's mercy she didn't kill me.

After the first race with Jake, I learned better than to run her against Jake's horse. If we decided to race, I had to have a big head start. One day we were about three quarters of a mile from my house and Jake wanted to race. I asked for at least a 100-yard head start and he agreed. The two-trail road to my house was straight most of the way, but came to a dead end and made a 90-degree left turn. Then the trail went on about three hundred feet to our barnyard gate in front of the barn.

The race started out okay except Jake lied. He didn't give me the head start he agreed to. He passed me about a hundred yards from the dead end and as he was making his turn, Maude decided to take a short cut. She headed through the woods and started for the barn straight as the crow flies. It was unbelievably thick through those woods. A normal horse couldn't walk through them much less run, but Maude did. I tried to turn her or stop her, but to no avail. I always rode bare back, so I lowered my head, got a handful of mane and hung on. I seriously thought we would hit a big tree and both be killed.

Somehow we made it through those woods and came out near the gate. She continued to run right up to the gate, suddenly put on brakes and I sailed over the gate into the barnyard, head first.

Jake, who had gotten there first, was laughing his head off. I was all scratched up on my face, arms, and hands. He accused me of trying to cut across and win the race. He didn't believe it was my horse's idea.

One day we were jumping ditches about two miles from home. We started off with small ditches. It became evident that Jake's horse was afraid of jumping a ditch, and I was elated because old Maude didn't mind and would jump. I went over a big ditch, and Jake was trying to get his horse to jump, and there was no way. I jumped back over and laughed while he tried to make his horse jump.

Finally he broke a switch, and seated on his horse he went up to the ditch and rapped the horse with the switch. Boy did that horse jump. The horse must have gone up ten feet higher than the ditch and sailed to the other side. When the horse landed Jake was not with him. There was a limb from a tree sticking out over the ditch really high up, but just low enough to catch old Jake under the chin and dump him into the ditch. I took off after his horse and left him lying in the ditch, crying and moaning.

Naturally the horse ran all the way back home and there was no way I could catch him until we he got back to the barn. I got the reigns and jogged back to where I left Jake. He was mad and dirty and called me some bad names for not staying to help him after he fell. I tried to explain, "Jake, I knew you weren't going anywhere but your horse was putting a lot of distance between us. I needed to catch him or we would have had to ride double back home."

Jake didn't appreciate my efforts. I couldn't wait to tell our friends how Jake looked as he took a swan dive from the horse into the bottom of that ditch. I imagine I got the same amount of pleasure he had telling about Maude dumping me. We were best friends and "pay back" just happened to be a part of that friendship.

I learned the same thing I did from the The Bull story above–a best friend can't be trusted completely.

Swimming

Before Jake and I got our horses we had to walk every place we went. One day we were down by the creek playing around and decided to go swimming. We both knew that was a "no-no" from both our parents because we were just learning to swim.

After discussing the situation and swearing each other to silence, we pulled off our clothes and went skinny-dipping. We had a great time because the water was cold, and it was really hot that day.

We finally started walking back to my house wearing our dry clothes. We were sure we had gotten away with a good one. When we got to my house, my mom was working in the yard. She looked at Jake and me and said, "You boys have been in that creek." We could not believe she knew, but we denied it. I don't know what happened to Jake, but she tore my butt up. I overheard her later telling my dad about the incident. He asked her the same question I had–how did she know? She told him our hair was still wet. That never crossed our minds.

We learned a valuable lesson that day. From then on, we dried our hair before we came home.

Childhood Pets

Joe watching me on Smokey, a horse my family acquired after my horse racing days with Maude, the plow horse.

Joe

Joe was a large red cur or mixed breed dog, and my faithful companion. My dad brought him home as a small pup. "Son, we are going to have us a catch dog for wild hogs and anything else that needs catching."

I was a small kid and Joe and I became best friends. Every place I went, Joe usually followed. He always raced ahead of me when I was walking or riding my horse. He never got too far away unless he jumped a hog or rabbit. I could always call him back and he cancelled the chase immediately.

When I set out catfish lines on Wrights Creek, he was my partner, protector and best friend, especially after dark. I was scared stiff after dark in the woods alone. Joe stayed close and we slept curled up in a washed out hole on a blanket when bedtime came.

I always carried my .22 caliber rifle with me and between Joe and my rifle I felt almost safe. My dad and I did a lot of wild hog

68

hunting after we harvested our crops. We always had a large field of peanuts that we used to fatten the hogs. There was no stock law in Florida at that time, so there were many wild hogs running loose in the swamps of Florida. If you raised hogs and lost some to the wild ones, you could register a claim in the county courthouse and legally hunt wild hogs with dogs or shoot them on sight.

Dad had a wild hog claim registered in the county courthouse and that gave him the right to catch any wild hog that did not have someone's mark on its ears and keep it. Each farmer had his brand registered at the courthouse and if you got caught with a pig with someone else's mark, you were in a heap of trouble. I'll never forget Dad's mark. It was a cross split in the right ear and two splits in the left ear. He gave me a mark that was the same as his but he added an under bit in the left ear.

When a farmer had a sow with a litter of pigs, one of the first things he did was mark their ears before they were old enough to go out in the field. Sometimes tame hogs took up with wild hogs and followed them off into the swamps.

We always planted twenty or thirty acres of peanuts and used the crop to make peanut hay for the cows and horses and to fatten hogs for market or for our own use. Once the crops were taken care of, Dad and I hooked the mule to a large sled, and took Joe along with Fanny to go on our annual hog hunt.

Fanny was our female mixed breed trail dog. All Dad had to do was find a hog track in the woods, lead Fanny to it on a leash, point to the track with his finger and take the leash off. She'd be off in a flash, barking about every third jump.

We caught many hogs that she tracked down. We kept Joe on a leash. Fanny continued barking and we tried to keep up as best as we could with the mule, sled, and Joe.

When she caught up with the hogs, she started baying them up. She changed from yelping every half minute or so, to a steady bark one after another. This meant the hogs had stopped running and had turned on her because she had them cornered. If they tried to run off, she nipped them on the back leg and they stopped, turned and charged her. She was quick and kept at a safe distance, but kept barking.

69

When Dad, Joe and I got close, Dad turned Joe loose and said "Get him, Joe," and Joe did just that. He caught the hog by the ear and as the hog turned, he kept his body next to the hog. Dad trained him to do this because the male hogs usually had large tusks running out each side of their mouth. If the dog got hold of the ear and stood in front of the hog, the hog lifted his head up quickly and ripped the dog open. A lot of hunters lost their catch dogs this way.

Dad had trained Joe well and he avoided the razor sharp tusks. When Joe caught the hog, Fanny usually grabbed the other ear. She never tried to catch a hog alone. She always waited on Joe.

Several people talked about a huge boar that roamed the woods and no dog could handle him. We were warned he was very dangerous and would kill a dog and attack a person if they got close. This hog was estimated to weigh between 300 and 400 lbs.

The day finally came when we met the big bad boar. Fanny tracked him up, with a small herd of other hogs. He turned on her, allowing the other hogs to continue on their way.

He stopped on a high bank overlooking Wrights Creek. When a dog bays up a hog like that, the hog will immediately start chomping his mouth open and closed. It makes a loud noise, clicking his teeth together, and means he is ready to fight. That was the biggest hog I had ever seen. He was black with a white stripe around him, just behind his shoulders. Each time he tried to take off, Fanny bit him on his hindquarters and he turned and tried to attack her. She stayed just out of his range.

Dad decided to try and catch him. He wanted to tame him and take him to market after the fattening process. Naturally the boar had plans of his own.

When Dad turned Joe loose, Joe did his usual thing. The hog started spinning around trying to get his large tusk into the dogs. Fanny stumbled over some vines, after grabbing an ear. The boar caught her in front of him and immediately hooked her with a tusk ripping her belly open. He threw her up into the air off the bank and into the creek several feet below.

Joe stumbled over some vines and fell off the hog's ear. The hog made a quick pass at Joe. He knocked one of Joe's eyes out and fled the scene. I grabbed Joe and Dad jumped out into the creek and grabbed Fanny who was trying to swim with most of her guts trailing along behind her.

Dad gathered her up in his arms and brought her back to the sled where he gently placed her guts back into her stomach. We picked up Joe, and headed home.

When we got home, Dad took an old spaying needle in the barn and sewed Fanny back together. He put burned oil all over the wound and made her a bed in the corn crib out of the weather. Believe it or not, Fanny lived and hunted again. There was not much Dad could do for Joe, so he had to live with one eye.

The next year we encountered that huge boar again. Fanny trailed him and Dad put a bullet between those big mean-looking eyes. That hog made us a lot of sausage and some good smoked ham and ribs. Joe continued to catch hogs and Fanny continued to trail them for several years to come.

Joe was king of the barnyard until Goosey came along.

 From Joe, I learned loyalty.

Goosey

Our next door neighbor, who lived on a farm about ¼ mile down the dirt road, had several geese. I thought they were beautiful. He knew I loved his geese and offered to give me one.

Mama and Dad said, "No way." Their reasons were that they made a mess of the barnyard, made a lot of noise and might fight the chickens. I was broken-hearted. The farmer told me to ask my mom if I could have an egg to put under one of our hens and raise a goose of my own. I was delighted and took the egg home. I neglected to tell Mama, assuming she would say no.

I climbed up in the barn where a big red hen was sitting on a nest of about twenty-one eggs. I thought one more wouldn't be noticed, so I eased it under her. What I didn't realize was the

71

goose egg was so big that it was the only one the hen could completely cover and keep warm.

The day finally came and a beautiful golden fur ball baby goose was hatched at the Pitts' farm. Not one of the chicken eggs hatched since she wasn't able to keep them warm. I think Dad saved my life when Mama realized what happened. Dad thought it was funny and talked Mama into letting me keep the goose. I named her Goosey.

That big red hen walked around the barnyard with that little fur ball running around behind her. The other chickens were truly concerned and kept their distance. After they determined there was no danger, they started picking on the little thing. The old hen did a good job protecting her baby and the baby stayed close to his adopted mom.

This baby kept growing. She was blue-gray in color and soon started going through the fence of the barnyard to catch bugs and grasshoppers in the fields. She never bothered the garden or our crops, so Dad was okay with her travels. I was afraid a hawk would catch her, but somehow she survived.

Besides loving that old red hen, Goosey loved me and we got along great. When I came home from school, she spotted me, squawked and ran to me with her wings spread out wide and tried to climb up in my lap.

As she grew larger, things started changing around the farm. All the chickens stopped picking on her and even the rooster stayed clear. Her mom, the big red hen, grew fearful of her and tried to steer clear of her, but that didn't work. Goosey chased her down and spread her huge wings around her mom and started squawking. The hen learned to just stop and lie down close to the ground and not move.

When the hen went to the laying mash trough, the goose made sure no other chicken came close. She and the hen ate alone. That goose could scoop up gobs of laying mash with her big beak. Mama was furious and got after Goosey with a broom. She said, "We have to get rid of that goose. We can't afford to pay all that money for laying mash that she won't let the chickens eat. She eats enough for ten chickens."

In those days, we had a bad problem with hawks catching our small baby chicks. Almost daily, a hawk swooped down from the big trees, grabbed a chick with its claws, and was gone in a matter of seconds. We always kept a shotgun close by, hoping to get a shot at a hawk. It was very seldom we actually killed one.

Goosey had gotten really big and now ruled the barnyard. We had a large female sow that was a good breeder and raised a large family of pigs each year. The bad thing was, the sow loved to eat chickens as much as any preacher. As a result of this we had to keep her penned away from the chickens in the barnyard.

One day the sow got out of her pen and immediately started chasing the chickens. They were screeching and squawking. Mama and I heard and ran to the barnyard. My goose also heard from the field where she was feeding and arrived about the same time Mama and I did.

Goosey came flying in, swooped down, and lit on top of that big sow. I just knew that was the last of my goose, but she stayed on top of that hog with her wings spread out wide, balancing herself. The hog spun around and around trying to dislodge her. That didn't work.

Goosey, in the meantime, was beating the stuffings out of the hog with her huge wings and squawking in her loud, shrill voice. Those wings had spurs on the inside and were very sharp.

Mama and I just stood and watched, not knowing what to do. Goosey kept whopping the sow with those spurs. The hog finally gave up and started squealing and headed back to her pen. The goose then lifted off her and dropped down to the ground in the middle of the barnyard and squawked real loud with both wings outstretched. She now had a wing spread of about five feet. She ran to me. I loved on her and told her she was a good girl.

Each night all the chickens went into the chicken house and hopped up on the roost Dad built for them when they slept. It was a small frame building that held thirty or forty chickens. It had a roof, walls and one open door for the chickens to come in and leave as they wanted.

This presented an ongoing problem for Goosey and her mom, the hen. The goose wanted to sleep under the old hen's wings as she did when she was a baby. She tried to crawl under her mom. The problem was she was several times larger than the hen and the hen was deathly afraid of her.

The goose got up on the roost and kept trying to get under her mother. Finally, the two ended up falling off on the ground. Then Goosey snuggled next to the hen. That is how they spent each night. Goosey had to be that old hen's worst nightmare.

When the goose was in the barnyard, no other chicken dared come close to that mother hen, especially the rooster. Even old Joe steered clear of my goose.

We had a mule, Jim, that was a good plow mule but mean as a snake. He tried to bite or kick me every chance he got. Dad tried to tell me that an animal could sense when a person was afraid of him. He told me not to show fear or the animal would take advantage. I told Dad the mule had guessed exactly right. I was afraid of him.

If the mule somehow got out of the barn and into the barnyard, he killed every chicken he could run down. We never let him loose in the barnyard and made his stall chicken-proof. If a chicken somehow made it into the mule's pen, it was dead in seconds.

One day the mule got out of the barn into the yard and started after the chickens... I probably left the gate unlatched when I fed him. The chickens shrieked and we all ran out thinking a hawk was after them. My dad was not home and I wanted nothing to do with that mule, because he and I did not like each other.

Suddenly, we heard a loud squawk. It was Goosey. She sailed into the barnyard from the field and onto the back of that mule. It was fun to watch. That mule bucked, farted, kicked and must have thought the devil had dropped out of the sky and lit on his back. He did everything in his power to dislodge that goose. Like the hog, Goosey stayed on top and beat him with the spurs of her wings.

This went on for some time until the mule finally raced to the other end of the barnyard and sailed over a high fence and into the corn field. The goose then left him and sailed back into the barnyard. She strutted around with her wings spread wide squawking loudly as if to say, "The winner and still champion." I was very proud of Goosey, the hero.

The goose did not just attack other animals. We had some visitors one Sunday afternoon and the kids made the mistake of chasing the chickens. Here came my goose. She nailed one of them good. They ran back to the house crying and telling their parents about the big chicken that had attacked them.

Mama had finally kind of accepted the goose. At least she had stopped threatening to have fried goose and dumplings for Sunday dinner. She was still upset about her eating habits, however. I had to guard the laying mash.

For a week or so we had lost several small chicks to the hawks. Mama sometimes sat outside with her shotgun to try and get a shot at the hawk, but never did. One morning as my goose was about to leave for her daily jaunt to the fields, the hawk struck, picked up a large chick and started flying out to the woods. When the hawk reached the power lines that ran by our house, my goose met him in the air.

The fight was on. Hawk feathers flew, the chick was released and the hawk was last seen headed toward the swamp. As far as I know, that was the last chick we lost to a hawk.

Mama witnessed the entire event and she couldn't wait to tell all her friends about the encounter. From that day on my goose was the most welcome critter on the farm as far as my mom was concerned.

She was a good home guard also. When night came, she always stayed with her mom in the chicken house. If any kind of varmint came around like a coon, fox, stray dog or family visitors, she alerted everyone at the house with loud screeches of alarm.

We went out to check the uninvited visitor. She made believers out of all our friends who visited our home. Word got around to beware of the goose at the Pitts' home, especially if you came by after dark.

You may have heard of the old saying about the fox getting in the hen house, but that was never a problem on our farm, not with Goosey around.

From Goosey, I learned love and faithfulness.

Jim

When I was seven or eight, my Dad bought Jim, a young

untrained black mule. He said, "We need a plow mule really bad. This one is cheap because he's never been trained to pull a plow or work the field."

All this was true and we soon found out Jim had a mind of his own. He was only afraid of my Dad and my goose. He never crossed either of them.

The first time I met Jim, I didn't like him. I had wanted a horse to ride for a long time and Dad said we couldn't afford one. So instead we got a mule. I was told I could break the mule to ride, and ride him with my friends. I could just see myself riding a long-eared jackass while my friends rode their sleek beautiful horses.

We stood and stared at each other for a few minutes. Probably the only thing we ever agreed on was that we disliked each other. But my dad saw him as his pride and joy. Since Jim was bigger, stronger and much smarter than me, it placed me at a great disadvantage.

When Dad and I were plowing in the field, Jim was a model plow mule with a halo over his head. If Dad went to the house or left the field for something, Jim changed into a beast with horns or the devil himself. He would not listen to my commands. If I walked by him and got a little close, he tried to bite me.

One day Mama sent me to the barn to get something. I ran to the barn door, opened it and found myself staring into the north end of that mule while he was looking south. Before I could back out the door, he cut loose with a hind foot that caught me in the middle of my stomach. I remember flying out of the barn door and landing on my back. I wanted to yell for my mom, but couldn't get breath to yell. I started thinking I was going to die on my back in the barnyard. And one of my biggest regrets was that I was going to die before I could figure out a way to get rid of that mule.

When I got a little breath, I yelled at the top of my voice, which brought Mama flying out to me. All Dad said was, "Son, walk up behind any animal sudden like, and they might hurt you." Some of the words of wisdom from my father I never forgot.

As I mentioned earlier, Big Jim loved to kill chickens. Dad had to patch holes in Jim's stall frequently so a chicken couldn't accidently wander into Jim's place. One day Dad was down on his knees driving stakes in a hole under the wall in Jim's stall.

Jim was standing behind Dad watching just like me. Dad was packing dirt around the stakes with a hammer handle when Jim, real easy like, reached down and got a mouth full of Dad's shoulder. Dad didn't say a word. He just turned slightly and cracked Jim between the ears with the hammer. Old Jim hit the ground flat on his back. I thought for sure he was dead.

But just when I thought I could celebrate, that sucker revived and stood up. He staggered across the pen and leaned against the wall and never took his eyes off Dad. He never offered to bite him again either.

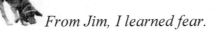 *From Jim, I learned fear.*

Ruth, Mama, Dad and LaVelle, 1942

Spooky

My sister, Ruth, had a goat named Spooky. The two things I remember the most about him was that he loved my sister more than anything in the world. The other thing was he hated me as much as he loved my sister.

When Ruth came home from school and got off the bus, that goat ran to meet her like she was his mama. When I walked out of the house, he came after me like I had a target painted on my bottom.

We had a smokehouse in our backyard, and it had a small chicken house built next to it. When that goat caught me and flattened me, he raced over, jumped on the chicken house, and then on top of the smokehouse. He stood up there and brayed like a mule.

I wish he had come along later when I had Goosey. I had no one to protect me except Mom or Dad. When they were with me, he didn't dare come close. When I wanted to go outside, I peeked out the window and tried to locate that goat. I had to make sure he was far enough away from my destination, so I could make it before he caught me.

My dad kept saying that we had to get rid of that goat, but my sister begged him not to and he kept putting it off. One day when Mama and Dad were busy, I ventured out and raced for the barn. The goat was hiding. He raced out from some bushes and caught me halfway to the barn. As usual, he flattened me out and I screamed.

Dad looked out and came outside with his shotgun. The goat raced to the smokehouse and went up on top and started braying. Dad cut loose with his shotgun and blew him off the top of the house. He was dead before he hit the ground.

You would have thought my sister had lost a best friend, and I guess she had, but I was glad to see the old boy go. I don't think she ever forgave my dad.

 From Spooky, I learned caution.

Flossie

My dad was a holiness preacher and pastored a church called New Smyrna Assembly of God. This church was located near Wrights Creek. It was about two or three miles from our farm. Occasionally, he loaded the family up in the 1940 Ford and went on an evangelistic trip. This usually occurred after the crops were gathered. I remember changing schools two or three times a year. I didn't study very much because we were in a different book at every school I entered.

On one of these trips we stopped at a service station and gassed up. There was a baby coon tied to a stake in the ground with a sign that read, "For Sale, $1.00." I started jumping up and down, begging Dad and Mama to buy that coon for me. They told me no, but when we started driving off, I really started boo-hooing. Dad stopped, turned around and went back and bought that coon for me. Mama was furious and Ruth remained neutral for the most part.

I don't remember what age I was, but it was before I started to school. I named the coon Flossie. Mama and that coon had a relationship like Jim and I. Neither one liked the other. Mama really disliked Flossie, and Flossie was scared to death of my mom and her big broom.

I found out that coons are very curious and very smart. I walked outside one day with food in my hand. Flossie was tied to a tree on a long rope. She came to me and I put the food in my pocket so I could pet her. She climbed up my leg put her front paw in my pocket and took my food out. She got down, carried the food to her water dish, washed then ate it.

This started a big game between the two of us. I brought something out in my pocket. She raced to me, climbed up my leg and dug it out. If I didn't have food in my pocket, she took whatever I had–knife, change, keys, etc.–washed it and tried to eat it. If she couldn't eat it or if I didn't have anything in my pocket, she bounced up and down squawking and throwing a temper tantrum like a little kid. It was dangerous to get too close to her when she got mad. She was subject to bite you.

We were staying in a little town near Pensacola where Dad was preaching. No one paid much attention to Flossie but me. I fed her, watered her and walked her around and no one else bothered with her.

Mama and Dad laughed at how she took food from my pocket. It was real cute until a visiting preacher stopped by our house for dinner. He walked over where Flossie was lying. She was not tied that day, because she wouldn't leave the yard.

Before anyone could warn him, Flossie captured him by the leg and started climbing up. This was a tall long-legged preacher. He hollered real loud and danced around, shaking his leg, trying to loose himself from that coon. The more he shook his leg and hollered, the tighter Flossie hung on. I think Flossie was about as scared as the preacher and afraid to turn loose.

Dad raced out to help rid the preacher of the coon. He had trouble catching him as he was circling the yard at a rapid pace. As for me, I was doubled over laughing like crazy. For this, I got a serious reprimand after the preacher left our house, which wasn't very long. I was also ordered to put the leash back on Flossie.

Flossie really loved cats and tried to play with them or hold them, but they were deathly afraid of her. She had a long rope on her where she could wander around about twenty feet from the tree. If Flossie saw a cat coming, she hid, keeping the tree between the cat and her. When the cat was real close, Flossie jumped out, grabbed the cat and, like the preacher's leg, she hung on for dear life.

That cat went completely bananas—screeching and fighting, biting and yelling. You thought the cat was dying. This wasn't true because Flossie never tried to hurt the cat. She just wanted to love on him. Flossie hung on until the cat clawed and bit her to the point she let the cat go.

With dogs it was different. She knew the dog was her enemy. When she saw a dog, she immediately climbed the tree and stay there until the dog went away.

A coon will always try to wash their food before they eat. I got the bright idea of putting a piece of light bread in my pocket and letting Flossie take it out. She ran over to her big pan of water and put the bread in and dipped it up and down two or three times. The bread dissolved after the first or second dip. Flossie took her front paws out of the water, looked at them and reached back in the water to feel around for the bread. Then she really got upset.

When Dad finished his preaching assignments, we finally made it back to the farm. By this time, Flossie was a full grown coon. We didn't have a dog at that time, and she had the run of the farm. I think Mama agreed to that in hopes Flossie would leave and find another home in the woods.

Each morning I had to go out to the barn and milk two cows and tend to the other stock. When I got through milking, I brought the milk back and placed it on the kitchen table near the back door. Mama strained the milk, put it in a large jug and let it down in the well at the end of the porch to keep it cool.

81

One morning I set the milk on the table and walked over to the other side of the kitchen for something and heard Mama yell. I turned and saw Flossie sitting by the milk bucket with her arm in the bucket feeling around for some food. Mama grabbed a big wood handle broom and swung with all her might. It caught Flossie as she was jumping off the table and sent her on a line drive through the open back door into the yard.

This wasn't the first time Flossie had been expelled from the house with that broom. I think Flossie finally had enough. She never came back after that. I guess she went into the creek swamp where there were a lot of other friends like her and none of them had brooms.

Flossie taught me that you better not mess around in Mama's kitchen.

Junior the Big Bully

When I was five, my family moved from the farm in Bonifay to Panama City in the Millville area. My dad worked at the Wainwright Shipyard during the day and worked on building a house at Highway 98 and Maple Ave in Millville at night. I

Home in Millville on Hwy 98.

held a light while Mom and Dad built.

Dad's sister was divorced and lived next door. She had four boys. The three older ones were fine boys. The youngest, Junior, was about five or six years older than me and mean as a junkyard dog. He delighted in whipping up on me anytime he caught me outside alone.

I checked as best as I could when I went outside to determine if he was anywhere around. Sometimes I got carried away and forgot to check the area every few minutes and he slipped up and cut me off from the house. He usually clobbered me before I could get past him.

One day he worked on me and I raced into the house crying and wondering how long it would be until I got big enough to whip Junior. While I was thinking along these lines, I happened to notice my Daisy 500 BB gun I got for Christmas sitting in the corner. The idea hit me, with my BB gun I just might be big enough now. I grabbed it and raced outside.

Junior was walking out of our yard and turned and noticed the BB gun. Instead of running to his house, he climbed a big sycamore tree in the back yard. He went up about ten feet, laughed and said, "Come and get me."

I just leveled off and plunked old Junior on the big part of his tail end. He screamed like a panther and climbed another ten feet straight up. I took another shot and he really started screaming. After a couple more shots for good measure, I told him, "If you hit me again, I'll wait for you every day with my gun. Every time you come out of your house I'll shoot you." He made all kinds of promises and agreed to abide by my rules.

I returned to the house and knew when my parents came in and my aunt told them what happened, I would get a good whipping. They did, and I did, but it was one of the few whippings I got that was worth every lick I received. Junior never hit me again either.

I learned that a Daisy BB gun is more powerful than a big bully.

Early Schooling

I failed miserably in school as I was growing up. Though Mama and Dad had very little education, they did their best to encourage my sister, Ruth, and me to take advantage of school and get a good education.

Ruth did exactly that. I remember her sitting up late at night and studying by an old kerosene lamp. Mama and Dad were always worried she would damage her eyes, but she paid no attention and studied all the time.

They didn't have to worry about me hurting my eyes, I went to bed with the chickens and got up with them before day each morning to do my daily chores. I loved to use the excuse that I had to do my home chores and had no time to study. That was not true and deep down inside I knew that. I did everything I could to keep from studying my books.

I went to a little country school about three miles from our farm. The school was known as the New Smyrna Elementary School. There were two large rooms identical in size with desks for the first through the fourth grades in one room and the fifth through the eighth in the other room.

Each room had a 55-gallon barrel in the center of the room with a stove pipe running up through the top of the ceiling. There was a teacher's desk in the front of the room and a big closet behind her desk. She used this as the spanking room. If she didn't want to walk that far and was really upset, she tuned our engine right where she grabbed us in the classroom.

On the wall was a large blackboard where I learned to hate school. I have a vivid memory of trying to learn multiplication tables. The teacher, Ms. Sapp, stood at the board with her big paddle. It looked more like a boat paddle than a school paddle. She called each of us up to the board and told us to recite our multiplication tables starting with twos and going to twelves. When we missed one, she'd hit us on the butt with that big paddle.

When she called me up to the board, I knew what was coming. If she started with me no one else got a lick, because by the time she got through with me she was worn out and my bottom felt like a raw piece of beef.

I never told my mom or dad because I feared another whipping. They always told me if I got a whipping at school, I would get another when I got home. They believed the teacher was always right. I think my old bottom was by far the toughest part of my body. If my mom and teachers had heard of the "time out" system used today, it could have saved me a lot of wear and tear.

The teacher taught spelling the same way. She gave you a word and you had to write it on the blackboard. If you misspelled the word she whacked you with that paddle. I did everything I could to sound the words and spell them, but to no avail.

My mom and dad taught me many things about life and hard work, but they didn't know much about books, only the Bible. My dad could not read very well. When he preached, my mom sat near him, read a verse out loud, and he expounded on the scripture. They were a good team.

Dad went to the fourth grade and had to drop out of school because his dad died. He and his older brother had to farm full-time to support his mom and the other seven kids. My mom completed the eighth grade.

During the first years of my schooling, our family traveled all over the state while Dad ran revivals. I went to a lot of different schools. I never attended a school that used the same books or taught the same thing I was studying at my prior school. That killed my motivation, but apparently made my sister study even harder.

I could never seem to understand how to spell or do my multiplication tables. I was embarrassed to ask for help, because I didn't want people to think I was dumb. In my math I had to rely on my fingers. I understand that many of the teachers I had were only high school graduates, so I guess they lacked the skills to help me.

I should have asked Ruth to help me, but didn't. I know I tested her patience and figured she wouldn't want to help me, but one thing I did learn from her was to run fast.

This was crucial in dealing with her, especially when Mom and Dad were gone. For a time Mama and Daddy worked in

Panama City at the Wainwright Shipyard on the Liberty Ships during World War II.

Mama was a tacker, and Daddy worked as a finish carpenter. An old man had a pick-up truck with a homemade wooden top and bench seats underneath. For a few dollars a week he transported several people to work each morning and brought them home each night. They left before daylight and returned after dark.

This 1943 photo would have been taken during the time Mother and Daddy worked at the shipyard. The Germans destroyed a number of our supply ships. As a result, extra workers were called in to work around the clock. The pay was good and a lot of the farmers and their wives were grateful for the work. My mother, who had always worn dresses, put on overalls for the first time. This ship is number seventeen of the 102 ships that were built at Wainwright Shipyard during WWII. (Photo from *Along the Bay: A Pictorial History of Bay County* by Marlene Womack, 1994)

That meant Ruth and I had to handle things at home. I did the outside chores and she did the inside. If I made her mad, I turned on the "after burner" and usually escaped to the hay loft. I knew she wouldn't follow me in the barn. If she cut me off from the barn, I headed out for open country. She kept me in good shape. I could run like a deer, so she never caught me. If she had, I probably wouldn't be writing this story now.

Ruth taught me the importance of speed.

The Assembly of God Church we attended in Millville

I often say I got hooked on drugs at an early age. From the cradle until I graduated from high school, Mama drug me out of bed Sunday morning, drug me to Sunday school and church and then drug me back on Sunday night. She drug me to Wednesday night service and when we had a revival, she drug me to church every night.

I obtained Bible education in church and another kind of education outside the church, listening to the older boys talk. Most everything I learned about sex, getting drunk, smoking and wild women was from older boys standing around talking in the church yard. Sex was considered a very bad word and was never used in our home. Mom and Dad never talked to Ruth or me about such things.

When God Spoke to Me

The farmer who gave me the goose egg was a good man and always had time to talk to me. He spent a lot of time answering dumb questions. Almost every visit he somehow brought Jesus into the conversation and he did it in such a loving way. I never resented him telling me things God had done for him, and how great it was to know he was going to heaven. I can't even remember his name, but his witness made a real impression on me.

Not long after my twelfth birthday, I had an experience that I will never forget. I walked to and from school each day, about three miles each way. I took a shortcut and crossed Wrights Creek to save about one-half mile. If we had lots of rain the creek was

87

too full to cross and I had to go around by the bridge, which took a lot longer.

Rev. D.E. Pitts and his congregation. Mama is 3rd from left on 2nd row. Ruth is in front and to the right of Mama. I am in a white t-shirt, front middle.

On this day as I was coming home from school, I really felt God was speaking to me about getting my life straight with the Lord. My dad was a pastor of the New Smyrna Assembly of God Church. I heard him preach many times and saw a lot people go forward when he gave altar call. But all his sermons never impacted me like the witness of our farmer neighbor. How could that be when I loved my dad with all my heart? More likely I was touched by the influence of both men.

I knelt down on the creek bank and started crying as I prayed. I asked the Lord to forgive me of my sins. I suddenly felt a strange and great feeling come over me. I experienced a great peace that is hard to explain. It was like I was almost walking above the ground about two or three feet.

I went on home and wanted to tell someone, but I got cold feet. As time went on, I gradually drifted back to my old habits. Throughout my life I can look back now and see many times when I was in a life and death situation, and somehow I managed to do the thing that kept me alive. I chalked it up to luck. Now I see it was not luck. I believe God was just not through with me, and intervened on a regular basis as I grew up.

I may have put God on the "back burner," but thankfully He never left me.

HIGH SCHOOL YEARS
(1949-1953)

Bay County High School
(Photo from *Along the Bay: A Pictorial History of Bay County*
by Marlene Womack, 1994)

My dad let me try out for the football team in Bonifay when I was in the 7th grade. The coach looked me over and said, "Son, you are too small. Come back next year." The same thing happened in the 8th grade. The beginning of my 9th grade year in Bonifay, the same Coach Davis said the same thing. He never gave me a chance.

I went home broken-hearted and Dad said, "Son, we are thinking about moving back to Panama City and maybe you can make it there."

I finally did make the team. At Bay High, football became my one and only desire. Bay was a 3-A school and Bonifay was a Class C school. The big difference was the coaches. Bonifay was looking for big mean boys that had a lot of talent. The Bay High

91

coach was looking for a warm body that could take a hit and get up and keep going. This was easy for me with past experiences like my horse throwing and stomping on me.

Suddenly football became everything I ever wanted. All else was a distant second and took a back seat.

The day I started at Bay High School in the 9th grade, I knew no one. I was a little fish in a big pond. We rented a house just outside of Lynn Haven on Highway 77. I rode a bus to school and hitchhiked home after football practice. People were usually good about giving a kid a ride back then.

The Night I Met "Tree"

On or about October 12, 1951, on a Friday night I trotted on the football field in Phoenix City, Alabama. I was playing first-string left tackle for Bay High School–all 140 pounds of me. The reason for me being the first string tackle was that Pelham, the 250 lb. first-string guy, broke his leg the week before. I guess I was the only one on our team that was expendable so Coach McKinney moved me to tackle until Pelham got well.

BAY HIGH END — LaVelle Pitts has played good football all year as an end on the Bay High team. (Staff Photo).

Football photo in News Herald 1952

We received the kick off and when I walked up to the line for our first offensive play, I looked directly into the eyes of the ugliest, meanest, nastiest and biggest guy I'd ever seen on a football field. He weighed over 300 lbs., was about 6'5" and had a big chew of tobacco with a little running out both corners of his mouth. His teammates called him "Tree."

He kept looking around for the real tackle to walk up. When it dawned on him that I was it, he looked at me, grinned and said, "Shhh-it."

I started thinking, "Why me, Lord? Why couldn't it have been me who broke a leg instead of Pelham?"

When the ball was snapped, Tree swiped me out of the way with a big hand and grabbed our quarterback with his other hand before he could hand off the ball.

Back then we played both ways (offense and defense) and when they got the ball things didn't get any better. I tried everything I could to stop that guy. I held him, tackled him and clipped him. Nothing worked. My good friend, John Bynum, was linebacker that night. His position was directly behind me. John was much bigger than me, weighing about 200 lbs.

Bynum came over during a time out and said, "Pitts, you are going to have to do something about that tackle. He's about to kill me."

I said, "You should be grateful he has to run over me before he gets to you. At least that slows him down a little."

I offered to swap positions with Bynum but he said, "No thanks."

I wish I could say things got better, but they only got worse. There was a happy ending, however. The game finally ended and Bynum and I were still alive.

Things never get so bad that they can't get a little bit worse. If you don't know that, you never met "Tree."

The Tuscaloosa Black Bears

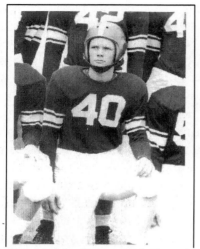

LaVelle, #40 for the Bay High Tornadoes

Playing linebacker for Bay High School was really tough in the 50s. We played some of the biggest schools in Alabama, Georgia and Florida. One such game was played in Tuscaloosa, Alabama, with the Black Bears. As I recall, they were the top-rated team in Alabama at the time. They had a quarterback who was "Mr. Everything" and could beat you almost single-handed.

We were warming up in the end zone when the Black Bears started running on the field. It was their homecoming and it seemed like everyone in Alabama showed up for the game. We all stopped warming up and watched as the crowd cheered, and they just kept coming on the field. We found out later they dressed out over 100 guys for the game.

You had to know our coach. He was a very tough taskmaster. He noticed we were watching the other team and yelled at us to stop watching and continue to warm up. He said, "Don't worry about numbers. They can only put eleven men on the field at the time."

Well that was true and every time we looked up they had a new eleven on the field and they were just as good as the last eleven or better.

Prior to the kick-off the coach told me, "Son, I have a special assignment for you. This quarterback that is supposed to be so good, I want you to hit him on every play. It doesn't matter if he has the ball or not. I want to see him on the ground."

I said, "Even if he's handed the ball off or passed it?"

He said, "Yes, I want him on the ground."

94

Well, the first play of the game the quarterback handed off the ball and I went right by the ball carrier and nailed the quarterback. He smiled and got up. The next play he threw a pass and while he was standing watching the flight of the ball, I nailed him good. He frowned at me as though to say, "Boy, you must be blind." This went on through the first quarter and it was really beginning to get on the quarterback's nerves. Even the crowd was picking up on it.

When the second quarter started, the quarterback ran an option play around the end and tossed the ball to his half-back who was following him. He looked over his shoulder and saw me coming like gangbusters so he headed for the sidelines, but he slowed down and I nailed him good right in front of his bench. His coach jumped up and down like a Cuban shortstop and yelled at the referee.

The referee came over to me and said, "Son, the next time you run that quarterback down and tackle him and he doesn't have the ball, I am penalizing you 15 yards."

I passed this information on to our coach and he said, "Well, use a little more discretion, but if there is any doubt hit him." I really felt stupid, but I guess it worked somewhat. Every time that quarterback handed off or threw the ball for the remainder of the game, he was twisting his head around looking for that crazy linebacker from Bay High.

It didn't help a whole lot, because the Black Bears were still number one when we left Alabama that night, even though the quarterback had a poor game of running the ball himself. We left there wondering if we played the Black Bears or the Crimson Tide.

For me, Coach's advice "not to worry" remains a classic example of understatement.

The Hanging of Stonewall

In 1952, Bay High was the largest of only two high schools in the county. The other was Rosenwald, the black high school. We were segregated in those days.

Since Bay High was the largest school in the area, we had to go a long way to play teams of comparable size. We traveled to places like Mobile, Tuscaloosa, Dothan, Eufaula and Phoenix City in Alabama. In Florida, we played in Jacksonville–Bolls Military, Miami–Edison, Tallahassee and Pensacola, Florida. We made some very long bus rides on a Greyhound bus. Going to a game was usually very quiet, with the exception of one or two guys who always wanted to be the center of attention. Coming back was usually quiet, especially if we lost. If we won, it was loud for a few miles and then everyone tried to sleep and rest tired bodies.

Again the same one or two never seemed to relax. One of the biggest violators of our quiet time was our center, Jackson, who nicknamed himself, Stonewall. He was a happy go-lucky guy who loved to pull pranks, tell jokes and never had a serious moment until…

We were coming back from Mobile, Alabama, one night after playing in Ladd Stadium. We were really tired and trying to sleep–all except Stonewall. He made the mistake of going to the back of the bus where the upperclassmen sat. They were usually the ones who played the hardest and were the most beat up.

One of our senior backs, J.J. McCrary warned Stonewall two or three times to go away and shut up. He would, but in a few minutes was back running his mouth, laughing, and telling jokes.

I noticed J.J. huddled up with two or three others. The next time Stonewall came back they grabbed him, lifted him off the floor and spread him across the top of the seats in the back of the bus. One held his hand over his mouth so he couldn't yell and others held him by his legs and arms.

J.J. un-zipped his trousers, took a shoelace, tied one end around his penis and the other end of the shoelace to the overhead baggage rack. They turned Stonewall loose and immediately all you could hear was a blood-curdling scream from Stonewall. He had to push up on the seats with both feet and both arms to get any slack in the shoelace. Then he had no way to untie the string.

Everyone on the bus was laughing except Stonewall and the coaches who were trying to fight their way from the front seat to the back of the bus through about 38 football players. The coaches finally got through and cut the shoestring. Needless to say no one knew who did this terrible deed. As I recall we did do some extra wind sprints, but it was worth the cost.

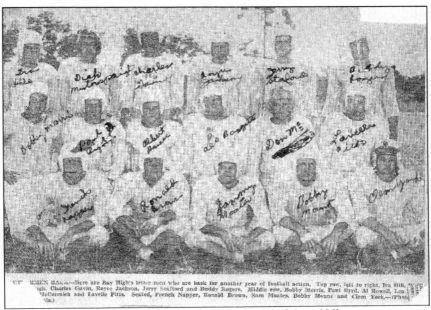

Bay High lettermen, LaVelle on right end of the middle row.

We had peace and quiet on the remainder of the trip home. But there was an occasional groan from Stonewall, and an eruption of laughter from the rest of the team that broke the silence now and then.

When a bunch of tired football players tell you to knock it off, pay attention.

Other Activities and Sports during High School

LaVelle, 1951

A Lynn Haven barber gave me my first barber shop haircut. Each week he gave a free haircut to the outstanding Bay High football player in the Friday night game. Up to then, my dad cut my hair so this was a special treat. I worked hard to earn the privilege of a "store-bought" haircut.

I especially appreciated the barber-cut if I had a date after a football game. My dad agreed I could drive his Studebaker pick-up truck, but insisted I be home by 11:00, or no future use of his truck. I was able to convince him to extend the curfew to 11:30 if the game lasted longer than usual.

So, after a game if I had a date, I rushed to the locker room, showered, changed, met my date at the goal posts and hurried to my dad's truck. The date usually consisted of driving to Tally-Ho at the corner of Harrison and Hwy. 98, where we chatted over a hastily eaten hamburger and shake. I dashed to get her home, with no time to tarry at her door, and headed home.

Tally-Ho Drive-In

98

My dad pastored the Assembly of God Church in Lynn Haven. After football season my first year at Bay High, my Dad finagled a job for me from a member of his church, Sister Holmes. Her family owned Holmes Fish Market on 6th Street in downtown Panama City. This was my first public job and I worked with an elderly black man in the basement of the fish house. The first floor had a large glass show case with ice spread from one end to the other. On top of the ice were mullet, grouper, snapper, sheephead, and shrimp.

Most of our business was mullet. The customer made his purchase, the fish were weighed, placed in a pan and sent down to us on a metal slide to the basement. This was accompanied by, "Dress them up," shouted by the upstairs clerk over the intercom. We scaled and filleted the fish, placed them in the pan and sent them back up where they were wrapped and given to the customer.

The black man, Joseph, was not only my teacher on how to clean fish and fillet them, but he also became one of my best friends. He was very good at cleaning the customer's fish. He insisted that I do the same. When we filleted the mullet, we cut the back bone out and he insisted that there be very little meat left on the back bone. He said, "It needs to be so thin you could read the newspaper through it."

One of the highlights of my job came at noon when all the walk-ins slowed down and we ate lunch. Joseph filleted two mullet, dusted them in cracker meal, sprinkled them with salt and pepper and placed them in an old frying pan on a two-burner hot plate he kept stowed away in the basement. We got a loaf of bread and a couple of drinks from upstairs and had a great lunch.

There was a dock next to the fish house and the fishing boats came in and off-loaded and weighed their catch right in the fish house. The crews on these boats were usually paid by the boat captains as soon as the fish were weighed. Then various crew members headed for the nearest bar for a good drunk.

The boats came in on Thursday or Friday afternoon and left again on Monday after the boat captains went by the jail and bonded out or paid fines for most of his crew. They were a sorry looking mess when they got back to the fishing boats. Food and cigarette supplies were loaded on the fishing vessels and they were off for another week or so.

Churches and civic clubs, as well as politicians, sometimes bought 500 to 1,000 pounds of mullet for fish fries. I hated to see an order like that come in. It meant staying real late, cleaning all the fish and icing them down before they were picked up. Preacher Hunt was our biggest customer locally for his church fish fries.

About one time each month, we sent out several barrels of iced-down mullet to New York. The first to go into the barrels were the older mullet. All the fresh fish was kept for the local traffic.

My paycheck was twelve to fourteen dollars a week. That was for working six days a week about ten hours a day, unless there was a big fish fry or shipment going out. In that case, we stayed until the job was completed. There was no such thing as overtime pay.

My second public job was Jitney Jungle Food Store #3 in St. Andrews. Mr. L.D. Lewis was the owner and I learned a great deal of good work ethics from Mr. Lewis. This man was a self-made successful business man. He demanded a day's work for a day's pay. He had store hours, but his policy was that as long as one customer was in the store you did not close up.

Mr. Lewis had several stores and visited them regularly. He later changed the name of the stores to Sunshine. One of the things that impressed me about him was that he jumped in and helped out if things were busy. He would run a cash register, stock the shelves and many times work in the produce department.

I was a bag boy and made about sixteen dollars a week. It was a much better job than the fish market and smelled much better. After I bagged groceries for about three weeks, Mr. Lewis came by the store one afternoon. When he visited the produce department, something was wrong and he fired the produce manager. He called me back and asked if it was true that I grew up on a farm. I replied, "Yes, sir." He said, "Well, you are my new produce manager."

He gave me a crash course on ordering produce and how to display it. I also went to $26 dollars a week. I thought I had hit it rich. This check, like the fish house check, was passed on to my mom when I got home.

I never cashed one of my payroll checks, but at the end of the summer my dad bought me a new Matchless motorcycle

Some of my motorcycle buddies, George Jordan, Jerry Reid, and Hugh Crosby

from money I had made during the summer. I now had a ride to school and home from football practice.

I also participated in community baseball teams made up of boys and some grown men from communities such as Southport, Callaway, West Bay, Lynn Haven or just anyone who could get up a team. We made a few phone calls and maybe had a game on Saturday afternoon in Southport or wherever we could find a field to play.

We had some wild games. We usually picked umpires from the crowd and the games really got rough. Most all ended up in a good fight or two and sometimes both teams ended in a free-for-all. (During football season we also had some community football games the same way.)

I played in one baseball game for Lynn Haven against Southport on the school grounds at Southport Elementary School. This was a real tight, hard-fought game. Going into the 9th inning Southport was ahead by one run and my Lynn Haven team came to bat.

Our first batter got on base with a single and the next two struck out. Don McCormick came to bat. He was our cleanup batter and could really smack the ball. He hit a ball into deep left field over the head of the left fielder and into some big oak trees on the edge of the woods.

101

Don circled the bases with the winning run while the left fielder located the ball hung up in a big oak. He was throwing sticks and rocks at it to try and get it down. We were gathering up our gear getting ready to go home when the guy knocked the ball out of the tree and caught it before it hit the ground. The umpire, who was from Southport, was standing around and noticed the guy knock the ball out of the tree and yelled, "The batter is out."

There was a large crowd gathered. A lot of people showed up to watch the fight that usually took place sometime during the game. When that umpire called Don out, the crowd got to see a really good fight. Most all the players were fighting and some of the crowd joined in. We still believe we won the game, but I have my doubts about who won the fight.

Another time we played Southport in a community football game. It was a tackle and hard-hitting game. There were several fishermen, grown men, on the Southport team. Most of the Lynn Haven team was made up of Bay High football players.

Needless to say we were clobbering them. The crowd started throwing oyster shells at our players and we finally had to stop the game. Those shells hurt when they hit you.

On some weekends, several boys went to the Panama City Country Club, hoping to get to caddy for some of the golfers. Occasionally, we hooked up with a big spender who tipped us two or three dollars in addition to the caddy fee of two or three dollars.

Panama City Country Club
(Photo courtesy of Bay County Public Library)

102

After the golfers were gone, the caddies chose up sides to have a tackle football game. There were about as many black as white boys, so we usually had both on each team. That's where I first competed with blacks. We never had any problems and even made some lasting friendships.

One black kid I met, I met again 25 years later. He was working at a large motel on the beach and remembered with fondness those football games and helped me in my campaign for Sheriff of Bay County.

There's another black man that I remember. He was well thought of in the Lynn Haven community. He had a mule and wagon with a plow in the wagon which he hauled around the Lynn Haven area and broke up small areas for gardens. He was a popular guy come garden time in Lynn Haven.

A group of kids, not ones that I ran with, got that wagon one Halloween night and pulled and pushed it across town to the Lynn Haven Elementary School. There they took the wagon apart, and piece by piece, carried it up a ladder onto the roof of the school and then put the wagon back together.

The next morning there were people from all around town at the school taking pictures of that wagon sitting on top of the school. The poor guy who owned the wagon was standing on the ground. He must have been wondering how he was going to get that wagon down. He was lucky they didn't find a way to put his mule on top of the school also.

Halloween was a day to remember in Lynn Haven. Four or five of my Bay High friends gathered together to go trick-or-treating. I was a kid just off the farm and kind of followed the other guys to try and fit in. Since most of the kids sort of looked up to football players, they accepted me.

We did things like soap car windows of people who didn't give candy or weren't at home. At that time Lynn Haven only had one policeman, Chief Cullifer. He chased us in his patrol car and we were on our feet and running.

There was a man who owned a large store in Lynn Haven and was very wealthy. He appeared to hate kids and yelled at them to get off his property. Late that Halloween night another group of guys came up with a bright idea to get even with the store owner for calling the law.

Lynn Haven Union Monument

One of them had a paper bag and two of the guys in the group managed to poop on the ground. The ring leader scooped it up with sticks and put the poop in the bag.

While the members of his group watched from the bushes, he took the bag and placed it on the store owner's front porch, set it on fire, beat on the door and ran. The store owner rushed out on the porch and stomped the fire out. I can only imagine the nasty mess and language heard from that store owner. It did accomplish one thing in his favor. Everyone avoided his house from then on, worried about the well-deserved retaliation he might have prepared for his next visitors.

Chief Cullifer stayed busy on Halloween night each year.

Lynn Haven, I am told, has the only statue south of the Mason-Dixon Line that honors the Yankee soldiers who fought in the Civil War. My buddies and I made it a top priority each year to tear that thing down. Attempts were made with sledge hammers, axes, and then reverted to paint. We painted it gray, yellow and any other color paint we could get our hands on.

Our last try for removal, one of the guys got his dad's pick-up truck. We placed one end of a steel cable around the statue and the other end around the rear axle of the truck. He floored it. The rear axle broke in half, but that statue was still standing–and still is.

I learned some things are stronger than the rear axle of a Ford pick-up truck.

LaVelle, Bay High Class of 1953

THE MARINE CORPS
(1953-1956)

Enlisting in the United States Marine Corps

Jake (LaVohn Price) and I graduated from high school in 1953. Since the Korean War was going on and the draft was in effect, we decided to join the Coast Guard to keep from being drafted into the Army. We didn't really want to get shot at by some people we didn't even know.

It seemed there were many others who had the same idea. There was a waiting period of six months to a year for the Coast Guard.

We discussed it and decided the Navy needed our service. The war was on the ground, so we thought it would be safe in the Navy. Would you believe they had a long waiting list too?

We tried the Air Force because we heard the Air Force was a cakewalk. Again we ran into a long waiting list.

We assumed the draft might get us any day, so we talked to the Marine recruiter. To our amazement there was no waiting line. The man in dress blues was very friendly and obviously missed his calling. He should have been a car salesman, because he really sold us. (That and the fact we had just watched a John Wayne movie, *The Sands of Iwo Jima*, in which he played a Marine.)

We were given a free bus ride to Montgomery, Alabama. There we caught a train to a small town near Parris Island. On the train we met two other idiots from Panama City who talked to that Marine recruiter–V.J. Nowell and Rodney Davis–good old Bay High grads.

V.J. was cool and minded his own business. Rodney was a fun-loving guy who tried most anything (most of which was wrong), and usually got caught in the act. We were convinced he would never make it out alive, but he was one of us from Panama City, so we stuck together. (As it turned out, we were wrong about Rodney. He is the only one who made a career out of the Corps.)

A big old bus picked us up at the train station and we lumbered across a large body of water to the "beautiful isle" called Parris Island. The word "island" brought visions of palm trees and sandy beaches, but this place was downright ugly with a lot of muddy water and marsh grass. Whoever called this a beautiful isle had never seen Panama City Beach.

When the bus stopped, we were met by a huge PFC Drill Instructor (DI). This guy matched the island–big and ugly. We found out later he played football for the Parris Island Marines.

He ordered us to get out of the bus. We found ourselves in a large area with big six-man tents set up. There were hundreds of fresh new recruits being assigned to stay the night. This DI used language that turned the air blue. Many of the words I had never heard. Playing football for four years with a couple of very obscene-talking coaches, I thought I had heard every bad word invented. This guy could have taught our former coaches a lot about profanity.

No one bothered us that night except the guys in the other tents. After every one settled down a little, they started doing cat calls out to other people in their tents. It became obvious that it was Yankees vs. Rebels. This went on all night, so we slept very little.

We found out the following day that this was the only freedom of speech we would have for the next 12 weeks. We no longer made decisions on our own and continued to not sleep much.

Orders were given about when to sleep (at least 3 hours a night); eat, including the exact number of minutes we had to eat; walk (mostly duck walk); run (which was almost all the time); shave; brush teeth; go to the head (bathroom); speak, including how to speak (the first and last word out of our mouth was to be "sir"); write our mother, including what to say and what not to say. They checked the letters to make sure we didn't write anything to upset our mothers.

The following morning, at about 4:00 am, we were rolled out and rushed into a chow line where we had a hurried breakfast and were herded off to a warehouse where we were put through a room filled with barber chairs. Notice I did not say barbers. The men that cut our hair were butchers.

Most of the guys from up North had those long, slicked down, "duck-ass" haircuts. The guy in front of me had a big head full of hair and the "butcher" asked him if he would like to keep his hair. He said, "I sure would," and thanked him. The barber (butcher) then took his clippers and started cutting off every hair on the boy's head. As he cut his hair, he piled it in the guy's lap so he could "keep" it.

I was next and had a neat flat top. He bragged on my hair and asked if I would like to keep mine. I knew what I had just witnessed, so I said, "No, sir. Cut it all off." He did. I looked at Jake. For a moment we didn't recognize each other, and then started laughing. We were really skin-heads.

The next stop was another warehouse they called the first aid station. They had Navy Corpsmen lined up on both sides of us with needles for vaccination shots. Each of them was hitting us with needles in both arms, many at the same time. One guy walked off with a needle still hanging from his arm. When he looked down and saw it, he fainted. They pulled him out of the way and kept the line moving.

I forgot to mention that we were butt-naked as we went through the medical building. These corpsmen called us names, made fun of us, and pushed us around to the point that when we left that building we hated Navy Corpsmen. Some of the guys in our platoon said they would re-enlist in order to find those Navy Corpsmen and "kick their butts."

From the medical building we went into the clothing area where we were issued a sea bag and all our clothing. We put on a set of fatigues and everything else in our sea bag. All our worldly possessions were taken from our bodies before going into the medical building, and placed in a box to be mailed to our family.

109

At this point we had divorced all our past life. We were now married to the United States Marine Corps.

Among the things we were issued were: an M1 rifle, backpack, bayonet, large brush and bucket, toothbrush, double edge razor, house wife (small sewing kit with thread, needles and some extra buttons), and other incidentals.

We were then marched to a large Quonset hut. This would be our home for the next twelve weeks. We became Platoon 243, 4th Battalion, USMC. Our new home was a large metal building that was real hot in the summer and real cold in the winter. We had stack bunks. It's hard to say if they were comfortable or not because we didn't use them enough to determine that.

VJ Nowell

Jake took the top bunk and I took the lower. I thought I had the best deal not having to climb up in the top bunk each night, but I was wrong. When we sat down to shine our shoes or fold our clothes it was always on my bunk. When we got up I had to straighten my bunk. Imagine jumping out of bed each morning and smelling too big feet hanging off the top bunk with old Jake tied to the other end. Rodney and VJ took the other two bunks next to us.

Finally in bed about midnight, we slept maybe three hours before being rudely awakened by one of the drill instructors. He gave us 15 minutes to get a shower, shave, dress, make up our bunk and fall into platoon formation outside with our rifle.

We marched to the chow hall where we were given an order to stack our rifles. This is no easy job. Three Marines take their rifles and hook them together near the end of the barrel so that they will stand on their own without falling when released. The DI then told us to take all the time we needed, but we better be in platoon formation when he got through eating and came outside.

He walked in and got his chow immediately while we had to wait in the chow line where the guys who put food on our tray got their jollies by screwing with our food. It was bad enough like it was, but when they finished dishing it up, it was really bad. (Sometimes we had ice cream for dessert. The last guy on the food line put it on top of hot mashed potatoes. Before we could get to our table it was almost all melted.)

Our group ate as fast as we could. When we finished, we raced to the garbage cans dumped our tray out, stacked it and raced outside to the pre-designated spot where our weapons were stacked and fell into platoon formation.

It was still dark after we had finished chow in the morning. It started breaking day as we were marching along an old road that had dolomite spread on top of it. The dust was so thick you could hardly breathe. In the distance, we could hear reveille being blown which signified the start of a new day, but our day had begun long before.

This was the procedure at the beginning of the day. At the end of the day, we heard taps being blown, which normally signified the end of a work day. However our drill instructors chose to ignore this. Instead they advised that medical science had proven the human body only needed three hours of sleep each day and they practiced this scientific rule. We trained with no break until lunch time where we did the whole process again the same as breakfast.

While standing at attention in 90-plus degree weather in the shade, the DI gave us a little "get-acquainted" talk. The speech was not nice. He explained he was going to do something our parents had failed to do for the past eighteen years. That was to make men out of us. He went on to say that from this day on he was going to be our father, mother and brother. "I will not be your sister, so don't try to screw me." I cannot recall all the names he called us, but they were not names you wanted to write home about.

Speaking of home, the DI advised we would write at least one letter a week to our mothers. To make sure we told her the "truth," he proofread them. He explained what would happen to the a–hole who gave his mother any wrong ideas about dear old Parris Island.

When addressing any of the drill instructors, we were told that the first word out of our mouth was to be "sir," as well as the last. Example: "Sir, Pvt. Pitts requests permission to speak to the Drill Instructor, sir."

Our weapon was a rifle and not a gun. He said our gun was in our pants. The rifle was for shooting and the gun was for fun.

Anytime a DI entered the barracks, the first one to see him jumped up and yelled "Attention!" Everyone else was to jump to their feet and snap to attention.

Anyone who failed any rifle inspection had to sleep with their rifle every night until they could clean the weapon well enough to pass inspection. This wasn't with the rifle lying next to you. It was field stripped (completely taken apart), and placed underneath the bunk sheet and you had to sleep on top of it. It was not unusual to see a recruit, who was supposed to be sleeping on his rifle, wrapped in a blanket and lying on the concrete floor next to his bunk after lights out and the DI left the barracks. In the morning this recruit in addition to the regular morning routine had to assemble his rifle and fall into platoon formation on time. Anyone who says this is impossible never had to deal with a Marine Corps DI.

We were issued two pairs of shoes–a brown dress pair and combat boots, which we wore daily. Both pairs had to be spit-shined to a glossy black. If you have never spit-shined shoes you have missed a major happening in your life. And if you have never spit-shined a pair of brown shoes into a glossy black, then you have never turned an impossible task into possible.

We washed our clothes once a week on a long concrete table using sand soap, a brush, and a lot of elbow-grease. We hung the clothes on a line to dry during the day and learned to put them between the springs and mattress and sleep on them so they would be pressed the following morning. These washed and "ironed" clothes were placed in our foot locker kept under the bottom bunk.

Every so often we had a clothing inspection which was called "junk on the bunk." All our clothing properly marked with our name along with other issued items and had to be laid out in the prescribed Marine Corps way. The DI walked by and inspected. He could always find something wrong.

Sometimes, usually after we had gone to bed, the DI ran in, turned on the lights, and yelled, "Air raid!" Everyone had to get off the top bunk and onto the bottom bunk. He then yelled, "Flood!" All of us had to climb on the top bunks. It got wild as the DI got faster and faster yelling, "Air raid, flood, air raid, flood," until we met our bunkmate going up or coming down.

Knowing our serial number, rifle serial number and general orders was a must. We had to memorize each one. There was no way, we thought, we could do that in a day or two. I couldn't even memorize my multiplication tables in grade school. It's amazing what one can do when it is a matter of life or death. We did it.

One kid, in answering a question by the DI, referred to his rifle as his gun and you would have thought he had committed a cardinal sin. For the next two hours he had to run around the company area holding his rifle in one hand and his penis, removed from his trousers, in the other hand. He had to raise his rifle in the air and yell at the top of his voice, "This is my rifle!" and then pulling on his penis say, "This is my gun!" Then holding his rifle back up say, "This is for shooting!" and holding his penis say, "This is for fun!"

We learned a lot the first few days. Speaking for myself, my greatest enlightenment was that Mama was right when she told me I should stay home instead of going to war. I also learned that being a Marine wasn't quite like John Wayne portrayed in the movies.

Platoon formation was arranged according to size, with the taller guys in the front and the shorter ones on the tail end. Jake, VJ Nowell and myself were about the same size and placed in the center of the platoon. Rodney Davis was very short and marched at the end of the platoon, called the "gooney bird" section. Rodney had to eat a lot of dust and was picked on by the DI.

I always wondered how my sister could march in step with her band members at Holmes County High. I thought I could never learn to march like that with 70 or 80 people, but I did. It was easy to learn to march with a big DI walking next to us. He used a swagger stick, which looked like a miniature baseball bat. When used on you, the swagger stick felt like a full-size bat and served well to keep us in step.

We wore a helmet liner a lot of the time. It was a very hard plastic helmet that fit inside the steel helmet. The DI loved to

113

catch someone doing or speaking something when he shouldn't, and rap his swagger stick on the head of the recruit. I've had my bell rung in football many times, been kicked by a mule and horse and it hurt but never like a swagger stick across the top of the helmet. The ringing continued for most of the day.

When one or more persons screwed up, we were usually punished by having to duck walk, holding our 9 1/2 pound M1 rifle over our head for a mile or so. There is no way to describe how much this hurts. Jake and I did okay because we were former athletes. It was city boys and others who came from easy lifestyles who fell out first. When the first two or three fell out, we had to duck walk over them. If they didn't move and were really out, the gooney bird guys had to pick them up or drag them to sickbay.

If we failed rifle inspection, there was another punishment. We were marched down near the water. We had to strip naked, stack our clothes up in a pile and then field strip our weapons into three pieces: the stock, the trigger group and the barrel and receiver. The three pieces had to be buried in the sand near our clothes. Then we marched to the water's edge and stood at attention while the mosquitoes and sand gnats ate on us. Anyone who moved got rapped on the head or the back side with the swagger stick.

One day the DI was really on a rampage and made us come to parade rest while he talked about us, our ancestors, various parts of our anatomy and our serious lack of intelligence. After he ran out of words, he said he was going to prove his point by calling us to attention and then he said he would order us to march off. But, he cautioned us severely that this was only a test and we better not move when he told us to march. He said, "I guarantee you that one of you shit birds will march off." He then called us to attention and cautioned that when he gave the command to march no one should move, not even bat an eye. Again, he called us to attention and said, "Forward March."

Not one person in our 73-man platoon moved except Jake. He just up and marched off alone. The DI screamed and cursed and said, "I told you so." The last time we saw Jake that afternoon, he was duck walking around the company area holding his rifle over his head and shouting "I am a shit bird. I am a shit bird." It took me two days to wipe the grin off my face.

Another morning, we had a shaving inspection. The DI walked down the line and rubbed his hand up the side of our face. If he could feel any beard, he sent the recruit back inside the hut to get his razor, footlocker and bucket. The DI took the razor and raked it on the concrete walk several times then ordered the recruit to stand on the footlocker, place the bucket over his head and hold the bucket down by the bale with one hand. With the other hand, he had to take the razor and start shaving. While he was shaving, he was instructed to double time on top of the footlocker and sing the Marine Corps Hymn at the top of his voice. Three or four guys in our platoon had to do this, including Jake. Jake had always had a heavy beard. Even though he shaved, it was heavy enough to feel it.

I could see blood dripping down on the necks of those guys singing on their footlockers. The DI stopped them now and then to check if they were clean shaved. During one of the inspections, Jake looked at me and noticed the big grin from ear to ear, and quickly pointed it out to the DI. Before I could wipe it off he looked at me and sent me to get my bucket and razor.

I had to go through the same program, but having seen the blood I kept the razor away from my face. I sang the Marine Corps Hymn and cursed Jake, while double-timing on my footlocker.

Parris Island had to be the cleanest military base in the world. Nothing was left on the grounds, not even a cigarette butt. The DI never let anyone smoke until he needed a smoke himself. He stopped the platoon and said, "At ease. Smoking lamp lit."

When the DI finished his smoke, he said, "Smoking lamp out." At that time each Marine smoking put out his smoke and field stripped what was left of the cigarette. This was done by tearing it from end to end, dumping the tobacco into the wind and rolling up the paper and putting it into his pocket.

One day a guy threw a cigarette butt on the ground. The DI made him get his shovel, dig a grave four feet by six feet, bury the cigarette, and say a prayer over the grave. The DI then asked the recruit which way the butt was pointed after he covered it up. The recruit did not know, so the whole process started again, with him digging up the butt and re-burying it. Needless to say no one ever threw a butt down again.

Swamp Training

As a recruit at Parris Island Marine Corps Base in South Carolina, I was an 18-year-old kid just off the farm and it was the first time I had been away from home. About half-way through boot training, we had to stay overnight in the swamp. It was raining and miserable. We wore water repellent ponchos that also served as half of a tent. Using the buddy system, two ponchos hooked together to make a small tent for us to sleep in with our M1 rifle.

My buddy was Lavohn Price (Jake). We put our tent up and some of the guys boiled coffee in a steel helmet. We all got our tin cups out for coffee. I never liked or drank coffee very often, but I had watched my dad drink many cups. He always added about as much milk and sugar as he did coffee. When I got my coffee, I looked around and asked where the milk and sugar was. Everyone stopped what they were doing and just stared at me with rain dripping off their helmets.

I wished it was possible to stuff those words back in my mouth. We were miles out in the swamps in a rainstorm and I was asking for cream and sugar. I kind of laughed it off and said I was just kidding. From that day to the present, I drink my coffee black.

Later, we crawled into our tent, hung our rifles between the two center tent posts to keep them clean and out of the water, and dozed off. We woke up to find our tent had fallen on top of us. I blamed Jake for not staking it down good enough and he blamed me. We got up, in the rain, re-staked the tent and went back to sleep. The tent fell again. This time I peered out, watched for a few minutes and saw the drill instructor walking around kicking the pins up and letting the tents fall on the two inside.

The next morning we found a bunch of mad Marines who had been up and down all night putting their tents up. Jake and I decided to sleep the remainder of the night with the tent and our rifles lying on top of us.

Rifle Range and Mess Hall Duty

Each platoon had to spend two weeks on the rifle range. One week was spent qualifying with the M1 rifle and the second week spent on mess hall duty.

During qualifying we stayed in wooden barracks. At the end of the week, we had to clean the barracks for the next group of recruits. Cleaning the barracks included five steps:

1) We each had to go out and get a bucket of sand, bring it back inside and distribute the sand equally around our bunks and the passage ways throughout the barracks.

2) We had to go back outside, get a bucket of water and pour it over the sand we just distributed.

3) Using our issued brush that we used to wash our clothes, we scrubbed every inch of that barracks on our hands and knees.

4) We then made several trips outside bringing in more buckets of water and squeegeed all the water and sand from the barracks.

5) Using our brush, we made sure all the sand was brushed from the cracks, swept into a dust pan and removed from the barracks.

6) A final inspection was made by the DIs. If they found any residue (which they did), or were unhappy with the clean-up (which they were), the entire procedure had to be repeated (which it was).

The following day we finally qualified with the M1 rifle. The top shooter of the platoon was given a new steam iron. I was blessed to receive that honor. From then on I was one of the more popular recruits in the platoon. All the guys wanted to borrow my iron so they could press their clothes after washing and not have to press them by placing them under their mattress and sleeping on them.

From the barracks we moved to four-man tents with cots to begin our required one-week of mess hall duty. We got up about 2:00 am each morning and had to start feeding the recruits at about 4:00 am. It was a very hectic time with several hundred troops rushing into the chow hall, eating like pigs and rushing out to the rifle range.

I was the lucky one. Since I was the only person in our platoon who could type, I was assigned to the mess sergeant's office where I typed food orders and miscellaneous things. I really learned to appreciate Ms. Henshaw who taught me first-year typing at Bay High. I regretted all the hassle I gave her trying to convince her to sign my football eligibility slip (which she always did) in order to play the Friday night game. Because of the extra time she put in with me, I was able to finish the course, typing fifty-seven words per minute with only three errors. This course ended up being more beneficial to me in my career than any other I took in high school.

As I mentioned earlier, Rodney Davis seemed to get in more trouble than anyone else, but somehow finagled, wiggled or lied his way out with minor damage. Jake and VJ Nowell were assigned to the food line and Rodney was put in charge of filling sugar dishes and salt and pepper shakers on each table before the troops were seated.

We had to listen to gripes from the other recruits about the food, service and anything else they could think of. Rodney came up with a brilliant idea. He got with us just before noon chow and, laughing like crazy, said, "Boys, I am getting even with those blankety-blank idiots for all of us. I put salt in some of the sugar dishes and sugar in some of the salt shakers. No one saw me, so they can never prove who did it."

VJ said, "Rodney, they don't have to prove anything. You are the only person in charge of the sugar, salt and pepper so they'll know exactly who did it." Rodney turned a little pale and said, "I didn't think about that."

The mess sergeant did think about it after a near riot in the mess hall. Quickly new salt and pepper shakers and sugar dishes were put out. After the recruits cleared out, all the suspect dishes were placed on a long table. Since about half of them were changed, Rodney was made to sit down and taste each salt and sugar dish until he returned all back in their respective places. Rodney staggered into the tent about two hours after we had secured. He had a yellowish tint to his face. He told us he had puked up everything he had eaten for the past week.

The following morning the DI opened the tent flap and yelled reveille as he did every morning. We always jumped up and got dressed in two or three minutes because he came back shortly and looked in. We had better be ready to go. On this morning we were finishing putting on our combat boots when he opened the tent flap and entered. We all looked at Rodney, who had not moved. He was sound asleep.

The DI went to his cot, grabbed it by the end, and threw it across the tent with Rodney still under the blankets. As I mentioned earlier this DI was huge and strong.

Somewhere between the take off and the landing of the cot, Rodney separated himself from the cot and crawled around on the floor grabbing for his clothes. The DI, without a word, left the tent. VJ, Jake and I doubled over with laughter. Rodney said, "It ain't funny. I could have fallen out of that bunk and broken my neck and you guys would have laughed." He was probably right. (I understand Rodney rose to the rank of Chief Master Sergeant and served 20 years in the USMC. This guy was a glutton for punishment.)

119

Parris Island Boot Camp Graduation

Our recruit training included a rigid procedure for rifle inspection. We were taught to stand at attention with our rifle by our side. When the inspecting officer–DI, Lieutenant or Captain–gave the order, "Inspection Arms," we brought our weapon up smartly, flipped the bolt open on the receiver, held it at a 45-degree angle in front of us across our chest and waited for the inspecting officer to approach.

LaVelle in Marine dress uniform, 1953

When the inspection officer stepped in front of us, we remained frozen in position until he reached for our weapon. When he reached out for the rifle, we immediately released the weapon. Our hands better not be touching the rifle when the officer caught it in mid-air. When he caught it in mid-air, he flipped it around, looked it over and stuck it back out. We were to reach out and grab the weapon as he released it. To drop a weapon to the ground was one of the greatest sins that could happen to you or to the officer doing the inspection.

I never saw this happen, but almost did on graduation day at Parris Island. The Base Commander, who was a General, was doing the inspection along with the company commander. The DI and other big wheels followed behind them. The wind was blowing at about 25 to 30 knots and I noticed out of the corner of my eye that the General was not taking any weapons, but merely looked at each Marine and smiled. Many families were on the side lines watching the ceremony which was going well until they got to me.

I was scared to death, like all the others. The wind was blowing very hard. We all had on our tropical worsted dress uniforms with ties. When the General stopped in front of me, my tie had blown around my neck across my shoulder. Trying to be nice, the General, with his seven rows of ribbons, reached up to straighten my tie and I thought he was reaching for my rifle. I released it. For a long moment it seemed my rifle was stranded in mid-air as a look of shock and terror shone on the face of the General. I am sure he saw the same look on mine. I have to hand it to him; he was fast. He caught that rifle about six inches from the ground. A long sigh escaped from each of the officers with him as the General handed my weapon back. I noticed he did not try to straighten any other ties as he continued the inspection. I can't help wonder what would have happened if the old boy had not caught that rifle before it reached the ground. I probably would have stayed in boot camp for my entire three-year enlistment.

On our final day before leaving Parris Island to go to our next duty assignment, the Drill Instructor spoke to us in a nice, human form. He said we were now Marines. To accomplish that, he and the other DIs had been very hard on us and he wanted us to understand why. He said, "Many of you will be headed to Korea. It is important to obey, without question, orders from your superiors. This is crucial for your safety as well as your fellow Marines and most of all for our country."

We left Parris Island feeling we were nine feet tall, and could whip our weight in wildcats if need be.

From boot camp, I learned that as a Marine, no assignment is impossible.

From Boot Camp to Quantico, Virginia

After boot camp, all four of us Panama City guys were sent to Quantico, Virginia, for training in small arms repair. A snowstorm covered everything our first night there. Being from Florida, it was the first snow we had ever seen. The sergeant woke us up at 0200 and took us out to clear the snow from the sidewalks so people could get around. We were given shovels and when we got off the truck we immediately fell down.

Everyone thought we were horsing around, but we couldn't stand up. We tried to explain to the sergeant that it was our first

121

snow, but he didn't believe us. He was a Yankee and thought everyone had seen snow.

After a while we started getting our snow legs and could walk a little without falling. The Yankee boys were having a good time making fun of us southern boys. As was bound to happen, someone got smacked by a big snowball and the war was on. We found some rocks to put in the middle of our snowballs and soon the boys from the south were winning the war. The sergeant returned from his coffee break and stopped all the fun.

The first weekend in Quantico, we got the whole weekend off. We were like birds out of their cages. Our company commander advised us of the places that were off-limits in Washington, D.C. The most emphasized location to stay away from was 9th Street where large gangs gathered. Under no circumstances were we to visit that area.

So when we rolled into D.C. that night, the first place we went was 9th Street. There was a large group of us and we were all in uniform. We thought we were real bad because our DI had told us that a good Marine was equal to at least five other persons in a good fight. (However, during the almost four years I was in the USMC, I met some Army Air Borne, Navy sailors and Air Force people that I bet my old sergeant never knew about.) We saw some large groups of gangs, but God was good to us and nothing happened.

The next place we stopped was a restaurant where we ordered a large steak. We had not had a steak since we enlisted in the Corps. That steak was beautiful, but the toughest piece of meat I had ever eaten. One of our guys stuck a fork in his steak and was sawing away with his knife trying to cut a piece off when his fork slipped. He shot that steak off his plate, down the aisle by the other tables and when it quit sliding, that Marine was right behind it with his fork in his hand. He stabbed it and walked back to his table, brushing it off as he walked. He plopped it down on his plate and started cutting again. We all ate our tough steaks, but it was a long time before I got steak-hungry again.

After eating steak, we, of course, had to visit a local bar. There must have been a hundred or more service men from different branches of the service in the bar and all in uniform.

There seemed to be roughly an equal number of Army, Navy, Air Force and Marines. A small country band played on a stage. Some people gave them money to play special requests.

Rodney had been quiet most of the night and hadn't done anything to embarrass us. But by this time he had had several beers. He took up a collection from our table, went to the band and requested they play *Dixie*.

While he was walking back to our table, Rodney yelled, "All you m--f–ers stand at attention." Slowly guys started standing in different areas of the lounge, but not the Yankee boys. As Rodney passed a table full of Navy guys he shouted, "Swabbies, stand up."

One told Rodney where he could stick old Dixie and Rodney immediately punched the sailor, knocking him out of his chair. World War III broke out. It was not the North vs. the South but Marine vs. Navy, Army, Air Force. It seemed all the people gravitated to the uniform of their kind and hit anyone who had on a different color uniform.

Fortunately we were at a table nearest the front door. Someone hollered, "Call the MPs!" Jake and I got down on the floor and crawled out the door as the MPs, SPs, APs and others came pouring through the front doors. (This reminds me of the remarks of a Marine Corps general who was asked about his retreat from a strategic hill. He replied, "We did not retreat, we were merely attacking from a different direction." Therefore, when the MPs arrived, we decided to make an exit out of the entrance.)

We made it back to the base and somehow Rodney also made it back without getting put in jail. We still don't know how he got out of that place. He was so drunk, he didn't remember.

Learning to Drive in Snow

My dad somehow scraped up enough money to buy an old '46 Dodge automobile for me.

The first time Jake and I took the car out, we went on a double date to a drive-in theatre. Everything was fine until it started snowing about half way through the movie. It was so pretty, we just sat there and enjoyed the movie and the snow. When the movie was over and we started out, the railroad track between the

Mama, LaVelle and the '46 Dodge

theatre and main highway was concealed under the snow. Earlier, we noticed that trains travelled very fast on the track.

We had to cross this track to get on the main highway. The problem was, we couldn't find the road out. So we guessed and we guessed wrong. We missed the road and went over the tracks and there we were two wheels on one side of the tracks and two wheels on the other side. We knew if a train came along we had lost the car.

I took the insurance papers from the glove compartment. We all got out and just stood there, not knowing what to do. Suddenly a car pulled off the highway and four Marines got out and asked if we needed help. They stopped because they saw our uniforms. It gave me a new sense of pride in being a Marine.

They got around the vehicle and picked up the rear end and dropped it on the other side of the tracks. We had not been over the tracks more than 10 minutes when a fast train blasted through. I believe those Marines were heaven-sent for a couple of old farm boys who were real dumb when it came to snow.

We started on to the girls' homes. When we got to the first stop sign, I slowed down to stop, but the car continued on. It felt like every short Marine-cut hair on my head stood up a little straighter. I had no control over the car. The girls had to coach us on how to drive in a snowstorm. Fortunately, we got them home and made it back to the base safely.

I learned a truth behind Semper Fi (Always Faithful). Not only are you faithful to your country, but also to your Marine brothers.

Jake and Skating

Another memorable event in Quantico happened when Jake and I were invited to go to a skating party with a Baptist youth group. The place was called America on Wheels. The group was really nice with several pretty girls. (Jake wound up marrying one of them later.)

The skating rink was housed in a large frame building and the rink was on the second floor. Everything was fine, except for the fact that Jake and I didn't know how to skate. The girls were very helpful and held on tight and eased us around the floor. I started getting the hang of it and asked to try it alone. That was a mistake.

I built up speed, got to the end of the floor and couldn't make the turn. Instead I ran into the fire exit door. It burst open. I flew out over the parking lot, hanging onto the bar of the door. I could see the cars below me.

Keeping my grip tight, the door swung back shut, depositing me back inside the rink. The people around the door looked surprised at seeing me back so soon and gave me a standing ovation.

When all else fails, hold on tight and maybe things will change for the better.

Knee Injury and the Webleys

The guys in my platoon and I had just received orders for Korea. But during physical training, I injured my left knee and ended up in the Navy Hospital. The doctors had to remove a cartilage. The rest of my platoon was shipped out to Korea, and I was left behind. It took several weeks to get over the surgery.

During my recuperation, I visited my sister, Ruth, on weekends. She was working at the Pentagon in Arlington and lived with the Webley family. I could never say enough good things about the Webley family. They took me in like I was one of their kids. When Mrs. Webley bought her kids something, she bought me something also. They would not let me pay for anything. When I didn't have money to buy gas to drive into Arlington from Quantico, they came and picked me up.

Mr. Webley was in the Navy. When he got out, his best friend, Darr, and he went into the plumbing business together. They really got along well. The two of them bought a large two-story house on the Chesapeake Bay. The families alternated weekends using it. They had a large 32-foot cabin boat and a 14-foot fishing boat that Mr. Webley and I took fishing or surf boarding.

LaVelle on weekend leave in Virginia, 1954

One day Mr. Webley let me operate the boat. He was going to show me how to ride a surfboard because each time I tried, I fell off. Mr. Webley climbed up on that board and with the large motor on his boat, I had no trouble getting him up on top of the water. He could really ride that thing.

There was one big problem, we did not get our signals straight before we took off. I started making big circles and he started waving one of his hands around in a circle. He was trying to tell me to make a larger circle and I thought he wanted the circle tightened. I fired the boat up, thinking he was going to really show off his surfing skills.

The tighter circle I made, the harder he waved. I couldn't believe he wanted to turn any sharper than we were, but being used to doing what I was told, I opened the motor up full speed and made a sharp U-turn and met him coming back. With eyes the

126

size of coffee cup saucers, he had a look of horror on his face when we met each other.

A picnic with Ruth, Jimmy & the Webleys, 1954

I looked back just in time to see him make the turn. It was like popping a whip. All I could see was him go high into the air off the board. His hands held tight to the rope wrapped around both wrists several times. The surfboard came down first with Mr. Webley following close behind. Both went out of sight by the time I got the motor turned off.

Suddenly the surfboard surfaced, then Mr. Webley popped up with Chesapeake Bay sea weed wrapped around his neck. We were in deep water and it was pretty obvious Mr. Webley got a piece of the bottom.

Naturally, I thought it was funny. I said, "Was that a small enough circle for you?" I won't repeat what he said. I discovered that some of his Navy words were the same ones I heard at Parris Island. That ended our surfboard riding for a long time.

From the Webleys, I learned that I was blessed to have a home away from home.

127

Wedding Bells for My Sister

During my stay at Quantico my sister, Ruth, was dating a young man named Jimmy Morris. They decided to get married. My mother flew up for the wedding, but Dad refused to go, saying he couldn't give one his children away. I couldn't understand his line of thinking because I'd been wanting to give her away for years.

Ruth asked me to walk her down the aisle. It was an honor to stand beside her on the happiest day of her life.

LaVelle escorts his sister, Ruth, on her wedding day, June 12, 1954

When I could walk well enough after the knee surgery, the Corps transferred me to the Marine Corps Supply Depot in Albany, Georgia. After a very sad farewell to the Webley family and my sister, I loaded my car and headed for Georgia.

Marine Corps Supply Depot, Albany, Georgia

I Knew a Hero

While stationed at the Marine Corps Supply Depot, Albany, Georgia, I was initially assigned to a weapons repair company. We rebuilt and modified rifles and pistols for the troops. There were a large number of civilian employees who worked with us. They were sort of looked down on by the Marines, because they were mostly retired military and we felt they were double-dipping.

One older worker, in particular, appeared to be mentally off. He was always smiling and you had to repeat several times anything you wanted him to do. Sometimes the guys yelled at him and some even cursed him. He just smiled, shuffled on and tried to do what was asked.

One day our First Sergeant happened to be on the floor and heard what was going on. He yelled for all of us to get into his office. We could tell by the bluish tint of his face that he was mighty upset. When we all crowded into his office, he closed the door and lit into us. After boot camp we had not had very many butt-chewings. Some of those gathered in his office were decorated veterans of many battles in Korea and even World War II.

After he calmed down a little, he finally got to the point. He told us the "old dumb idiot" we had been making fun of was a better man than all of us combined. "For your information this guy is a former Marine. He fought through World War II, and was decorated with most every medal you could win. He was a prisoner of war and even survived the Battan Death March in which thousands of prisoners died. Even if you can overlook all that, remember one thing. This guy, which you call a dumb ass, was decorated by the President of the United States with the Congressional Medal of Honor."

There was nothing but silence. Two or three of the veterans, who were ready to whip the first Sergeant a few minutes earlier, were almost in tears now. Everyone walked out and not another word was spoken by anyone for quite some time. From that day on a great deal of respect was given to the former Marine. Guys got him coffee, asked him to sit and rest while they did his chores and always said, "yes, sir" and "no, sir" when talking to him.

He still smiled and nodded his head like always, but I really think he knew there was something different about his life with his fellow workers. I know there was a great deal of change in our attitude. From that point on, there was not a Marine there who wouldn't intervene for him if someone treated him the way we used to. It's amazing how a little information and education can change a person's outlook.

This story drives home a truth my dad taught me. You should never judge, make fun of or mistreat anyone less fortunate than yourself.

Paratroopers from Ft. Benning

One evening I was recruited as designated driver by a Sgt. Malki and four other Marines. They had been drinking in a local bar in downtown Albany, Georgia, the afternoon before Armed Forces Day. I was parked by the curb. The Marine group came out of one bar and had to walk past the Albany Police Department to get to another bar. Just then, two busloads of paratroopers from Ft. Benning, Georgia, pulled up and started unloading. They were there to march in the Armed Forces Day parade.

Sergeant Malki, who had about one too many drinks, took one look at the Air Borne guys and yelled something like, "Men are we going to let these ground pounders take our town?"

The fight was on. Of all people to pick on, the 82nd Air Borne should have been way down on the list. But not to some inebriated Marines. The fight didn't last long because the police were changing shifts. They quickly joined the scrap and two busloads of Air Borne and about 20 Marines ended up in the police station.

There was a lot of confusion as the police were trying to sort out who did what. The desk sergeant had piled all the ID Cards on his desk while they discussed where to start. Sgt. Malki straightened up his uniform, walked over to the desk and picked up his ID card, dropped it in his pocket and walked out of the station. He was the only Marine who was not booked as far as I know, and I think all the Air Borne guys were cut loose.

Alcohol can make even a Marine do stupid things.

Becoming a Part of the USMC Rifle and Pistol Team (1954)

Until I enlisted in the Marine Corps, I had never fired any weapon other than a .22 caliber rifle, a shotgun, my slingshot and a BB gun. With the .22 and shotgun, I was a fairly good shot when it came to squirrel shooting. My dad always preached about how good the Pitts were when it came to marksmanship. I heard many stories of how my grandfather was the finest marksman in the whole community. There were also many stories of my dad's triumphs with weapons while he was growing up. Many of these I had witnessed myself as a kid.

In the Corps they handed me an M1 rifle and it was love at first sight. I won a new steam iron for being the best shooter in our platoon.

About a year later, at the supply depot, I applied for a tryout with the U.S. Marine Corps Rifle and Pistol Team. They sent me to Camp Lejeune, North Carolina, from my duty station at Albany, Georgia, to try out. I was surprised to see three or four hundred Marines there to try out for about thirty positions on the rifle and thirty on the pistol team. There were more good squirrel shooters in the world than me. Those guys were good.

The USMC Rifle and Pistol Team

Being very nervous, I shot slow fire from 500 yards. My target was littered with holes but very few were getting in the bull's-eye. I knew it had to be the rifle, because I was a much better shot than that.

Walking to the armor repair tent behind the firing line, I asked the Gunny Sergeant to check my weapon because it wouldn't hold a group. About ten minutes later he called me over and handed me the rifle back. I asked if he found the problem and he replied that there was a loose screw behind the butt plate. I took the weapon and walked away about ten steps when it registered that he was talking about me. I turned and looked back to see the Gunny looking at me with a big grin on his face. The sad part of the story is that what he said was the truth.

The Marines trying out for the rifle team shot every morning and in the afternoon picked up the empty brass from the morning shoot. This was a backbreaking job—even worse than picking cotton. I noticed some of the guys were going over to the pistol range and shooting pistols in the afternoon. I inquired about this and was told the people who were good with a pistol could try out for the pistol team and did not have to pick up brass. I made my way to the pistol range and advised the first sergeant I was a pistol shooter and wanted to try out for the team. He gave me the old, "yeah, that's what they all say" look, but checked out

131

a .45 accurized automatic pistol to me. I was instructed the following morning to pick up ammo and pick any target that was unoccupied and start shooting from the 50-yard line.

The only time I had ever fired a .45 was in boot camp, where we shot a 50 round familiarization course from 15 yards. The trigger pull on a regular issue .45 is 9.5 pounds. You really have to squeeze that trigger for it to fire. The match conditioned .45 that the team shot was a 4¼ pound, or less trigger pull. You can almost breathe on the trigger and it will go off. I knew I'd better improve greatly or I'd be picking up brass again.

I watched Lt. McMillan, who I had heard was possibly the best rifle and pistol shooter in the Marine Corps. He was standing on the 50-yard line shooting slow fire which consists of firing 10 rounds in 10 minutes. McMillan picked up his .45, loaded it with a five-round clip, and fired them all in about 10 seconds. The target was run in (electrically) and all five were in the bull's-eye. I thought this was the way to shoot—in a hurry and they would all go in the center of the target.

So the next day after shooting the rifle in the morning, I ran to the pistol range and checked out my ammo and Lt. McMillan's ammo and placed it on two target stands side by side. When McMillan arrived, he called out, "Who picked up my ammo?"

I raised my hand and replied, "Here, sir."

He walked down, smiled at me and said, "Thanks," and started loading his clip. I watched him shoot the same way he had the day before. When the target was brought in to score, all 10 shots were in the bull's-eye and most shots were touching each other.

So I tried copying his technique. I didn't even hit the target much less the bull's-eye. I did hit the rail that the target ran on and the target metal frame itself. After trying one or two other methods, with the same luck, my weapon was suddenly snatched from my hand and behind the hand was a very irate lieutenant who demanded, "Who in the hell told you that you could shoot a pistol?"

Lt. William McMillan

I knew it was over and I was headed back to picking up brass on the rifle range. I thought up several things I could have said, but I decided to tell the truth. I told him about the brass, how I hated picking it up and thought this might be my way out. He stood there a moment and then burst out laughing. He confessed that was exactly how he started shooting the pistol.

He then said, "Okay I'll show you a couple things, so you don't kill someone out here and shoot up all the target frames." That was my introduction to Lieutenant William "Bill" McMillan, USMC.

I was going to make sure he did not get rid of me that easy, so each morning after I finished shooting the rifle I ran to the pistol range and picked up the lieutenant's ammo and mine and signed for it. When he came by to get his ammo, he was told someone had picked it up. He yelled from the ammo shack, "Who has my ammo?" I answered, "I do, sir." He laughed and came down where I had him set up next to my target stand.

I was a terrible pistol shot and why he didn't kick me off the team I'll never know. I will always be grateful for his patient instruction and teaching me the art of pistol shooting. My teacher was the best and he proved it by winning a gold medal in the World Olympic Games. He became known as the best pistol shooter in the world.

LaVelle, a member of the USMC Rifle and Pistol Team

After we got to the next stage at Parris Island we had a big match between all the shooters who had been picked for the last training phase before the last team cut. There were about a hundred rifle shooters and about the same for the pistol. Some of the shooters shot both rifle and pistol. Lt. McMillan was one of those.

The big match lasted about four days and the combination of the four days' scores produced winners for the pistol and rifle. Lt. McMillan advised he would shoot both rifle and pistol for the last time and after the matches stick to the pistol. He did shoot both and won both matches. He was the most amazing marksman I have ever seen.

134

The Men of the USMC Rifle and Pistol Team

Along with Lt. McMillan (more on him follows), some of the

Col. Walsh & members of
Rifle and Pistol Team

people I met who really made an impression on me were Captain Tom Mitchell from Texas, SSgt Houser, PFC Townsend, Tiny, and Col. Walsh.

Capt. Mitchell, of Texas, was one of the coaches. He held the Marine Corps record and the world record with the 1903 bolt action 30-06 rifle. (That record will never be broken because they discontinued shooting the 1903 rifle.) He helped me more than anyone in learning the finer points of shooting a rifle. I would never have made the cut had it not been for him.

Following are stories of some of the men who became my teammates:

SSgt Houser

I became friends with SSGT Houser who was short, about 5'5", with a paunch belly. He looked anything but a Marine, however he was a 14-year veteran.

SSgt Houser, alias Sgt. Barnsmell

There were two things Houser was very good at–his marksmanship and women, all seemed to love him.

The first big match against the Army, Navy, Air Force and Border Patrol was really a big deal with a lot of pride between the different branches of the military. Houser was entered in the rifle competition, which consisted of 200 yd. off-hand, 300 yd. rapid

135

fire and timed fire, 600 yd. slow fire and 1000 yd. slow fire.

The course was shot for two consecutive days. A large board listed the scores of the top 20 shooters at the end of each day and their branch of service. At the end of the competition, the man at the top of the scoreboard was SSgt. John Barnsmell, USMC. The rest of the names were recognized as they were the normal ones on the score board.

Some of the big brass were scratching their heads and asking who this new shooter was that shot the incredible score. They finally ran him down and found it to be Houser. Demanding an explanation, Houser told them he had started the match and after a couple of shots his rear sight fell off his rifle. He got it fixed, and knowing he was out of the competition, he went back and re-entered as SSgt. John Barnsmell of the USMC.

The Marine big brass were amused but not the other military branches, so Sgt. Barnsmell's name was removed from the scoreboard.

McMillan at the Hialeah, Florida Pistol Matches
We fired many matches around the country getting ready for the national championship match in Camp Perry, Ohio. One such match was in Hialeah, Florida, against the regular teams from the Army, Navy, Air Force, Marine Corps and Border Patrol.

McMillan's wife was about to have a baby. The Marine Corps team captain, Col. Walsh, was trying to get the pistol matches started on time so McMillan had time to shoot and catch a plane back to Parris Island.

Just before the matches were to start, McMillan got a call to get back to Parris Island if he was to be there when the baby arrived. The Marine Commander quickly asked the other commanders if McMillan could shoot the course alone, all timed fire and rapid fire, before he left. The other branches were eager to do this because they knew he could not possibly win shooting timed fire with the .45 at 50 yards. The firing starts at 50 yards and in a match you have to shoot 10 rounds with the .45, the .38, and the .22 calibers. You have one minute per round or ten minutes to shoot ten rounds. At 25 yards you shoot the same amount of rounds with all three weapons but you have 25 seconds for each round. At 25 yards you shoot the same number of shots with each pistol but have two five-round sets within 10 seconds. That is where most matches are won or lost.

McMillan was told he had to shoot the 50-yard course at timed fire, and then the 25-yard course at timed fire, and the rapid fire at 25 yards at the same rapid fire time or 10 seconds. As you can image all participants crowded around and watched.

McMillan walked up to the firing line as calm as if it were just a practice round, picked up his .45, and waited for the targets to turn. He fired his required shots and immediately moved to the 25-yard line and did the same. Then the rapid fire.

When he finished you could almost hear a pin drop. The sound had gone from the continuous roar of the guns to dead silence. McMillan put his weapons back in his shooting box and headed for the vehicle waiting to take him to the airport. I don't remember the final score but he had the individual high score for the day. It kind of put a damper on the matches because everyone was shooting for second place. No one would have believed it happened if they hadn't witnessed this impossible feat.

McMillan Against the Army's Best

We started shooting matches against the Army, Air Force, Navy and Border Patrol. These were highly contested matches. Each branch of service had two or three teams. Usually the Blue Team, Red Team, and Yellow Team. Naturally each branch knew the shooters on the other teams and placed their best against the other's best.

The Army had a shooter by the name of Sgt. Benner. He was a lot like McMillan. He was the best they had and both he and McMillan were great friends. They always looked each other up, and shot next to each other. They did everything to mess each other up.

Lt. McMillan on the shooting range

Sometimes you could find a single bullet up on the side of the target of one of the shooters and all the rest in a tight group cutting each other in the bull's eye. They always blamed the other for putting an extra round in their weapon and shooting it into their target. The judges had a tough time judging who did what.

McMillan and the Target Number Trick

Any time we had a match with another branch, their best shooter tried to get next to McMillan to shoot against him. McMillan seemed to have ice water in his veins and nothing bothered him. Pressure was not a word he was acquainted with. In one match, the guy shooting next to him had a bad habit of calling out his target number, real loud when the targets turned so he was sure he was on the right target. On this day McMillan was on target #8 and the other guy on target #9. They were shooting the rapid-fire match where they have ten seconds to shoot five rounds after the target turns. Going into the final five rounds, McMillan and the guy next to him had not dropped a single point. All through the match the guy yelled "nine" as the targets turned.

When the targets started turning on the final five round of rapid fire, McMillan immediately yelled "nine." The guy shot his first round into the ground thinking he was about to shoot the wrong target. McMillan won the match. The other guy told

McMillan that if he had one more round he'd have used it on McMillan. Everyone thought it was hilarious except the guy who lost the match.

McMillan Becomes an Officer Against His Will

Lt. McMillan was one of the greatest rifle and pistol shooters in the Marine Corps. He was equally great with the pistol and the rifle. As an enlisted man he simply won most all the pistol and rifle matches he entered. The World Championships in shooting were coming up and the Marine higher ups thought it would look better if McMillan, a staff sergeant, was an officer. Thus the Commandant of the U.S. Marine Corps ordered McMillan be sent to Officer Candidate School (OCS) in Quantico, Virginia, to become an officer.

The one thing they overlooked was that McMillan did not want to be an officer, and like most of the enlisted men he didn't even like officers.

Some of this story I heard from McMillan himself and most of it from various Marines who had been stationed with him for a number of years.

The story goes something like this:

SSgt. McMillan was approached by his Company Commander and advised he had been selected to go to OCS at Quantico, Virginia. He said, "No, thank you. I don't want to be an officer. I don't even like officers." The company commander said, "I don't care what you like or don't like, the Commandant of the Marine Corps has ordered you to report to Quantico and you are going."

McMillan arrived at Quantico, skipped classes, got drunk at night and involved in disturbances. He thought this surely would get him kicked out of school and back home as a sergeant again.

He thought wrong. He was brought up before the base commander and asked what his problem was. He again reiterated what he had told his company commander about not wanting to be an officer and not liking officers.

The base commander called in the military police. Two MPs put McMillan in cuffs. The commander told him he did not care about McMillan's opinion of officers or what he wanted or did not want. He said he had his orders and McMillan would be an officer.

The MPs were ordered to lock McMillan up each night and pick him up each morning and take him to class. After the last class at the end of the day, they were to take him back to the stockade and lock him up until the following morning. This would continue until McMillan graduated from OCS or decided he wanted to be an officer.

After a period of time, McMillan accepted defeat and decided to finish school just to get out of the stockade. He was taken back to the training quarters for the remainder of the school.

McMillan, much to his disdain, graduated as a 2nd Lieutenant.

USMC Rifle & Pistol Team, Parris Island, SC, August 23, 1954. The arrow is pointing to MSgt. Huelet Benner, rapid fire pistol winner at Camp Perry, Ohio match, 1954. LaVelle, 10th from left, standing.

McMillan Wins Gold

McMillan always seemed to be calm when shooting, so I asked him if anything ever shook him up or made him nervous. He replied that he had been nervous on one occasion when he shot in the World Championships in Venezuela. They were shooting in a mountain region and when all the shooting was completed there were three perfect scores. A Russian, a Venezuelan and McMillan.

140

The three shot the course again and the Venezuelan dropped a point. McMillan and the Russian shot against each other two or three more times before the Russian finally dropped a point and McMillan took gold. He said he was kind of nervous because when they were shooting, you could look around and see hundreds of people all around the sides of the mountains watching the matches and he really felt alone out there as the only American.

McMillan did lose some matches, but you could never tell if it bothered him. He was happy go lucky either way—win or lose.

This guy was the hero of all the enlisted men. He hung out with them on liberty, poker games and such. Sometime after the World Championships, he was made a 1st Lieutenant and then a Captain in charge of the rifle and pistol range at Parris Island, South Carolina.

In 1960, he went on to win the gold medal in Rapid Fire Pistol in the Olympic Games in Rome, Italy.

(I googled him when I was writing this and found that he retired as a Marine Lieutenant Colonel and was a weapons coordinator for the San Diego County Sheriff's Department. Sadly McMillan died in 2000 at age 71. In my opinion, he was the greatest marksman in the world and my friend. Semper Fi, Mac, I sincerely hope to see you again in Heaven.)

Townsend and Tiny
While we were trying out for the team at Parris Island, everyone stayed in one barrack—enlisted men and officers. There was no such thing as rank, it was just the team.

Townsend & date, Kathy Walsh, on Virginia Beach. (Kathy was a Marine, a master shooter, and daughter of Col. Walsh, the team's commanding officer.)

Two good friends were PFC Townsend and Tiny. Townsend was from New Jersey. He was about 6'6," weighed about 250 pounds, and was the Amateur Heavy Weight Boxing and Wrestling Champion of New Jersey.

Tiny was a farm boy from Georgia. He was about 6'6" and weighed about 300 pounds. These guys were big. I never knew why they liked me, but the three of us kind of hung out together. When we went out on liberty, I sat in the rear of Townsend's convertible and the two of them sat in front. It must have been a lopsided sight. I measured 5'11" and weighed about 170 pounds soaking wet.

We went into town one night on liberty, went to a bar full of Marines, and sat at the bar. Townsend and Tiny ordered a beer. I ordered a coke. The bartender stopped in his tracks and said out loud, "This boy wants a what?"

Everyone looked around and Townsend leaned over the bar and said, "My friend wants a coke. Do you have a problem with that?"

The bartender took one look at Townsend and Tiny, who had stood, and said, "No, sir, not at all. No problem." This brought some laughs from the crowd.

We were cautioned at the base about a military policeman who was a Staff Sergeant and very mean. Everyone said he could tear your head off with the club he carried and to stay away from him.

Tiny, Townsend, and I were at a bar again for only a few minutes when a Marine at a table in the back jumped up. He picked up a beer bottle and broke it and held the jagged edge up to another Marine's face and threatened to kill him. There were about eight other Marines at the table and they finally got him calmed down and made him sit down.

Someone must have called the MPs because two of them came in the front door and looked at the back table. One was the SSgt we had heard about. He pointed his club at the back table and said in a loud voice, "You at that back table. Come out and get in the van."

They all looked at each other and all eight got up and walked out to the van. He sorted them out and took the guilty one and let the others go. We just sat there like all the others did and Tiny said, "That guy must be mean."

One day we were leaving the island on liberty and a baby coon ran across the road in front of us. We stopped and the little coon climbed up a tree next to the road. Townsend and Tiny wanted to get the coon and make a pet out of it and asked if I would climb the tree and get the coon.

They lifted me up to the first limb, and I had no problem getting to the little coon. Coming from the farm, however, I knew what damage a coon could do if you grabbed one. About the time I was reaching for his tail an MP vehicle pulled up and two MPs got out and wanted to know what was going on.

Townsend and Tiny told them. About that time I got hold of the tail and said, "Here he comes." I pulled him loose from the tree and in the same motion threw him in the middle of the four Marines on the ground.

Townsend and Tiny grabbed the little coon and they had a lot of trouble turning him loose. Finally they dropped him and he stood up on his little hind legs and hissed at them. The four big Marines went off in four directions. That little fellow whipped all four and trotted off into the woods–a free coon. I couldn't wait to get back to the base and tell the other guys about the little coon that took on Townsend and Tiny.

Tiny Learns to Box

On one of our rare days off for the rifle and pistol team, a group went to a very elaborate gym on Parris Island. Townsend told Tiny he would teach him to box, so they put on gloves. No one in their right mind would put on gloves with Townsend. They all knew he was the Amateur Heavyweight Boxing Champion for the State of New Jersey.

Tiny knew and made Townsend promise he wouldn't hurt him. They were out on the gym floor and Townsend started dancing around and reaching out and tagging Tiny lightly on the head with his left hand. Poor Tiny kept saying, "Don't hurt me."

Townsend grew tired of tagging Tiny and told Tiny to hit him. Tiny said, "No way, I don't want to hurt you 'cause you're my friend." Townsend kept saying, "You are not going to hurt me. I will block all your punches."

He continued on and started tagging Tiny rather hard on the chin and head with his left and finally Tiny started swinging big haymakers with his right and then his left hand, which Townsend

143

easily blocked. Townsend was putting on a show for all the guys standing around and smiling and dancing around and looking around to be sure all were watching.

One of the times he looked out at the crowd, Tiny brought up another wild swing. Townsend didn't see it and Tiny connected on the point of Townsend's chin. Townsend literally left the floor and came down on the back of his head on the mat. He did not move. Tiny snatched off the gloves and fell down beside Townsend. He gently picked up his head and started crying, saying, "I didn't mean to hurt you. I'm so sorry. Please forgive me." Finally Townsend started to revive and everyone breathed a sigh of relief.

Townsend said later that he had never been hit so hard in all his life. This ended the boxing lessons with Tiny.

Pranks in the Rifle and Pistol Team Barracks

Some members of the USMC Rifle and Pistol Team, 1955

The rifle and pistol team stayed in a large barracks with single bunks and all members of the team could pick the bunk they wanted. There were Officers, NCOs and rookies like myself. There were many pranks pulled in that barracks. Most of the time the victim never found out who did it.

Each morning at 0500, reveille was blown in the hallway outside our barracks. Everyone, or most everyone, hit the floor and got dressed for chow. Some waited for the second and final call at 0530 and that meant you had 5 minutes to be in the chow line or you did not eat.

There were always two or three who waited until the last minute and just made it in time. Usually we had an empty bunk next to our bunk and we laid out our fatigues on the unoccupied bunk with our boots and socks sitting next to the bunk. After all the practice we had, we could put on our clothes and be in line in about two or three minutes.

One sergeant always waited until the last minute and just barely made it into the chow line each day. He went on liberty, got in very late and was dead tired when it was time for chow. He always laid his gear out on the bunk beside his prior to going on liberty. The following morning he waited for the last call and made his late mad dash for his clothing and raced into the chow hall as they were closing the doors.

One night, after he left on liberty, a couple of Marines got their "housewives" (sewing kits). They stitched his clothes to the bunk where he had laid them out the night before. Everyone knew who did it, but they would die before telling anyone who the culprit was.

The sergeant, true to form, came in very late after lights out and went to bed. Almost everyone waited outside in the hallway and peeped in the windows when he leaped out of bed and grabbed his fatigues the next morning.

He snatched them up and along came the mattress with his trousers. Realizing what had happened, he raced to his wall locker for another set of clothing. His lock, that he never locked, had been replaced with one that was locked.

When we got back from chow, he was sitting on the other bunk with his pocketknife cutting each stitch one by one. I dare not print the language he used on each of us or what he said he would do if we had the guts to admit who pulled the trick on him. All you could hear was roars of laughter, but no confessions.

***

The night following a prank, we all slept lightly because the victim might retaliate. Since no one ever told on a guilty person, no one knew where the phantom retaliator might strike next. One night I was sound asleep and had crawled down under my

145

blankets that were tucked in so I didn't have to spend much time in making up my bunk the following morning. Most of us did this. I have no idea what I was dreaming but I suddenly felt something warm and fuzzy moving around my feet. It was not uncomfortable, but it suddenly dawned on me that there was something else in my bunk other than me.

I was wide-awake and leaped from my bed with a screech and a big house cat flew out from under the covers and raced away across the barracks. I don't know who was scared the most, the cat or me. I could hear the laughter throughout the barracks. I got my blanket and went back to bed. I made no threats or comments, but didn't sleep much the remainder of the night. I was planning my get-even move.

I had a pretty good idea who pulled the cat trick considering who went on liberty the night before and the ones who did a lot of the dirty tricks. I let a few days go by to give them a feeling of security and then struck. After this group went on liberty that night and just before lights out, I got a bucket and started filling combat boots with water. You could put about six inches of water in a boot and it wouldn't leak out.

The next morning I was up in a flash and out of there. As I was leaving I started hearing a roar of profanity and laughter both at the same time. The guys emptied their boots and had to put them on wet. I had worn wet boots at Parris Island in July, it really gets hot. We shot from 0700 to 1100 and the guys moaned and groaned plenty during the morning as those boots started shrinking up.

***

About four bunks over from mine was Sgt. Petragast, an old salt Tech Sergeant. (That is what a person was called who had been in the Corps for a number of years.) This guy was a large Pollock with a big black moustache. He also had been on the rifle team for a number of years. He was kind of a loner and no one bothered him. He looked really mean and from all his combat ribbons and medals it was evident he had been in many battles. Most of us were really surprised that the phantom picked him.

He had a habit of getting out of his bunk each morning and picking up his big pipe, which he had packed prior to lights out the night before. He lit up and leisurely smoked his pipe as he got dressed for chow.

Someone got the bright idea to do a number on him. After lights out, a prankster took his pipe and dumped out the tobacco and put gunpowder in the bottom and finished filling the pipe with tobacco. I have no idea who did this. They must have been drunk to take such a chance.

The following morning there was no mass exodus for chow. I knew something was in the air, so I hung around. The sergeant finally lit his pipe. When the fire hit the gunpowder, there was a hissing noise and fire shot straight up about four feet high. It took about half of the Sergeant's moustache off as it traveled skyward.

Petragast let out a yell that was more animal than human. He knocked the pipe from his mouth, breaking it and sending it across the barracks. There were howls of laughter throughout the barracks, and a mad exodus for the doors at the same time.

Sergeant Petragast shaved the remainder of his moustache off. For two or three days he walked though the barracks talking to each Marine, telling him what he thought of the low life who did this and begging the guilty one to be man enough to admit it. He talked about each Marine's ancestors, wives, children and anything else he could think of to get a reaction. There were no takers. No one wanted to cross that angry Pollock.

***

Sgt. Duncan was probably one of the top rifle marksmen in the nation. He took his shooting seriously. He sat by his bunk at night and reloaded each round of ammo he was going to shoot the following day. For the 200 yards he loaded a light load. For 300 yards he loaded with a little more powder. For 600 yards he had a heavy powder and for the 1000-yard line he really had a powerful load of about 200 grams as I recall.

Marine Corps Marksmen–Sgt. Duncan, left, Petragast, right

We always had several cases of ammo from major companies sitting out at the range each day to pick from. Some swore by one brand and some another.

Sgt. Duncan always used his own. He didn't watch TV at night or go to a movie for fear of damaging his eyes. He didn't drink any alcoholic beverages or coffee. This guy was serious about his training. On top of this, he was about the nicest Marine I ever met. He was nice to us young guys and the older ones alike. One night the phantom struck and took Duncan's ammo and changed it around. Duncan had a shooting box with 20 bullets on a row marked 200 yards, 20 bullets on a row marked 300 yards, 20 bullets marked 600 yards and 20 bullets marked 1000 yards. The phantom put some 1000-yard bullets in different holes from 200 to 1000 yards and the others the same way. Naturally the word got around and everyone stood quietly waiting for Duncan to start firing.

His first shot went high. He looked at his sight and turned them all the way down and counted the clicks up and fired another shot. This one was out also. He was really getting concerned and fired one more shot. He must have got the 1000-yard bullet because it just about drove him backward off the line.

He knew he had been had. He frowned for the first time I had ever seen him frown and then smiled and walked over to the ammo cart and drew factory ammo for the remainder of the practice round. He never said another word and so far as I know never tried to get even. He was too nice a guy to be a Marine, but next to McMillan he was the best rifle shooter on the team.

While working on this book, I happened to see this news article on the sports page of The News Herald, May 2, 2014, about Col. Walsh, who was the commanding officer of our Marine Corps Pistol and Rifle Team. It reads:

Walter R. Walsh, the world's oldest Olympian, has died. He was 106. USA Shooting says Walsh died Tuesday–six days before his 107th birthday–at his home in Arlington, Va. Walsh finished 12th in the men's 50-meter free pistol event at the 1948 London Olympics. He had already demonstrated his marksmanship working for the FBI and the Marine Corps. During the Depression, Walsh was instrumental in the capture and killing of several gangsters, including discovering the body of Baby Face Nelson and catching Arthur (Doc) Barker. Walsh spent more than 20 years as a shooting instructor before his retirement in 1970. He later served as the team leader for USA Shooting in several competitions, including the 1972 Munich Olympics.

Page C4 | The News Herald | **Friday, May 2, 2014**

SPORTS Briefs

Sharpshooter Walter Walsh dies at 106

ARLINGTON, Va. — Walter R. Walsh, the world's oldest living Olympian, has died. He was 106.

USA Shooting says Walsh died Tuesday — six days before his 107th birthday — at his home in Arlington, Va.

Walsh finished 12th in the men's 50-meter free pistol event at the 1948 London Olympics. He had already demonstrated his marksmanship working for the F.B.I. and the Marine Corps.

During the Depression, Walsh was instrumental in the capture and killing of several gangsters, including discovering the body of Baby Face Nelson and catching Arthur (Doc) Barker.

Walsh spent more than 20 years as a shooting instructor before his retirement in 1970.

He later served as the team leader for USA Shooting in several competitions, including the 1972 Munich Olympics.

I was blessed to be associated with some of the best marksmen in the world.

My days of service came to a close. I had a recommendation for the U.S. Naval Academy, but I was twenty-one and missed the age cut off by a couple of months.

One of my buddies from high school told me about a football scholarship opportunity in Mississippi. I took a ten day leave and drove to Ellisville, Mississippi, where Jones Junior College is located, and tried out for a football scholarship.

I had stiff competition. Some were All-State and others were All American high school players. These kids had trained to play football while I had been learning how to kill people. I have to give credit to the good Lord, Marine training and Coach Jim Clark for being selected for a scholarship. (Having three friends who were returning first string players from Panama City supporting me helped.)

JONES JUNIOR COLLEGE
(1956-1957)

College, Football, and Pranks

1956 ELLISVILLE BOBCATS

The 1956 Ellisville Bobcats, LaVelle, #56, 3rd row up, middle

Libby

In September of 1956, I was in training for football season at Jones Junior College in Ellisville, Mississippi. I had been released from the USMC a few weeks early to attend college. My roommate, Don York, and I were freshmen. Our nearest neighbors across the hall, were Sherrill Balkon, the fastest man on our team, and Sammy Burkett. Burkett was a guard on offense and defense

151

that could whip his weight in wildcats. Both Balkon and Burkett were sophomores and we were all from Panama City.

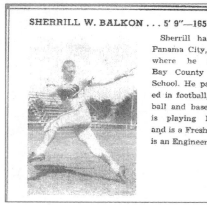

SHERRILL W. BALKON ... 5' 9"—165

Sherrill hails from Panama City, Florida, where he attended Bay County H i g h School. He participated in football, basketball and baseball. He is playing Halfback and is a Freshman. He is an Engineer major.

SAM B. BURKETT ... 5' 10"—185

Sam comes to us from Panama City, Florida, and he attended Bay County High School w h e r e he played football t w o years. He is a Sophomore and is playing Guard a n d Tackle. Sam has chosen Engineering as his major field of study.

From time to time Sherrill and Sammy talked about this young, beautiful woman who lived a few miles from the campus. She was supposedly free with sexual favors when her husband was at work. They offered to set it up for Don and me to meet her one night when her husband was gone.

Don asked me what I thought of the idea and I blew it off thinking it was some kind of a trick. After all I had just gotten out of the Marine Corps where dirty tricks were born. Sammy got me off to the side and confessed the truth. It was a sham and he was afraid I was going to blow it for Don.

There was an old house about five miles from the campus off the main highway and no one lived there. The set up was that one of the football players, a boy named Pete Flemming from Pensacola, Florida, would be dropped off at the house with a double barrel shotgun. Later, when the unsuspecting freshman arrived, he would come out with the shotgun and yell and fire the gun up in the air.

Well, it sounded workable to me, so I was instructed to go along with the prank. They would drop Don and me off on the highway and we were told to walk up to the house on an old dirt road. When we got near the house we were to call out, "Libby." She would be inside with no lights on and would answer saying to come in.

When the gun fired I was to yell, "I'm hit, I'm hit," and fall on the ground. Like I said, the more I heard the plan, the more I got into it. My roommate was really enthused and could do nothing but talk about Friday night and our date.

Come Friday night we started out. Don wore a black t-shirt, blue jeans, black socks and loafers. All the football players dressed much like this around the campus so the girls could see our muscles. I think everyone on the campus knew what was going down except my roommate. I had the hardest time keeping a straight face all day when Don talked about it.

Shortly after dark we left the campus with Sherrill and Sammy in the front seat and Don and I in the back seat. We got to the dirt road and they dropped us off in the dark. We had no flashlight. They just said follow the little dirt road, it will take you to Libby's front door.

We started walking. It was really dark, with no house or light anywhere near. All the way down the road, all Don talked about was who was going to be first and if she was really as good looking as they had told us. I told Don he could go first, if he liked, and he said, "I owe you one." (If he only knew.)

We finally got close to a large dark house about 200 yards off the highway and Don called real low, "Libby."

No answer.

"Maybe she's not home," Don whispered.

I said, "Call a little louder."

He called, "Libby," and then a real loud, "LIBBY!"

Suddenly a door slammed and a deep bass voice yelled, "You must be the SOB who has been screwing my wife!" With that, a shotgun blast went off and I yelled, "I'm hit!" The second blast went off and I lay on the ground. For a moment I heard feet running and then nothing. I lay there for a few minutes unable

DONALD C. YORK . . . 6' 3"—205

Donald hails from Panama City, Florida, and he attended Bay County High School where he lettered in football two years. He is playing Tackle here and is majoring in Physical Education.

to get up because my stomach was cramping from laughter. Pete came out of the house with several football players and you could hear everyone laughing.

Sherrill and Sammy drove in and called for Don to come back. There was no answer. Everyone started calling Don. Then we started getting worried, because he was in a strange area and we had a ball game the following Saturday afternoon. Don was a big star on offense and defense. If something happened to him, the coach probably would run all of us off.

We drove up and down the highway calling and blowing the car horn, but no Don. Where Don had been standing by the house when the shotgun went off was one of his loafers, pointed toward the house. About 30 feet down the road was the other loafer pointed the other direction. So he was barefooted except for his socks. After about an hour and half, we went back to my room on campus to quietly organize a search party and hoped the coach didn't find out.

Just as we were about to leave, someone said, "Don just ran on to the campus." I got in the closet and Don came up the stairs breathing real hard and yelled, "We've got to go get my roommate! He's been shot!" They started asking him what happened and he said, "When we got to the house her husband was there. He ran out and shot Pitts."

They asked what he did.

He said, "Man, I took off to go get help. When I got to the highway and started back toward the campus a big dog ran out from a house and I flat outran him. Then I saw a car coming up behind me and figured it was the husband trying to shoot me, too. I jumped off the road into what I thought was a ditch. It was really off a hill and I rolled for a long time before I stopped. I heard the car go up and down the road and when it finally left I crawled back up to the highway and ran all the way back to campus."

I could stand it no longer and stepped out of the closet. I'll never forget the look on Don's face. He said, "Roommate, are you all right?" Then it dawned on him. He had been had.

He really took it well considering the condition he was in. Both of his socks were shredded on the bottom and ends. Poor Don had a blister on all ten toes. There was grass, mud, dirt, stickers, and sand all over his body.

After everyone calmed down, we suddenly remembered he had a tough football game the next afternoon and it was doubtful Don could play. I must say there were a lot of home remedies tried that night to get Don ready.

All I can say is Don was a good sport. He could have refused to play the next day and all of us would have been in a mess of trouble, but he never said a word. He dressed out and played a heck of a good game on both offense and defense. The coach never knew.

I began my football career playing third string end. Of all the positions I could have tried for, I had to go with the one I played in high school and my competition was two guys who were about a foot taller, 50 pounds heavier and both could run like deer. Needless to say, I sat on the bench the entire first game.

But there were two incidents that happened in that first game that did end up affecting me. The first string, all American High School center was injured and the second string center got his butt kicked really bad in the third and fourth quarter.

The following Monday when we reviewed the game film the coach asked if anyone had any experience playing center in high school. I quickly raised my hand and said, "Coach, I did a little."

He said, "Good, you're center as of right now. Learn the plays."

I did okay snapping the ball to the quarterback, but I had real problems on punts. Robinson, our punter, stood twelve to fourteen yards behind me. My snaps might bounce on the ground, be high over his head, or one or two steps to his right or left. The guy was a great punter after he got hold of the ball.

This was Robinson's second season at Jones Junior College, and apparently he was kicking the ball much better than the year before. He was questioned one afternoon about his punting because he was the top punter in the conference. He said, "Last year my primary concern was punting the ball. This year I don't worry so much about my punting–I can credit my center for that. I just worry about where the ball is going to end up so I can field it for the punt." As I recall Richardson's punting average was a little over 50 yards per punt. With dubious pride I'm thankful my imprecise ball placement contributed to his impressive record.

Raising the Old Flag

Jones Junior College was a very old school that had a high school on one side of the campus, with the college taking in a large area on the south side. A football stadium was on the east side of the school where the high school played on Friday nights and the college played on Saturday afternoons. The stadium held about 12,000 fans, as I recall. We had a very good team and usually filled the stadium on Saturday.

After the game, we just kind of hung out around the campus until Monday morning classes. Most of us were from out of state and had no place to go and no money to spend when we got there. So we sat around telling stories and trying to entertain ourselves. The guys who had cars could not leave the campus because the coach had all car keys.

One Sunday, we came up with a great idea. We should scale the side of the administration building to the second floor, enter the auditorium through a window, get the Rebel flag, and run it up the flagpole on the front of the campus. There were some risks involved like climbing up the side of a building to the second floor and through a window into the auditorium without getting caught and keeping the flag flying until all the students arrived on Monday morning. We knew the first professor to arrive would take the flag down.

I was selected to climb up and steal the flag because I was a former Marine and was supposed to be able to climb mountains and jump small hills and the like. I made the flag trip without too much trouble, but putting the flag up and keeping it up took some planning.

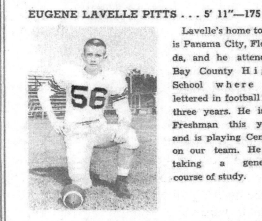

EUGENE LAVELLE PITTS . . . 5' 11"—175

Lavelle's home town is Panama City, Florida, and he attended Bay County High School where he lettered in football for three years. He is a Freshman this year and is playing Center on our team. He is taking a general course of study.

Some farm boy came up with an idea that he witnessed at a carnival. They put a ten dollar bill on the top of a long pole, stuck in the ground, greased the pole and anyone who could climb the pole got the ten dollar bill.

Sounded like a winner to me. We raised the banner of the Old South on Sunday night and a small guy got on Don's shoulders and tied the pull-rope for the flag high up the pole. The pole was then greased as high as the kid could reach from the top of Don's shoulders, all the way to the ground.

Monday morning we got up early and rushed outside to see a large number of the student body crowded around the flagpole laughing. A very mad caretaker was staring at the pole with a lot of grease on his clothes. It took two or three hours for the college brains in power to figure out a way to get the flag down. Someone finally got a long ladder and that did the trick. An investigation took place with threats of expulsion from the president of the college when the guilty party or parties were identified. I think most every student knew who the guilty parties were, but no one ever told.

The Turkey Detail

Most of my teammates would have made good Marines. They could come up with some great ideas and then think up some way to accomplish the desired goals without doing the dangerous part themselves.

One great thought came from Gene Mosley, a high school senior, who took a liking to us Panama City boys. Many times he took us to his mother and dad's farm on weekends. The farm was not far, and his mom could cook some great meals.

He suggested we go to a place where a lot of wild turkeys roosted, sneak up and snatch one, cut his head off and have his mom cook us a turkey dinner. The dinner idea won out and we set out about midnight.

Not only were we breaking curfew but it ended up the turkeys were not wild turkeys but tame, and belonged to a farmer. When all the facts came out we were miles out in the country and had made arrangements for a turkey dinner the next day.

We decided to go through with our original plan and naturally they decided that the former Marine was the logical one to do the deed. I had to crawl across the field to the barn and snatch a turkey off the fence within 30-feet of the farm house. That is good gun-shot distance. I was beginning to wish I had never been in the Marine Corps.

It was a hair-raising experience but I managed to get to the fence. The turkeys were getting mighty nervous and making noises. I finally grabbed one and took off across the field expecting a gun to shoot any minute. I made it and everyone enjoyed the turkey dinner except me. I kept remembering my Dad preaching that:

An idle mind is the devil's workshop, and an idle brain is the devil's playground. I seemed to fit both categories.

Ending My College Career

We finished the football season and were rated the top Junior College team in the Southeastern United States. We were invited to the Junior Rose Bowl in California to play a team from Missouri. There was a lot of rejoicing on the campus for a few days until the powers that be found out there was a black player on the Missouri team. The College Board met immediately and voted to decline the invitation.

I voiced my opinion because I had worked with black kids most all my life. I caddied on Panama City Country Club with them all the way through high school. In the Marine Corps, I fought with blacks and would have laid my life on the line for them as they would have for me. I couldn't understand what the big deal was, and was very vocal on the campus. I got the word to be quiet or I could possibly lose my scholarship. I finally did quiet down but my scholarship was given to someone else the following year.

I attended a Jones Junior College homecoming game almost 50 years later and to my amazement there were nine black and two white players on the starting line-up. To a small degree I felt vindicated.

LETTERMEN'S CARD

Jones County A. H. S. and Jr. College

ELLISVILLE, MISS.

LAVELLE PITTS

College Football | Season of 1956
Sport | Date

Jim Clark
Coach

Ath. Director

159

LAW ENFORCEMENT
(1957-1989)

Becoming a Deputy Sheriff

I left college, got married to a Mississippi girl, Sarah Allman, and came home to Panama City to find a job. My father introduced me to Sheriff M.J. Doc Daffin, the very popular Sheriff of Bay County. As a result, in 1957, instead of snapping a football and backing up the line on defense, I pinned on a badge and become a law enforcement officer.

Doc looked me over and said there were a few things he required of someone to work for him–to be a citizen of Bay County, a graduate of Bay High School, a Democrat, and a jailer until you were twenty-five years of age. Doc said no one under twenty-five had sense enough or was mature enough to be a patrol deputy. Since I fit all the above criteria and my father was well-known in Bay County as a pastor of a local church for some years, it was a good political move for the sheriff to hire me.
Doc sent me upstairs to see Mr. Maxwell, the chief deputy, who did the honors of getting me on the payroll. I was very excited, knowing I was about to be sworn in as a deputy sheriff.
Mr. Maxwell was a tall, gray-haired man who seldom smiled. He looked me over and wrote down my name, social security number and address. Then he handed me a small silver star badge and said, "Go to Sears and buy some green work trousers, gray shirts and snap on ties. There's a store on Harrison Avenue where you can find some gray ribbon. Get your wife to sew a stripe down each leg of your trousers." He advised the only things the sheriff's

office furnished were a badge, a commission card, one Stetson hat and arm patches.

I asked about a weapon and he suggested that I check at one of the two pawnshops in town for a .38 Special revolver and gun belt. He said my black Marine Corps issue shoes would be okay to wear to work. I was to see Charley Wilsdorf, the chief jailer, on Monday and he would put me on a schedule.

**Mama, LaVelle (a new deputy),
little brother Larry and Daddy, 1957**

My starting pay was $275.00 per month. My work hours were 12 hours a day, 7 days a week. If I was needed when I was off, I would be called out. There was no such thing as overtime, vacation time or sick leave at the sheriff's office.

I found an old .38 Special Colt revolver at Woody's Pawn Shop on east 6th Street for $29.00. I purchased green work trousers and gray wash and wear work shirts from Sears and gray ribbon from The Ribbon Store on Harrison Avenue. Sarah sewed the ribbon down the outside of both legs. They looked okay, but nothing like the dress trousers the Marines furnished. The first time the trousers were washed, the ribbon shrank and pulled the pant legs up about two inches on the side. And that was my start at the Bay County Sheriff's Office.

Early Events at the Bay County Sheriff's Office (1957-1961)

Uncle Custer

After leaving Mr. Maxwell's Office the day I received my badge and commission card, I walked back downstairs looking at my small badge. As I passed the coffee table, a small older gentleman was sitting there sipping a cup of coffee. He asked me to sit down. I did, because I didn't know who all the bosses were yet and I wasn't going to take a chance.

He said, "You must be the new man Doc just hired."

I said, "Yes, sir."

"Son," he said, "I'm Custer Russ, the uncle of Doc Daffin. Most people call me Uncle Custer."

(I didn't know then, but later realized this was probably one of the best things I did–making friends with Uncle Custer.)

Uncle Custer said, "I'm going to give you some free advice. You probably won't listen or remember, but it's free so I'll tell you anyway. That badge you have there just made you a son of a bitch."

I was shocked. "I thought I was one of the good guys."

He said, "In the eyes of a lot of people you are just another young hot head running around the county trying to find someone to put in jail." He emphasized two things. "First, remember when you stop a car, and ask the driver for his driver's license, take a good look at that driver and always remember but for the grace of God it could be you sitting under the steering wheel and the other person looking at your license. Next, if you treated that person the way you wanted to be treated, you wouldn't go wrong too many times."

I never forgot this and repeated it numerous times to new officers and employees that eventually came under my command.

**Uncle Custer Russ on left, with a catch of fish
behind the jail, around 1957**

This was the first of many meetings with Uncle Custer at the coffee table. He was always cheerful and gave advice when I asked, and sometimes when I didn't ask. More than one time, I believe, he interceded and saved my job with Doc Daffin when I screwed up. Doc had a quick temper and would fire someone at the drop of a hat, and sometimes he dropped the hat.

If you had a confrontation with someone, you had better get to the sheriff first with your side of the story. If not, you might not have a job the next day if that person got to him first. I learned quickly, that if I couldn't find the sheriff, to go to Uncle Custer and explain my side of what happened. He always came through for me.

Uncle Custer was a great and knowledgeable man. He was one of the few people who could tell Doc Daffin he was wrong and get away with it.

Bloody Bucket
(This is one of the first law enforcement stories I heard when I became a deputy.)

In the early 1950s there were several small jukes scattered around Bay County. Five dollars could get you drunk, a woman, a real fight (if you were looking for one) and your butt whipped on top of all the above.

164

Most of the trouble happened on the weekends. The commercial fishermen fished all week and usually brought their catch in on Friday afternoon. After the boat was unloaded, fish sold, and crew paid, the fishermen usually headed straight for one of the local jukes.

Two brothers took their pay and went to a juke on Highway 22 about two miles east of the City of Springfield. There were several customers there, most being fishermen. The customers lost no time drinking beer and trying to make out with the females present.

The two brothers were getting very drunk when they apparently got into an argument over a girl and this led to a fight. One of the brothers ordered the other to leave and threatened to cut his head off and put it in the mop bucket sitting near the bar. This did not seem to discourage the other brother.

According to witnesses, soon after the threat, the fight between the two started again. The one brother that had made the threat, pulled his fishing knife out and literally cut his brother's head off and dropped it in the mop bucket.

When a deputy arrived, the head was in the bucket and the brother was sitting at the bar drinking his beer.

From that day on, the juke was called the "Bloody Bucket" by officers until it was torn down. When we stopped to check a business or bar or got out of the patrol car for any reason, we had to sign out and give our location. Many times you heard an officer sign out with, "Car 27 will be 10-6 at the Bloody Bucket." Later you heard, "Car 27 will be 10-8 from the Bloody Bucket."

Twigs the Wonder Dog

Twigs came into my life in the early years of my career. I was a jailer at the Bay County Jail and Twigs, a pure-bred bloodhound, arrived as a gift to Doc Daffin from a doctor friend who lived some place up North. Doc said we were going to train this dog to track escapees.

LaVelle with Twigs, 1958

We had both a county and state prison camp in our county. Unfortunately some of the inmates grew tired of their environment and left without permission. When this happened we had to call the state prison camp in Chattahoochee, Florida, for bloodhounds. This was about 60 miles away and it took quite some time for them to arrive. By this time, the escapee was long gone. Sad to say, most of the escapes were successful.

Doc Daffin in his infinite wisdom, knowing I was a farm boy, decided I was the one who would be the expert dog trainer to catch escapees. I had no idea how to train a bloodhound. Twigs was the first one I ever saw.

Doc decided that I should continue to work my 12-hour shift plus come in each day for at least two additional hours and train the dog. Needless to say, there was no extra pay for the training time or for the many times I had to come out on my off-duty time and chase a prisoner.

The training started when Twigs was about six or seven weeks old. I copied some of my dad's old methods of training hog dogs. I took a prisoner (trustee) out and let him pet the puppy and then run a short distance and get behind some bushes. I turned the puppy loose and told him to find him. He did.

Twigs ran to the bushes and jumped on the trustee who petted and praised him. This went on for several weeks. We kept extending the distance until the trustee ran about a mile, hid and the puppy would find him. Each time the trustee petted and praised the dog, and that was the only reward he wanted.

When Twigs was 6 months old he caught his first prisoner who escaped from a work gang. The catching of the prisoner was the easy part. The hard part was making the prisoner pet and praise the dog after being caught.

This became a standard problem when we captured a prisoner. But before we came out of the woods the escapee concurred with our way of thinking and petted the dog. I always let the dog ride in the back of the patrol car with the prisoner, who had his hands handcuffed behind him. The prisoner could do nothing but use foul language and talk bad about the dog and me.

Twigs accepted the prisoner's chatter as praise and every now and then licked him across the face with his big tongue. That really brought out some bad language. The prisoner was briefed before he was placed in the patrol car and told what would happen if he hurt the dog in any way, so we had an understanding.

By the time Twigs was a year old, he had caught thirteen escapees. He got more press than the sheriff. The head dog trainer for the state prisons came by one day and wanted to see Twigs. After looking at him he asked how old he was. When I told him one year, he was amazed and said you're not supposed to start training a dog until he is two and a half or three years old. Twigs and I didn't know that.

Tracking with bloodhound, Twigs

There was a big redheaded kid serving a year on the county road gang. He escaped five times and got extra time after each escape. Twigs caught him each time and I really think the dog started to love this guy.

The escapee hated to pet Twigs and one or two times we had to hold a little "prayer meeting" in the woods before he agreed to pet the dog. Twigs loved to ride in the back seat with

167

"Red." The guy called Twigs names all the way to the jail, while Twigs gave him wet kisses and wagged his tail.

Marvin "Big Mo" Freeman

Marvin Freeman, or Big Mo as many people called him, was a name that was known as well as Doc Daffin. Marvin was a deputy sheriff when Bay County was a part of Washington County. At one time, only one sheriff and Mo policed the entire area. Marvin Freeman was indeed a legend in his time. I was fortunate enough to have him as one of my training officers when I went on patrol. Being a young officer, I was looking for excitement, fights, robbers, burglars–somebody to arrest. Marvin didn't feel that way. Putting someone in jail was his last resort. In fact, it was almost impossible to get Marvin to lock anyone up. He always tried to settle problems by talking to a subject, taking him home or threatening to put him in jail if he had to come back. I never remember him having to go back.

Marvin Freeman standing on the far right. This photo taken shows the BCSO in the early 1960s with a group of Junior Deputies, a program Doc Daffin started for youngsters.

One time, while I was jailing, they sent Marvin on a call in which a drunk was causing a problem at a bar outside Springfield. Marvin signed out and later called in and advised he was 10-12 and 10-8. That meant he had someone with him and was back on the air. About an hour later Marvin called back and said he was 10-15 (prisoner in custody) and en route to the jail.

Several of us were at the coffee table, along with Doc Daffin, when the dispatcher called down over the intercom that Marvin was 10-15. Doc said, "I don't believe it. That guy must have done something really bad for Marvin to bring him to jail." He got up and went to the back door in time to see Marvin getting out of the patrol car.

He opened the back door and this guy jumped out, raced in the back door and back to the booking desk. He started putting personal items from his pockets on the table. Needless to say he had been there many times and knew the routine.

Doc asked Marvin what this guy did that was so bad. Marvin was thoroughly upset. He told the sheriff that he took the guy home from the bar and told him to get out. The guy refused and demanded to go to jail.

Marvin drug him out of the patrol car and up to his front porch. When he released him, the guy ran back and jumped in the patrol car. Marvin took him out again and the same thing happened. He said he had to bring him to jail because his shift was ending and he needed to go home himself. Doc said, "Well, I knew it had to be something unusually bad."

***

Law enforcement in the 50s and 60s always referred to spring break as AEA (Alabama Education Association), when Alabama schools were out and kids flooded the beaches. Marvin, with his frequent riding partner, Tommy Smith, handled problems that occurred at the hot spot on the beach–the Hang-Out.

Of the thousands of high school and college kids gathered on Panama City Beach each year, most of them made an appearance at the Hang-Out. Some spent the entire summer in or around the Hang-Out. The Hang-Out was comprised of three large concrete pavilions with one juke box in each pavilion. There were all kinds of games, rides, snack bars and souvenir stands and a large building called the casino, where it was rumored to have housed slot machines in the old days. The fights and problems always seemed to start on the dance floor.

Tommy and Big Mo broke up the fights, arrested the disorderly and called for patrol cars to transport subjects to the jail.

Tommy loved it when someone resisted. Big Mo told me one Friday that they had an incident with a college boy and he hoped nothing came of it. A group of huge guys, real clean cut, came down to the Hang-Out and the larger of the guys asked where he could find a deputy called Hondo. Tommy said, "That's me."

This guy said he was a football player from Auburn University and so were the others with him. "We aren't looking for trouble and don't even drink, but we heard you were the meanest, toughest guy on the beach. The last thing I want is to go to jail, but I'd really like a friendly, no holds barred, fight to find out if you are as bad as they say."

This guy apparently had the same kind of reputation at Auburn as Tommy did on the beach.

Tommy told the young man, "There's no time like the present."

He unpinned his badge, handed it to Deputy Freeman along with his pistol and invited them to the beach.

Freeman tried to talk Tommy out of it and said he'd get fired. "Besides, there's five of them and only one of you."

The college guy said, "No problem. My friends are just watchers and will not interfere."

Marvin said he didn't see the fight but in a few minutes the Auburn players came back carrying their friend and took him out to a car and left. Tommy put his badge and gun back on and never said a word about what happened. Freeman said he saw very little sign on Tommy's face and he didn't seem to be hurt in any way.

The fight took place on a Friday afternoon and Sunday afternoon the same five guys showed up at the Hang-Out again and went where Tommy and Freeman were standing. The one in the fight had very visible signs of the fight on his face and head.

He stuck his hand out and shook hands with Tommy and said, "No hard feelings, Hondo. You are truly the meanest SOB I have ever met." Word got out and I never heard of anyone who challenged Tommy again.

***

The first time I rode with Marvin, we visited three or four jukes located on SR 22, just outside the City of Springfield on the edge of Callaway. The deputies called it "22 Sunset Strip" (after the TV show *77 Sunset Strip*).

The strip was one of most popular hangouts on the east side of the county. You could park and visit all the jukes without moving your car. If you got thrown out of one juke, you could just walk a few yards and be in the next one. If you couldn't pick up a girl or guy (as the case might be) in one, just keep walking. There were those who got their butts kicked for trying to pick up someone else's girlfriend. That's when we normally entered the picture.

I was in high hopes of action when we entered the first juke. To my surprise, everyone saw Big Mo and it was like old home week. Everyone started shaking his hand, slapping him on the back, and the girls were hugging his neck. We sat down at the bar and were handed a cup of coffee, on the house. I sat there, a rookie deputy looking for action, and found a family reunion instead.

We were only to be out of the car for five or less minutes, unless there was trouble, so I figured we wouldn't be there long. I still didn't know Marvin very well. He marched to his own drummer. After about 45 minutes, Marvin decided we had to move on, so we headed out to the next juke.

I thought this surely would be the fighting juke from all I had heard from the other deputies. Wrong again, same reception from the second, third and fourth jukes. I learned that if you wanted action, you did not want to ride with Big Mo. Dale Carnegie would have been proud of Marvin because he knew how to win friends and influence people.

I learned a valuable lesson and did not realize it until later in my law enforcement career. In many cases what's most important is not seeing how many you can put in jail, but solving problems, keeping the peace, and helping people stay out of jail.

As Marvin explained, the guy or gal we locked up was usually not the one who got hurt as much as the family members at home and little children who looked to the person for their support. I have tried to pass this concept on to many young officers just starting out.

***

But there was another side to Marvin, when he started drinking (off-duty and sometimes on-duty) he could be bad news. I remember one afternoon Sheriff Daffin got a call that Marvin was at a Cook's Bayou juke on the east side of the county and very drunk. He was off-duty and on his old pick-up truck. He had reportedly shot up the place.

All the deputies were at the jail changing shifts. Doc said he needed someone to run out to Big Orah's juke to bring Marvin in and lock him up until he sobered up. It got very quiet and the deputies started looking around at each other.

Doc said, "Are all you guys afraid of Big Mo?"

Some admitted they were and others lied and said they just didn't want to hurt him. Doc turned to the smallest deputy there, Walter Ellis. He said, "Ellis, go get Marvin and put his ass in this jail."

Ellis smiled and got in a car and headed out. Some believed this would be the end of Ellis, but no one volunteered to go with him. Not a deputy left the jail. They waited to hear what happened. About 45 minutes later, Ellis called in and said he was en route to the jail.

Everyone tried to get a good location to watch the excitement when Marvin was put in jail. Ellis pulled in and got out of the patrol car. Big Mo got out from the passenger side and he and Ellis walked in with their arms around each other singing some old country song.

Doc Daffin almost started a war as they were walking down the hallway. The sheriff said, "Marvin, you drunken fool. You are an embarrassment to the sheriff's office."

Big Mo turned around and all the good humor left him. He pointed his finger at the sheriff and said, "Why you sorry old bas- - - -. How many times have I hauled your drunk ass around this county in the backseat of my car, hiding you from the governor's investigators? How many times have I hid you and watched after

1957 Christmas party at BCSO: Front : LaVelle, Sheriff Doc Daffin, Helen Haggerty, Row 2-women in uniform- Dutch Sirmons, Helen Breedlove, Ginny Cobb, Behind starting on left W. A. Stewart, B.D. Culver, Leonard Finch, Cade Pearson, W.A. Browning, Marvin Freeman-with glasses on.

you while you were trying to sober up? And you call me a drunk? Why I will just kick your ass right now in front of your whole department."

Doc immediately left the area. It took some real talking from Ellis to get Marvin back to his cell. Ellis is probably the only one there who could have done that without someone getting hurt. Marvin slept about ten or twelve hours and a deputy took him home. The sheriff fired him. I found out this was the normal thing Doc did when Marvin got drunk.

When payday came along, I was working the east side of town where Marvin lived. Doc handed me a check and said, "Take this to Marvin's wife. Don't you dare give it to him. Give it to his wife to buy groceries."

This went on for about a month. Doc told us to check on Marvin and see if he had dried out enough to come back to work. He had and he did, just as though nothing had ever happened.

A short time later, Doyle Connor, the Agriculture Commissioner for the State of Florida, was in town campaigning for re-election. Being a good friend of Doc Daffin's, he came by the jail and was drinking coffee at the table during shift change and Marvin came in. Doc introduced Marvin and said, "This is a good old boy, but sometimes he'll mess up. I've fired him 12 times, but he somehow works himself back in when he straightens up."

Marvin looked at Doc and said, "Doc, that's a damn lie."

Doc turned red as a beet and said, "What do you mean?"

Marvin said, "It's 13 times."

Doc smiled and said, "Okay, 13 times then."

Marvin was back in good graces with the sheriff.

***

There was another time Marvin got on a drunk at Big Orah's juke. This place was miles from a phone on the east side of Bay County near the Gulf County line and Cook's Bayou. When they had problems someone had to drive into Callaway to get a phone to call the sheriff's office.

Marvin had a day off and bought a sack full of BBQ chicken and decided to share it with big Orah. Marvin furnished the food and Orah the beer.

I guess every town has a few really tough bullies, or some who think they are. Three brothers (I will call them the Waltons), who lived on the east side of the county, were bullies and especially bad when they traveled together drinking. They were big, mean, had several confrontations with the law and in particular with Freeman. They had one very large friend (I'll refer

175

to him as Gus) who usually traveled with them. He was almost as bad as the brothers.

I never knew why, but these guys had at least one thing they all seemed to agree on, they did not like Marvin Freeman. They drove up to Big Orah's juke on the afternoon Marvin was there getting drunk and eating chicken with Big Orah. No one else was present at the juke when they walked in.

They looked around and quickly took in the situation. They saw that Marvin was alone, wasn't on duty and didn't have a gun. They closed and locked the door and one said, "Well, Big Mo, we finally caught you alone and off duty. We hope you enjoyed your dinner because you're going to get the worst ass-whipping you've ever had."

Marvin said, "Okay, but if you don't mind I'd like to go in the bathroom and wash my hands first." They laughed and told him to go ahead, there was plenty of time.

Marvin went in the restroom and out a back door the brothers didn't know about. He went to his pick-up truck, grabbed a Carbine with a 15-round clip and re-entered the juke after kicking open the front door.

As he came in, he fired several shots off into the ceiling. The brothers departed through the back door and a window.

Some passer-by called the BCSO and a deputy was dispatched to the juke. The deputy dispatched to Big Orah's said when he entered the juke only Marvin's old truck and one car were in the parking lot. Inside he found Marvin sitting on one side of the bar and Big Orah on the other side. Both were eating BBQ chicken and drinking beer. Leaning on the bar next to Marvin was an M1 Carbine rifle.

After hearing the story from Orah and Marvin, the deputy went outside and started calling the brothers to come back out of the woods. No one took him up on his offer. The night shift said that sometime that night the brothers came out of the woods, got their vehicle and left the area. They never filed a complaint.

***

A riding partner of Marvin Freeman told this story and swore it to be the truth. A rash of burglaries had been going on at various businesses for several months and both the local police department of Panama City and the Bay County Sheriff's Office had worked many hours of overtime staking out various locations. This was in addition to their regular shift. Back then there was no such thing as overtime or days off.

Someone called Sheriff Daffin and gave him the name of an ex-con who lived just off Cove Boulevard. He said this guy was the burglar he was looking for. Doc ordered him arrested and put in jail for investigation. During that period of time in the 1950s, you could hold a man in jail for 72 hours for investigation and question him. This guy had been there and done that many times and knew all the ropes. He would not admit to doing anything wrong. He laughed and said, "Prove it."

Just before the 72 hours expired, Marvin pulled behind the jail and told the jailer to bring this suspect out. The sheriff was not present and the jailer did what Big Mo asked him to do. His riding partner kept asking Marvin what he was doing, and Marvin just smiled and said wait and see.

They put the cuffs on the prisoner, sat him in the back seat of the patrol car and headed toward Wewahitchka down Highway 22. Going through Springfield, Marvin pulled into the Shell service station and took a five gallon can out and filled it full of gas. He put it back in the trunk and drove off toward Wewahitchka. His partner said he was really beginning to wonder and the prisoner was getting worried.

Several miles out of town Marvin pulled off on a two-trail dirt road and drove out in the woods on the Gaskins Reservation. They stopped in a cleared area where the pulp wood people had been cutting trees. Marvin picked out a pine tree that had not been cut and took the prisoner to it. He backed him up to the tree and handcuffed him with his hands behind the tree.

By this time the prisoner was begging Freeman to not beat him up. Marvin told him he had no intention of beating him, he just wanted him to tell him all the places he had burglarized in the past few months. The guy started yelling that he had not broken into any place.

177

Marvin opened the trunk and took out the can of gas and started splashing gas on the prisoner and the tree. Marvin's riding partner begged him to stop. The prisoner yelled and cried.

Marvin took a big box of kitchen matches from the patrol car and struck one and flipped it high in the air. It went out before it reached the gas fumes. The prisoner, by this time was screaming bloody murder and begging. Just as Marvin started to strike the second match the guy yelled, "Okay, okay. I'll talk."

He did and they wrote down all the places on a pad. Marvin took him back to the jail and told him he best tell the investigators everything he told them. The prisoner did and pled guilty.

***

One day Marvin gave me words of wisdom when we were talking about an officer who had messed up and gotten fired by the sheriff. Marvin explained that sometimes Doc was too hard on the officers.

"Doc messes up, I mess up and so do others. You can't unshoot a gun. Sometimes you just need to work around a situation." As an example, he related this story.

When Marvin started in law enforcement he worked for the Sheriff of Washington County. There was no Bay County at that time. Most of the time, Marvin worked the entire area on patrol.

He received a call one day from the sheriff, who sounded very excited. He advised Marvin that a bank robbery had just occurred in Tallahassee. Marvin was instructed to get on U.S. Highway 90 and be on the lookout for a late model black automobile, no other description. The suspects left Tallahassee on U.S. Highway 90 and were expected to be entering Jackson County any time, headed toward Pensacola. The sheriff advised the people in the vehicle were armed and should be considered dangerous.

Marvin drove to the bottom of a hill on Highway 90 and blocked the highway with his patrol car. He said he had only been in place for a few minutes when a big black limo topped the hill and was moving at a high rate of speed. The limo started breaking immediately and slid all over the road from side to side and finally came to a stop a few feet from his patrol car.

It scared Marvin because he thought the guy was going to hit his patrol car. He ran over to the suspect car, opened the driver's door, snatched the driver out and threw him on the highway. He started to pull out the guy in the back seat. He was wearing a suit and derby hat and yelled, "What the hell do you think you're doing?"

Marvin said, "I am a deputy sheriff, who the hell are you?" The little man said, "I happen to be David Sholtz, Governor of the State of Florida and I want to know what the hell you think you're doing?"

Marvin snatched the little skinny driver up, who was still laying on the highway, brushed him off and sat him back into the car under the steering wheel. He said, "Y'all go ahead."

A short time later he received a call to come to the sheriff's office and see the sheriff. Marvin said for the second time in less than an hour he faced a really angry person when he walked into the sheriff's office. The sheriff said, "If you were not the only deputy I had, I would fire you on the spot."

"This," he said, "is an example of a situation that just had to be worked around."

The Coffee Table

The coffee table in the Bay County Sheriff's Office was a legend in itself. This was an old oak table about 4-feet wide and 8-feet long. There were four straight back chairs on each side and one on each end. The chair on the south end was for Sheriff Daffin. There was no sign to indicate this. Everyone just knew.

This chair faced the back entrance of the jail which saw all kinds of activity. It was where all prisoners were brought in, visitors came in to check on people in jail, people got out on bond, filed complaints or came in to visit Doc.

LaVelle sitting at the famous coffee table, 1972

Anyone who needed to see Doc, could usually find him at the coffee table. The "who's who" in Bay County and many in the State of Florida came through those doors and sat at that table. Some of the state officials who visited Doc were: Doyle Conner, Commissioner of Agriculture; Thomas Burton Adams, Secretary of State; Dempsey Barron, State Senator; Bob Sikes, U.S. Congressman; U.S. Senator George A. Smathers; Ed Ball, St. Joe Company; Judge Lewis; Judge Bailey; J. Frank Adams, State Attorney. There were many others at this level. The local regulars and close friends of Doc were: Uncle Custer Russ; Bruce Collins, Clerk of the Court; Fred Turner, attorney and later judge; Attorney Mayo Johnson, Doc's attorney; Gerald Conrad, Property Appraiser; Gladys Chapman, Supervisor of Elections; Pop Woods; Bunk Williams; Uncle Mark Conan, the only court bailiff; Circuit Judge Fitzpatrick; Circuit Judge McCrary; Tullis Easterling, FBI Agent; Woody Smith, Smith's Funeral Home; John Christo, Bay Bank; Bubba Nelson, Commercial Bank; Hugh Sikes, Sikes Concrete; J. R. Moody, Florida Asphalt Paving Company; Rev. J.W. Hunt, Springfield Community Church; Isaac Byrd, Pepsi Cola Company; Toby Moore, truck driver; Ralph Coleman, motel owner; Jessie Cogburn, Cogburn Clothing Company; Woodrow Gainer, owner of a bonding company; Pat Patterson, bondsman. They came, along with many others, to have close ties with the most powerful man in Bay County. And another reason they came was that Doc had one of the best cooks in Bay County running his kitchen. Everyone who visited at meal time could eat at that table with Doc for free.

Riding with Ellis

Walter Ellis and I were bad news when we worked together. I don't know why, but everyone we got a call on or stopped on traffic violations seemed to want to fight. Ellis was a small person and one of the nicest guys you ever met, but he didn't know the meaning of back down. If challenged, he was ready to scrap.

One night we were working the booking desk together and two of the deputies brought in a drunk from Southport. Ellis also lived in Southport, knew everyone who lived there, and was related to most.

The drunk was a big guy and apparently had been giving the two deputies a hard time or vice versa. As Ellis was searching him and going through his pockets, one of the deputies started saying, "I wouldn't let that guy put his hands in my pockets. He doesn't have any business doing that."

The guy was, by this time, very flustered. He turned suddenly and cold-cocked Ellis upside the head. Ellis hit the concrete floor and slid a few feet on his back.

I grabbed the guy and before I could do anything, Ellis bounded off the floor and rapped him in the head with the jail keys he kept hooked to his belt. There were about 15 very large and heavy keys on the ring that fit all the jail doors. Ellis caught the guy on top of the head and blood went everywhere as he hit the floor. We pulled Ellis off and put the guy in a cell. Naturally the two deputies were out of there in a hurry.

Ellis knew the guy and his family. I'm not sure how he explained the lump on the guy's head to his father. As usual, he had to talk his way out of trouble with the sheriff as well.

***

One night, during spring break when the beach was flooded with college students, Ellis and I were assigned to the beach. He was driving first and said his uncle had just come in with a truck load of peaches from Georgia and we needed to run by Southport and get a few. Southport was out of our work area, but he said it would take only a few minutes. Peaches sounded good, so I agreed.

181

We pulled up beside the truck and Ellis climbed up to the top and started throwing those big Georgia peaches down. I was catching them and putting them in the patrol car when a call came on the radio and said a riot had broken out in the Hang-Out at Long Beach. We were to proceed 10-18 (red lights & siren).

Ellis jumped down and we left in a cloud of dust. The station called back and asked for our 10-20 (location) and Ellis advised them the FHP station, which at that time was on the east end of the Hathaway Bridge. We were at least ten miles from the FHP station. We flew through Lynn Haven and got on very crooked Highway 390. Two things you could say truthfully about Ellis, he loved to fight and drive fast.

We were traveling about 80 to 100 mph on that crooked highway. Each time we came to a curve the tires screeched as we slid sideways. He kept cutting his eyes over at me. I was scared silly, but I wouldn't have admitted it, even if he flipped that car two or three times.

The station called back every few minutes for our 10-20 and Ellis blamed our location on heavy traffic. We finally got to the Hang-Out and I was glad to face a few hundred kids fighting just to get my feet safely on the ground again.

When we got there Marvin Freeman and Tommy Smith had arrested a bunch and placed them in the large shower room. They told them if they tried to escape they would probably be shot. Those arrested were all present and accounted for when we got there.

***

Walter Ellis and I started work at the sheriff's office at about the same time. We soon became best friends. We were the two youngest officers in the department and took a lot of crap from the older officers.

One day Ellis was working day shift on the beach. At shift change, we were supposed to be at the jail at 5:30, unless we were on a call. Something happened and Ellis was late getting to the jail. He came in the back door and all the rest of us were standing there. Doc Daffin was talking on the phone.

He yelled at Ellis and said, "I've got a man on the phone that says you came through St. Andrews at 60 or 70 mph and almost ran him over."

Ellis, quick as a flash, took the phone from Doc's hand and said, "You no good, lying SOB. You come down to the jail and say that and I will whip your ass..."

About that time Doc had recovered and snatched the phone back and told Ellis to get out. Ellis and I went back to the coffee table.

"Ellis, you're crazy. You know you'll probably get fired."

"I don't care. I'll go back to commercial fishing."

"What possessed you to cuss that man on the phone?"

"Hey. I did what he said. The guy just had no business telling the sheriff."

So far as I know Doc never said another word about it. I think he was in shock, just like the other deputies, that Ellis snatched the phone away from him.

Ellis and I loved to ride together. It seemed each time we were riding partners on the night shift and arrested someone, we had to fight.

One night when we were jailing, we had a guy in custody who had given us a lot of trouble. He was drunk and a regular visitor to the jail on the weekends. He kept screaming and talking about our ancestors, so we decided to put him in the tank. This was a round metal tank where we could put mentally disturbed or out of control people, temporarily, so they couldn't hurt themselves.

I was wearing a cast and heavy bandage around my left hand that I had injured a few days prior. With my one hand and Ellis with two good hands, we finally got this guy to the tank. He knew what the tank was and putting him in was like trying to drop a cat in a board well. He fought us tooth and toenail.

As we finally pushed him inside the tank, he grabbed Ellis and pulled him inside with him and slammed him down on the floor and started kicking the daylights out of him. I went into the tank and with my one good hand I grabbed the guy and kicked his feet out from under him. As he fell, he took me with him and nailed me a few times. In the meantime, Ellis got his second wind and took care of business. We were in bad shape, but the guy was in much worse shape.

We left him and didn't hear another sound. An hour of two later, we climbed up on a ladder that's attached to the tank and looked in. The guy didn't look like he had moved since we left him. Ellis said he might be dead. I agreed.

After watching him a while, Ellis said, "Maybe we should dump him in the bay and say he escaped."

I said, "You know that won't work. Let's check him and then call the sheriff." About that time the guy started moving, and we were two happy dudes.

We charged the man with two counts of assaulting an officer– one on Ellis and one on me. When it went to trial, the jury convicted the man for assaulting Ellis and the judge directed the verdict of not guilty for the assault charge on me because the judge said I was the aggressor when I went in to help Ellis. The convicted man served several months on the road gang.

One good thing that came from the incident, was when the drunk served his time, he never got locked up again as far as I know. As for me, I still remember getting the crap kicked out of me trying to help Ellis and the judge said I was the aggressor.

Ellis thought it was funny. I told him next time I wouldn't intervene. I'd just stand back and enjoy watching him get his butt kicked so I wouldn't be accused of being the aggressor.

***

One time when I was riding with Ellis, we got a domestic call. A man had beaten his wife and kicked her out. When we got there, she said he had a gun, but she hadn't heard him move around for awhile. She believed he was probably passed out in the bedroom and she wanted to get back in her house.

Ellis suggested we sneak in there and see if we could see him. If he was on the bed we would go in and grab him, get his gun and take him to jail.

I said, "It sounds like a good idea and since it's your idea, go ahead." He said he would, but insisted I go with him.

184

The house had real slick hardwood floors. We eased down the hall and got pretty close to the bedroom door. The door was standing wide open. Just as Ellis was leaning over and trying to peek around the corner, I just nudged him a little bit in the back. He slipped on the floor and went sliding into that room, waving his arms and trying to stop. He did stop, right next the bed.

Thankfully the guy kept sleeping. We jumped right in the middle of him and got the gun away from him.

I laughed and commended Ellis on handling the situation very professionally.

He said, "Yeah, I'd made up my mind when I got that gun I was gonna' turn around and shoot you. You could'a got me killed!"

***

When Ellis and I were riding together on the night shift, we usually tried to entertain ourselves during the slack hours. The slack hours were when no one needed a deputy and there were very few calls to answer. These hours were usually from 6:00 pm until about 10:00 pm and again from 3:00 am until 6:00 am. At this particular time Ellis and I were working the 10:00 pm to 6:00 am shift.

Our usual route when we left the jail on 4th Street and Harmon Avenue, was to drive east on 4th Street to Cove Boulevard, then north on Cove Boulevard to U.S. 231 if we were working the center of the county. There were two black juke joints on Cove Boulevard–the Little Savoy and the Harlem Bar. These places were usually packed out and generated many calls due to drunks, fights and just plain disorderly conduct.

As soon as we gassed up our patrol car, Ellis told me he had come up with a great idea. He pulled a large cherry bomb, with a fuse in the center, out of his pocket and explained how we could drive by the two black jukes, throw the cherry bomb in the door, and watch everyone evacuate.

I said, "Yeah, and get fired for our trouble."

He said, "No. You haven't heard the rest of my plan." He then pulled a sling shot out of his back pocket and said, "You

185

drive by real slow. When I tell you, you light the fuse with the cigarette lighter. I'll fire it right through my window and into the open door of the juke. It's cold. They'll be inside. They'll never know where it came from."

At first I wasn't convinced, but the more I thought about it, the more it sounded like a plan. Sure enough the place was full, the door was open as usual, and the weather cool enough that everyone was inside.

I drove slowly. Ellis rolled his window down. He placed the cherry bomb in the sling and pulled it way back. I pushed in the cigarette lighter and got ready. He said, "NOW."

I held the lighter to the fuse. He watched until the fuse started sizzling, turned quickly, and fired. Everything was fine and went according to plan except one thing.

Ellis missed the window. He hit the window frame with the cherry bomb and it immediately went ricocheting all around the patrol car. Since it was cold outside, all the windows were rolled up except the one on the passenger's side, which he missed. It seemed that cherry bomb went all round the car three or four times but never out the open window.

I sped up and must have been three or four blocks past the juke when it finally went off.

I was trying to cover my ears, drive the car and get my feet out of the floorboard where the cherry bomb had come to rest all at the same time. It went off and I thought it blew all the windows out of the car.

I pulled off the road to the edge of some woods and got out of the car. I didn't know if my ear drums were busted or not. I stood there and called Ellis every name I could remember. Suddenly it dawned on me that I wasn't hearing the words I was saying. I looked at Ellis. He was trying to talk, but couldn't hear.

After a few minutes, we started yelling back and forth and began to just barely understand what the other was saying.

The rest of the night, we had to watch the police radio. When the little red light came on indicating the station was broadcasting, the one in the passenger's seat had to hold his ear down next to the speaker in order to barely hear the station with the volume turned all the way up.

Thank the Lord we didn't have any calls for the first three or four hours and most of our hearing gradually returned. So much for Ellis's bright idea.

***

When I rode with Ellis, trouble seemed to follow us around. I could ride for weeks and never get into a scrap. I could ride one night with Ellis and everyone wanted to jump us and fight. There was something about Ellis that seemed to bring out the worst in drunks. I have never been able to understand that. Actually Ellis was nice and polite, but if you wanted to fight he was ready to rumble. The same thing happened when the two of us jailed together. Finally, Doc Daffin gave the chief deputy orders that under no circumstances were we to ride or work together again.

That decision probably saved both our lives. I had more uniforms torn, cuts and bruises, bites and scratches and was just generally banged up whenever Walter Ellis and I worked together.

One time (before we were not allowed to ride together), we were on patrol on Panama City Beach during AEA (Alabama Education Association). This is when 100,000 to a 150,000 kids invade the beaches of Panama City Beach in the spring when school is out. At that time there was no City of Panama City Beach and no policemen, so the sheriff's office handled patrol and protection on the beach. Usually there was just one patrol car with two deputies, if we were lucky to have a partner, to work from the Hathaway Bridge to Phillips Inlet, West Bay and down Highway 388 to Burnt Mill Creek.

Naturally we tried to stay on the strip as much as possible. That was where all the pretty girls were hanging out and where most of the action was.

One Friday night we passed the Breakers Restaurant drive-in, a favorite eating place for the deputies. It had a patio where the kids danced. This was also where many fights took place. As we passed the restaurant, we noticed the big black Lincoln parked in front that belonged to Sheriff Daffin. He was standing with two or three girls and seemed to be having a good old time.

187

About an hour later, we passed back by and the sheriff was still out front with the girls–several of them this time. We continued on our patrol and kept hauling drunks and disorderly people to jail.

The following night we were on the beach again. We passed the Breakers and noticed not many people were present at that early hour and the sheriff was not there. Suddenly we were hungry, so we stopped and ordered some food. We stayed near our patrol car so we could hear our radio, ate hamburgers and talked to the carhops. They were always glad to see us, especially when trouble started.

We finished our supper and, since we had no calls, we continued to hang out for about 30 minutes. This was a "no, no" to stay in one place more than five or ten minutes, except to eat, answer a call, or write a report.

The following night the two of us were called into the sheriff's office and Sheriff Daffin started chewing us out for being in one place for more than 30 minutes. I finally spoke up and said, "Sheriff, we saw you there the night before for over an hour."

The sheriff stared at me with those bloodshot eyes of his and said, "Boy. You do as I say do, not as I do. You got that?"

I said, "Yes, sir."

I never forgot about the two sets of rules that govern an organization. (As I learned in the Marine Corps–there is the right way and the Marine Corps way, and you had better do it the Marine Corps way.) In this case, there was the right way and Doc Daffin's way, and you had better do it Doc's way.

My First Domestic Call

When I was a very young and inexperienced deputy, I was assigned to ride with an old deputy who had been around for many years. After riding with him a few times, I could see why he had been around so long and never got hurt. This guy never took chances. We usually rode with a partner for one month and then changed. The younger deputies rode with the old timers to "learn the ropes."

This particular officer talked very little unless he was around women, then he came alive and tried to impress them. Two things stood out about him. 1) He dressed immaculately in his gray and green uniform–there was not a wrinkle or piece of lint on it. 2) He was very careful and always sent the other officer in first. I determined this is why he had lived so long.

The first night we rode together, we got a call to go to a home near Cook's Bayou on the east end of Bay County. That area had dirt roads and very few homes. We found the house which was a large frame house with a big front porch.

It was a cold evening and a lady was standing outside in her nightclothes. She was crying and said her husband was drunk and had beaten her up. He chased her out of the house. She wanted us to go in and get him. She said he went into the bedroom at the far end of the hallway.

My riding partner said, "Well, let's go get him." We started down the hallway, which must have been thirty feet or more to the door of his bedroom. It seemed like a hundred yards as I slipped along quietly, hoping to make it to the door and surprise him. I was about two-thirds down the hallway when the lady said in a loud whisper, "Be careful, he has a gun."

I stopped and looked back. Standing with her at the front door was my riding partner. I thought he was right behind me. I had to make a quick decision. I could go back the way I came, or go on to the room and hope for the best. Since I was only a few feet from the door and a long way from where I started, I decided to go on.

I crept along carefully, taking easy steps. With each squeak of a floor board, my hair felt like it stood straight up. It was in times like this that I exercised prayer. I finally arrived at the door. It was partially open, and I peeked in.

The guy was huge. He was asleep lying on his back on the bed, fully dressed. He had a double barrel shotgun lying across his chest, his arms across the gun.

I eased the door open enough to slip in and it squeaked. He awoke. He started coming out of the bed with the gun and I made a mad dash toward the bed. As he was getting to his feet with the gun in his hands, I did a long flying tackle. I caught him and the gun.

We hit the bed, the frame broke and crashed to the floor. We rolled over and over across the floor, both of us trying to gain possession of the shotgun.

It was a pretty even match up. He was determined to shoot me and I was determined to survive until my partner arrived. After what seemed an eternity and we had almost destroyed the bedroom, my partner peeked in the door and finally helped me subdue him.

I found out later that this man with the shotgun had a very bad reputation and could have killed both of us. My partner knew this, but never mentioned it to me until we got back to the jail and locked him up.

 "Learning the ropes" can be tough.

The Old Dutch Tavern

An incident that could have cost me my job was a disturbance call to the Old Dutch Tavern on Panama City Beach one Friday night. I was working alone and the dispatcher said a man was causing a disturbance at the Old Dutch and they wanted him removed. What I didn't know, until later that night, was this man was a wealthy

businessman in Panama City and had a reputation of having killed two or three people in the past.

I arrived at the Old Dutch and walked in. The bouncer pointed out the man who was standing in the middle of the floor cursing and challenging any and all comers to take him on. I walked up to him and asked him to step outside and talk to me.

He said, "Make me."

I reached for his arm and the fight was on. We rolled around on the floor, turned over tables and chairs and he tore my uniform shirt and got in some good licks and so did I. Finally, I pinned him down, and with the help of the bouncer, I handcuffed him and got him to my patrol car.

As we were leaving for the county jail, he started telling me all about his bad reputation, all the places of business he owned and most of all what a good friend he was of Doc Daffin. I told him that was fine and maybe Doc would go his bond.

He also promised to have me fired and said he was going to kill me. What I didn't tell him was his threat about Doc concerned me the most. I had seen Doc react sometimes very negatively, when a good friend of his was arrested and he heard the story from the friend instead of the deputy.

**Photo courtesy of
Bay County Public
Library**

After booking him at the jail, I went to the Dixie-Sherman Hotel, where the Sheriff was living at that time, and knocked on his door. It was about two o'clock in the morning, but I knew it might be in my best interest to get to the Sheriff before the other guy did.

Doc, with bloodshot eyes and dressed in pajamas, opened the door and said, "What's up boy?"

I apologized for waking him and told him what happened with his friend.

He admitted the guy was very dangerous and could get mean when he was drinking. He said, "Don't worry boy, I'll take care of it."

I breathed a sigh of relief and went back on patrol. I understand Doc really chewed the guy out and didn't give him time to really tell his side of the story. Doc told the guy he already knew what happened and he "shouldn't have been drunk and showing his ass."

You had to present your case to Doc first. If you didn't, you might be driving a taxi for a living the following week.

The Rock House Juke

When Doc started getting complaints about an establishment from a number of people, in particular church or business people, he'd usually make a personal visit to the business in question. He took one officer along, and let the officer drive his Buick.

Doc told the business owner about the complaints received and in no uncertain terms what steps they needed to take. If they didn't straighten things out, he let them know he would handle it. That was usually all it took. But sometimes the love of money and greed overrode their fear of Doc, and they continued to operate.

This was a bad move on their part. When you bucked Doc Daffin he reacted in a number of different ways, none of which was good for the person and the place of business they ran.

I was with him on some of these trips. We went to a place called the Rock House on the west end of Panama City Beach. They had a country music band and packed people in every night. This place was way out on the beach. Every motel and other business was closed for the winter. This place really went wild. Normally we only had one deputy working the entire west end of Bay County during the winter. There was no beach police department back then.

To start, Doc had a meeting with the management. They ignored what he said.

He ordered the beach deputy to start arresting any and all drunk and disorderly persons and bring them to jail. The arrests increased each night. Doc ordered two cars to work the beach and put the heat on the Rock House. This didn't seem to help and more and more people were being booked each night.

Doc called in J. Frank Adams, State Attorney, and advised him that he wanted to close this place down. The state attorney advised he needed to document the problems in order to petition the circuit judge to close the place as a public nuisance.

The sheriff had a meeting with all his deputies and related the conversation he had with the state attorney. He said each time a car had to go there and pick up a 10-15 (prisoner) and leave for the jail, the next available patrol unit was to pull in and go inside and take over where the other car left off. At this time we only had four uniform patrol cars. With three of them on the beach, that only left one unit to work the entire rest of the county. He put one officer and one auxiliary deputy in each patrol car.

The Rock House held 100 plus customers and the band was in the very back on a raised platform. The lights were always turned down real low. We learned from experience that before we charged in to break up a fight, to go behind the bar and turn the lights up on bright. They were having three to five fights a night and we were putting as many as twenty to thirty people in jail each night.

One kid from Springfield, Mickey, seemed to get in jail every night and was always nearby when the fights started. Each time he got out of jail, he complained we were picking on him because of his reputation.

One night a fight started and there were five or six deputies present. This kid, Mickey, ran up on the band platform and held both hands up and started yelling, "I am not in this fight, I am not in this fight." About the third or fourth time he yelled that, a quart bottle of beer came flying through the air and connected on his head. He slowly slid down the wall onto the floor, out cold. When we got all the cars and paddy wagon to the jail, Mickey was one of those booked.

We had long whip antennas on all our patrol cars. Occasionally, a car was vandalized at the Rock House while the officers were inside. One night one of the deputies, Tom Sullivan, decided to wait in the shadows and watch the vehicles. A teen-age kid came out, looked all around and took the long antenna and rolled it up in a knot. He then got down and started letting the air out of the rear tire of the patrol car. As the air was escaping, Tom walked up. The kid, thinking it was his buddy who was supposed to be watching, looked up with a big grin just in time to get whopped on the side of the head with a slap jack. He also earned a trip to the county jail, along with a big headache.

Many stories could be told about the Rock House. One night there was a female stretched out on the dance floor passed out. I recognized her from the Springfield area. She was known as "paregoric Burkett," one of the town drunks who drank anything she could get her hands on, including paregoric, to get drunk.

I picked her up and threw her over my shoulder and started off the dance floor. She was limber as a rag and it took a while to get her over my shoulder. Needless to say, I got no help from any of the crowd. I was wearing a black leather uniform jacket and I had taken only two or three steps when she latched onto my back with her teeth. She got a real mouth full of my back through that jacket.

Everyone was laughing at me carrying her off the floor, and I could do nothing but grit my teeth and keep walking. I felt the blood start running down my back inside my jacket and uniform shirt. When I got out the door, I went to the nearest car and popped her head against the side of the car. She finally turned my back loose.

After locking her up, I went to Bay Medical Hospital and got a tetanus shot. The jacket I was wearing was not even torn, but there was an open gash on my back that had to be stitched up.

How to Break Up a Fight and Close a Business in Five Minutes

One night, while working with Deputy B.D.Culver, we received a call to go to the Breakers to break up a big fight. The traffic was so heavy that it took about thirty minutes to drive less than a mile. As we pulled into the parking lot, everyone was standing around. There was not a fight in sight. Two or three were bloody, but we witnessed no one fighting.

After looking around for a few minutes, we pulled off and were not a half mile down the highway when they called back and said the fight was on again. We had the same results the second time.

The car hop girls at the Breakers said trouble-makers watched down the highway, and when they saw us coming, stopped all the fights and just stood there until we drove off. The third time we drove off, I pulled into a motel about a 100 yards away. We got two tear gas grenades and ran back to the Breakers on the beach side.

As we neared, we could see the fight going on all over the patio. We tossed the two grenades onto the dance floor. The cans started jumping and bouncing around. They looked about the size of a can of beer. One guy looked down and kicked it with his toe saying, "Hey Gus, look at this crazy beer can." We spotted their look-out who was standing on top of a car in the parking lot. He was looking up and down the highway for our patrol car.

There was a breeze blowing in from the Gulf and when the grenades started spewing the gas out, it made a large cloud and started drifting toward the highway. This was the way most everyone was running. They were running over cars, each other and anything else that got in their way. We got a big laugh. However, the gas also went inside the Breakers and they had to close.

The following morning we were called in. Doc was going to fire both of us, but a sweetheart by the name of Maxine showed up. She was the owner of the Breakers and told Doc to leave us alone. She said it was well worth closing just to see all those people running and crying, instead of fighting all over her parking lot. Doc let us off the hook, but took our tear gas away.

The Sleeping Police Officer
We had a police officer in the City of Springfield who worked the night shift and patrolled Springfield alone. Barryhill was a nice officer, but had a real problem when it came to staying awake. He would find a place near US Highway 98, which ran through his city, park his patrol car facing the highway, sit up straight in his seat and go to sleep.

All the small cities in the county had their police radio hooked into the Bay County Sheriff's Office. After 5:00pm all complaints came into the sheriff's office. When a call came in, the BCSO dispatcher notified the police unit that was in that city. If the radio operator couldn't raise the police unit, then a sheriff's unit was dispatched. That's how we found out about Barryhill's sleeping problem. Sometimes we had to find him and wake him up to go on his call.

One morning, about 1:00am, two deputies working the east side of the county were dispatched to Mexico Beach to answer a call. They passed through Springfield and saw Barryhill parked in front of a service station at Everett Avenue and Highway 98, asleep. It was hot weather and Barryhill had all his windows down. One of the deputies reached in and flipped on all his emergency red lights. The patrol car lit up like a big Christmas tree. The two head lights and tail lights were blinking on and off along with the large red lights on top of the patrol car. The two deputies left and went on to Mexico Beach, wondering how long it would take Barryhill to wake up and turn off his emergency lights.

About three hours later, the deputies were returning from Mexico Beach and received a call from the dispatcher stating that Officer Barryhill was in a phone booth requesting a car with jumper cables to assist him in getting his patrol car started. He explained to the deputies that he must have a bad battery. He said he just stopped for a minute or two and then his car wouldn't crank.

The deputies jumped him off and never told him what really happened. They did, however, tell everyone at the sheriff's office.

Freddie Clark

Back in the 50s and 60s, warrants were given to a deputy working the area where the warrant was to be served. If the deputy couldn't serve it, the warrant was passed on to the deputy who relieved him on the next shift.

**Freddie Clark at recovery scene of a vehicle in
the water near the Bailey Bridge, 10-12-1959**

I was getting ready to go to my zone and Freddie Clark, a black deputy and fine officer, came to me and said, "Would you mind helping me a few minutes before you go to your zone?"

"No. What do you need?"

"I've got a warrant for this guy and I've been to his house several times to serve it. Whichever door I go to, he goes out the other one and leaves. I need you to help me."

We didn't have a bunch of law enforcement officers then. We only had four deputies to cover the entire county–one for the east side, center and the west side, and a black deputy who worked only the black sections.

He told me where the house was and I met him there. He said, "Give me about 10 minutes to get in place at the back of the house and then you knock on the front door. Beat on it real hard."

I said, "What if he comes to the door?"

"Grab him."

I went to the front door and beat on it and said, "Sheriff's office. We've got a warrant for you."

All I could hear were retreating footsteps reverberating from that old wood frame house set up on block. I heard the back door slam. I jumped off the front porch and ran around back. When I got there, Freddie and that guy were rolling over and over on the ground. They rolled up under the house.

197

I didn't know what to do. I just stood there and watched the fight. Finally, Freddie came crawling out. He had that old boy by the foot and drug him out. They were both roughed up and breathing heavily.

Freddie handcuffed the guy and put him in the back of his patrol car and said, "I appreciate the help."

I said, "Yeah, any time."

That's the easiest arrest I ever participated in.

***

Working as an investigator, I got a call to go to Bay Medical Center. There was a black female in there that Freddie Clark had shot.

I got down there and saw it was Rose. She was a big girl who had been in and out of jail a lot. She was mean, and when she got drunk, she was really mean.

I went and looked at her. She had one shot in the leg, one shot in the shoulder, one shot through the arm and her face was all busted up,

I took Freddie outside the emergency room and asked him what happened.

He said he had received a call from the dispatcher to check out a fight at the Sunset Bar and Grill. When he arrived Rose was standing in the middle of the grill with a butcher knife in her hand cursing and yelling at two people she had backed up against the wall. It was obvious she was drunk.

He told her she was under arrest to drop the knife. Rose told Freddie to come get it. As he started toward her she ran at him with the knife. He drew his weapon and fired. Apparently the bullet hit her arm. She dropped the knife and then reached down and picked it up with the other hand. He fired again and hit her in the leg and she dropped to the floor. She got back up again with the knife in her good hand. He fired again hit her in the shoulder. She dropped the knife again. Then she got down on her knees and was trying to rake the knife up with her hands. By this time there was blood all over her. As she was trying to pick the knife up again he walked up and kicked her in the face. "And that did it. I brought her down here to the hospital."

I said, "Freddie, I didn't know you could shoot that good."

"What do you mean?"

"You shot her in the arm and made her drop the knife, shot her in the other arm, shot her in the leg. I didn't know you could shoot like that."

Freddie said, "I wasn't trying to shoot her in the arm, shoulder or leg; I was trying to shoot her right between the eyes. I just hit her in those other places."

After the doctor patched her up at the hospital, Freddie brought Rose to the jail and charged her with aggravated assault. She could have received up to 10 years in prison had she been convicted of trying to cut Deputy Freddie Clark with a butcher knife. Sheriff Daffin got the judge to reduce the charge and give her a year in jail so he could use her as a cook. All the deputies who ate at the jail were delighted because she was one of the best cooks around.

The sheriff let the deputies eat at the jail when they were on duty. At breakfast you could tell Rose how many eggs, bacon, biscuits or whatever you wanted. She cooked it and brought it to the coffee table just outside the kitchen where everyone ate. When Freddie came in, he went in the kitchen and said, "Rose, fix me up a couple of eggs, sausage and biscuits. You know how I like my eggs."

She'd say, "You don't want none of my eggs." She stood there and glared at him, but then went ahead and fixed his breakfast the way he wanted.

I told Freddie he was crazy eating her cooking after he had tried to kill her. He just laughed and said, "She's all right. She'll get over all that."

And I guess she did. She spent her time in jail and got out. But all the officers and guests missed her cooking.

Of all the law enforcement officers I ever worked with, Freddie would rate as one of the finest.

 *Giving a prisoner who was a good worker maximum jail time, worked well for our department. It saved the taxpayers money on salary and helped the trustee in his or her determination not to return to jail again.*

USMC Rifle and Pistol Team Experience Pays Off

Little did I know that the shooting skill I learned on the USMC Rifle and Pistol Team would later fit into the field of law enforcement. Some of the ways it assisted me was in arresting fleeing prisoners. My reputation as an expert marksman was known by word of mouth shooting in pistol matches with other law enforcement officers.

One afternoon a jail trustee, posing as an escaped prisoner, was helping me train the BCSO bloodhound. We were returning to the patrol car after the bloodhound tracked him down. A small bird flew up in front of us and went about 30-feet away and landed on a stump. The trustee asked if I thought I could hit the bird, I said, "Sure," pulled my weapon, aimed and fired. The bird fell. The trustee said, "You missed him." I said, "No I didn't."

LaVelle, BCSO deputy, pistol match winner

He ran over and returned with the small bird. Its head was missing. I had aimed at the bird not the head, but he thought I had. When we got back to the jail, he started telling the story to the other trustees. Each time he stretched the story a little more. The distance got up to a hundred feet and one time the bird was flying. So my reputation spread all over the jail.

About a month after the bird incident, a prisoner fled the jail. I gave chase. As we were running down a sidewalk, I realized he was much faster than me and was about to get away. I yelled, "Stop or I'll shoot." He immediately stopped and put his hands up.

He told me later that the only reason he stopped was he heard of my shooting reputation from prisoners in the jail.

There are times when an exaggerated reputation can work to your benefit.

The Good Law Enforcement Officer with a Couple of Weaknesses

There was a really fine, well-respected deputy that everyone liked. Wallace had a farm on Callaway Bayou and lived alone. I stopped on occasion to visit him since we were both from Holmes County and knew some of the same people. I could sit on the porch and visit, but it was mostly a one-sided conversation. Wallace wouldn't say more than a dozen words, but commented on some of mine. He was real quiet. I don't remember him ever talking bad about anyone–even those he arrested.

Sheriff Daffin used to buy new Stetson hats from Cogburn clothing store once a year and present one to each deputy. On one occasion the Sheriff gave out the hats at shift change behind the jail. After he left, all the patrolmen stood outside admiring the new hats.

Somehow the conversation turned into how good some of the guys could shoot a pistol. Al Barron spoke up and said "I bet there is not a one of you could hit a bull in the ass with a base fiddle." Some took exception to that remark, so his challenge changed to, "I bet not one of you could shoot a hole in my new hat if I tossed in the air."

Somebody said, "Throw it." Al casually tossed his new hat about ten to twelve feet straight up in the air and prepared to catch it before it hit the ground. In a flash Wallace pulled his service revolver and fired. Al caught his hat and yelled, "You hit my new hat." Wallace calmly put his revolver back in his holster and said,

201

"It was your idea." I thought Al was going to cry as he poked his finger through a bullet hole in his new Stetson.

When he was off duty, Wallace had two weaknesses according to the scuttlebutt around the sheriff's office—women and poker. However, to my recollection no one ever actually saw him with a woman or in a poker game, and no one ever accused him of this to his face.

He was what I called a real loner. He didn't party with the guys or go out and get drunk. Most of the deputies, when they got together, liked to talk about their conquests with women, getting drunk, and close calls they had arresting someone. Wallace never bragged about anything he had done or heard. It was like pulling teeth to get him to talk.

He had a day off one time and the following day he didn't come to work. When he came back to work, he could barely walk. Of course, everyone was curious about what was wrong with him. The guys asked and he'd just shrug his shoulders and didn't say anything. I was his riding partner that night. It appeared he was in a lot of pain. I kept bugging him until finally he said, "I'll tell you, but keep it to yourself."

He explained he knew a lady who lived in the upstairs apartment of the checkerboard store at East Avenue and Highway 98. It was his day off, so he went down to see her that night. Her husband worked the midnight shift at the paper mill.

"I went to see her about midnight after her husband had gone to work. Everything was fine until about two o'clock. I heard somebody coming up the stairs and figured it was her husband."

There was only one way in and one way out—those stairs. Wallace said he raised the window and looked down. It was a long way down. About four feet from the window, there was a creosote telephone pole. There were spike holes all over the pole where power workers climbed up and down.

"I grabbed my clothes and shoes, dropped them out the window, jumped out and grabbed the light pole as the husband was coming in the door. I slid all the way down to the ground. The creosote splinters and spikes tore me up and almost castrated me."

Wallace drove to the emergency room and got the creosote splinters dug out of his skin. I was amazed he managed to get back to work as quickly as he did. The only person I ever shared the story with was Ellis. I had to tell him.

His other weakness was playing poker. He grew up in Holmes County and that's where he usually went for his poker games. One night, he came to work all beat up. I finally managed to get him to tell me what happened.

He said he got in a poker game in Bonifay with a bunch of old boys he had grown up with. He was really hot that night and won a couple hundred dollars. Back then, that was a lot of money. Knowing the type guys he was playing with, he believed they would try to intercept him before he got back to Panama City to get their money back.

When he left the poker game, he took a roundabout way to get to the highway and thought he lost them, but they caught up with him near Vernon. They forced him off the road and drug him out of his truck and demanded the money. When he told them he had left it at a friend's house in Bonifay, they searched him and his truck and beat the crap out of him.

They finally gave up and left him lying on the side of the road. He crawled back in his truck and came home.

I asked where he hid it. He kind of chuckled and said, "In my boots."

They did everything but search his boots. They took his clothes off, but never thought to look in the socks in his boots. I asked if the money was worth what he went through to keep it. He grinned and said, "Yeah, not so much the money, but the pain and embarrassment it caused them by not being able to get it back, made it well worthwhile."

Convict Who Almost Kept His Word

While working as a deputy sheriff, Bay County Sheriff Doc Daffin assigned me an additional job, training the blood hound, Twigs, and chasing escaped prisoners. This job entailed hours of training the dog in addition to my regular 12-hour shift. We had a state prison camp near the airport and some very bad convicts lived there. They worked each day in prison clothes with shotgun-bearing guards. These were, for the most part maximum security prisoners serving time for major crimes. They regularly escaped,

203

and when they did I was called out with Twiggs. So, added to my regular 12-hour shift as a jailer and patrol officer and the already added dog training time, was tracking escapees. I received a call early one morning that a convict, working on a chain gang near the airport, had escaped into a swamp near the bay. The prisoner was described as serving life for murder and should be considered very dangerous.

I placed Twigs on his trail that took us into a snake-infested swamp. Most escapees tried to work their way north to possibly steal a vehicle and clothes around the Lynn Haven area. This is the route he took.

About five hours later, Twigs caught up with the subject lying in some water under a bush. He was wet, muddy and in a very bad state of mind. I ordered him to stand up, while holding my weapon on him.

As he stood, he took his hand out of his pocket withdrawing a large roll of bills. Where he got the money, we never found out. He said, "No one knows you've caught up with me and it's almost dark. Take this money and just say you lost the trail. No one will ever know." I said, "You're wrong. I would know. Put your hands behind you for the cuffs."

On our long walk out of the woods, he got more and more angry. He said, "I'll come back some day and pay you back for making me go back to prison." I told him, jokingly, that if he served the remainder of his sentence, I wouldn't have to worry about it.

He was booked back into jail. Later he received an additional 10 years for escape to go along with his life sentence. He was sent back to the state prison in Raiford, Florida.

About a year later the sheriff called me into his office and showed me a teletype message he had just received from the state prison. It read in substance that this guy had escaped again from a camp in south Florida and had stolen a vehicle. A description of the vehicle was furnished. Inmates who knew him were questioned and they advised the escapee had talked about nothing but getting back to Panama City and killing that "dog man deputy" who had caught him the last time he escaped.

Sheriff Daffin cautioned me to be very careful and put me on the day shift, so I could be home at night.

About a week went by. Although I never publicly admitted it, I was getting very nervous. I lived in the Hiland Park area at the intersection of Game Farm and Transmitter Road. There was a huge wooded swamp area that bordered my backyard.

One afternoon I got home late, took my gun belt off and tossed it on the couch as I walked through the front room. I went into the kitchen. There was a quart jar filled with water and a sprouting sweet potato sitting in the window over the sink. The window faced the woods. I walked up to the sink and for some reason, turned back around. At the same time I heard a crash as the jar with the potato exploded. I knew immediately what had happened. I'd been shot at. I raced back into the front room snatched my .357 magnum from its holster and raced outside and into the wooded area.

It was a stupid move and had the guy sat tight for a moment he could have easily killed me. 1 could not find any sign of him. A number of officers came to the scene. In searching the entire area, we found the vehicle that was stolen in south Florida but no sign of the escapee.

As far as I know, he was never arrested or heard of again. This was another one of the instances where I believe God intervened. That bullet would have hit me had I not turned around. In checking the path of the bullet after it came in through the window at chest height, it continued on through three more walls and out the front of the house and into the woods across Transmitter Road.

Though I walk in the midst of trouble you preserve my life. Psalm 138:7

Another Story about the Three Walton Brothers (Earlier story under Marvin "Big Mo" Freeman)

One night in the middle of the week, the three Walton (alias) brothers, known as the "Bad A_ _ Brothers" and their friend, "Big Gus (alias)," visited the Bay Harbor Bar and Pool Room. There were only two or three people in the bar, including one small mild-mannered man who worked at the paper mill, and the bartender. The lone man sitting at a table was quietly drinking a beer. This man went by the name of Ronald and trouble seemed to follow him around.

I never went on a fight call involving Ronald that he was accused of starting. I don't know what kind of work he did at the mill, but I witnessed some of his work with his pocket knife and as a result he had built up a reputation as a real bad dude.

One evening the Walton brothers and Gus went to the bar and Ronald was there. I have no idea what the Walton brothers had against Ronald, but it was known they didn't like him. According to the bartender, Ronald was alone and no words were spoken until the brothers walked past his table. One of the Waltons slapped and knocked Ronald out of his chair. Big Gus went to sit at the bar and tried to stay out of trouble.

The brothers circled around Ronald lying on the floor. As they closed in, kicking and cursing him, he suddenly shot up off the floor with his big pocket knife open. The bartender said that in a matter of seconds all three of the Walton boys were on the floor, cut badly.

Ronald proceeded to the door. The investigating officer reported that as he passed Gus sitting on a bar stool, he sliced him also, and never stopped walking. He went out the front door and on to his house about three blocks away.

As soon as we heard about the incident, Doc Daffin told me to go to Ronald's house and pick him up. I drove to his house. As I was getting out, he opened the front door and said, "LaVelle, I'll be with you in a few minutes."

He went back inside and I waited. In a few minutes he came out with fresh clean clothes on and asked if he should sit in the front or in the cage. I told him to sit in the front and asked if he had his knife on him. He smiled and said, "You know better than that." I took him to jail and, as expected, the Walton brothers and Gus declined to prosecute.

Escape Attempt from Emergency Room

People in jail who are facing serious charges spend much of their time trying to come up with a way to beat the charges or escape if the opportunity arises. I was jailing one night when a prisoner, who had been complaining all day of serious pain, was ordered by the sheriff to be taken to Bay Memorial Hospital emergency to be checked out by a doctor.

Bay Memorial in the 1950s
Photo Courtesy of Bay County Public Library

The old emergency room was located in the back of the hospital. Just inside the door to the right was another room with an examination table and other equipment for the doctor on call. There was one window about six feet above the floor, overlooking the emergency entrance. The window was very high to provide privacy for those receiving medical attention.

Deputy Barron took the prisoner to the emergency entrance. He was told to have the prisoner lay on the table in the examination room and the doctor would be there shortly.

Al Barron was ticked off at having to come in off his zone and haul a prisoner to the hospital. He liked to smoke and he couldn't smoke in the hospital. To make things worse the doctor was late getting there. After waiting 30 to 45 minutes, Al was tired of standing in that small room with a complaining prisoner. He told the prisoner he was going to check on the doctor and took the opportunity to step outside the emergency door entrance to light up a cigarette.

The prisoner saw a way of escape. He thought the deputy was wandering around the hospital looking for the doctor. He stood up on the examination table, pulled himself up to the window sill, and jumped out the window into the darkness below. He landed squarely on top of one grumpy deputy, squatting down smoking a cigarette. When Al drug him back in the examination room the prisoner was indeed in need of medical attention. After getting patched up, the prisoner was brought back to the jail with an added charge of attempted escape.

Dr. Lingo, the Jail Doctor

My first job in law enforcement was as a jailer or "turn key" at the Bay County Jail. Sheriff Doc Daffin did not believe in anyone starting off as a road deputy and he also required you be at least twenty-five before going on patrol. Even though I had served a hitch in the USMC, that made no difference to Doc Daffin. As a jailer many interesting things happened. Dr. Lingo, our jail doctor, was very old and never got in a hurry. He had an office on the second floor of a building that housed the Bay Shore Bar on the ground floor. He came to the jail once a week for sick call. The sheriff had him examine prisoners who were in jail and claimed to be sick. (Most all claimed to be sick or hurting in some way.)

As jailer, I had to go to the cells and bring the prisoners to the bull ring–a large cell where drunks were put to sober up. Dr. Lingo didn't believe in a lot of conversation. If a prisoner said he had the flu or a cold, he took their temperature and gave me some pills in a bottle with their name on it. I had to give them the medicine at the given times he wrote on the bottle.

One afternoon an inmate, I think he was a commercial fisherman, started telling the doctor about a friend of his upstairs. He said the friend was embarrassed to come down, but wanted him to ask the doctor some questions. Dr. Lingo told him to go on and ask.

Doctor Lingo is seated with the cane.
(This photo, taken in front of Daffin Cut Rate Drug Co., features men who knew each other 50 years. Top L-R: Doc Daffin, Proctor Van Horn, Wallace Laird, Sr., Les Gilbert, John Phillips, Charlie Powell, Jimmy Daffin, Roy Laird. Bottom L-R: Bob Ennis, Harry Phillips, Custer Russ, Doc Lingo, Ross Phillips.)
Photo credit: *Centennial Stories, Celebrating the History of Panama City, 1909-2009*, Marlene Womack.

The inmate said, "Well my friend thinks he might have caught a disease or something." The doctor said, "Why would he think that?" The inmate replied, "Well, his penis is swelling up and running a little and he is just worried." The doctor looked at the inmate a moment and said "Son, drop your pants and let's have a look at your friend." Sure enough his friend had a problem.

Susie the Jailhouse Cat

An alley cat, Susie, lived at the jail. Doc Daffin loved that cat. She had free run of the jail and everyone knew to leave her alone. The third floor of the old jail was maximum security. Some real bad boys were housed up there. During the day we let all of them come out of their little two-man cells and go into a large day room where they could take showers, play cards and generally socialize with each other.

One day Doc Daffin was sitting around the coffee table with some of his old cohorts. That cat came flying down the stairs yowling. She raced by the coffee table and down the hallway into another cellblock. Doc said "What the hell is wrong with that cat?"

We finally rounded her up and found that someone had shaved her tail, nicked it in several places and rubbed after-shave lotion on the cuts. Doc was furious and immediately went to the maximum security cellblock with several deputies. Naturally no one told who did it. So the sheriff instructed the deputies to take the mattresses from their bunks, and advised the cook to feed them only bread and water. They asked how long they were going to be punished. Doc replied, "Until you serve your time in jail or until the hair grows back on that cat's tail."

Several years later I was picking up a prisoner at Raiford State Prison to bring back for court. One of the prisoners on the prison yard asked me if the hair ever grew back on that cat's tail. He said he was one of the ones who suffered the punishment of bread and water and sleeping on a steel bunk with no mattress.

Before he left the Bay County Jail, whenever Susie came around, the inmates made sure that no one touched or harmed that cat in any way. He claimed the greatest thing that ever happened to him was being transferred to the state prison.

Indian Fire Water and Drunk Driving

In the early 1960s, I was patrolling the center zone of the county. This covered the area from US 231 at the Bay County line, Jackson County line, Calhoun County line south to the Hathaway Bridge north to the Washington County line including Southport and west on Highway 388 to Burnt Mill Creek. This was a lot of area to cover for one patrol car and one deputy. There were only three zones in Bay County and three patrol cars working 12-hour shifts.

At shift change, I was at the jail at 5:30am and briefed by the deputy who had just worked the zone I would take over. At 6:00am, I climbed into the vehicle of the officer who had just gotten off, gassed the vehicle and started out on my 12-hour shift. The shift assignment lasted one month and then we changed zones.

On this particular month, I was working the center and had covered my entire zone. All was quiet. About midnight I started concentrating on bars and night clubs for drunk drivers and fights.

By this time, serious drinkers had usually been drinking four or five hours, and were trying to pick up a date or get the one they were with to a motel or home to bed. The ones who had struck out with the women were usually the worst ones to deal with. They were drunk, mean and ready to fight.

About 1:30 am I spotted an old vehicle going into Southport and moving erratically. I called in a 10-50, meaning I was stopping a vehicle. I gave a description of the vehicle, the tag number and the location. While I was giving the required information to the dispatcher, the driver turned off SR 77 and headed toward the old cemetery. I had my lights on and touched my siren. It took a few moments before the vehicle stopped. I got out of my patrol car and walked up to the other car with my 3-cell flashlight in my left hand.

I asked the man to step out of his car and for his driver's license. This guy started getting out and it took a while. He was very, very big and it seemed like he was never going to get all of his body out of that car.

It was obvious he was in a bad mood when he asked what the hell I had stopped him for. I told him, in my opinion, he had too

211

much to drink because he was on and off the road with his vehicle.

He told me what I could do with my opinion.

I was trying to be very nice. In the early morning hours there was no back-up available in the event I had trouble. He started to get back in his vehicle. I told him he would have to go with me; he was under arrest. He stopped looked down at me and said, "Shh...it."

I reached out and put my hand on his arm and he immediately ripped my badge off and took most of my shirt with it. I took a swing at his head with my 3-cell flashlight. It caught him on the edge of his eye and blood went everywhere.

He dropped to his knees holding his hands over his face. I felt bad, so I told him I was sorry I had to hit him, but he was still going to go to jail with me. I tried to help him up and he let me. As he regained his feet, he exploded and worked on ripping off the rest of my uniform shirt, along with my head.

I used my flashlight again and hit him with all my might. The end came off my light and I heard the batteries flying out through the woods.

We then went down on the road and were rolling over and over. He was hollering at the top of his voice. I could do okay in a scrap with most people, but after about 3 minutes, I was ready for someone to ring the bell for a brief rest. Needless to say the fight was a little one-way, his way.

Suddenly someone yelled out, "What's going on here?" I looked up and saw a grand sight. It was one of my old classmates, Wendell Gainer, standing there in his night clothes. I asked Wendell to help me get the cuffs on this guy and he did. I had gone to school with Gainer and never realized how special he was until that morning.

I took the subject to the emergency room at Bay Medical, had his eye stitched and then left him at the county jail.

Some of these stories sound bad, but actually in my years of law enforcement I can count on both hands the fights I had. I really tried to talk the person I was arresting into coming along peaceably. It was better for them and much better for me, my body and my clothes. (We had to furnish our own uniforms.)

212

After an arrest like this, there was usually no more trouble with the person arrested, but not so with this guy. A couple of days later, Sheriff Daffin called me in his office and advised me that this guy, of Indian descent, was putting the word out around Southport that he was going to kill me. The sheriff was very concerned and offered to move me to the beach zone for the remainder of the month. I thought about it, but knew if I moved to the beach, the word would be all over Southport that the Indian had run me off. That's what I told the sheriff and asked him to please leave me in the Southport zone. He did, wished me luck, and advised me to be very careful.

On my first night out I drove straight to his house, located near the graveyard in Southport, and pulled up in his front yard. He was sitting in a rocker on the front porch. He just sat there and stared at me, and I at him. I had my weapon, so if he started anything, we could just finish it there in his front yard. I realized later that this may have been a stupid move, but thankfully nothing happened.

The next thing I did was check all my jukes. I parked as near the front door as possible and waited until two or more people started in, and quickly got out and went in with them. His threats were that he would wait in the bushes somewhere in my zone, and shoot me when I started in or came out of one of the jukes. When I left the juke I did the same thing–exiting with a group of two or more people and leaving quickly.

This went on for several days until I completed my month and was moved to the beach. The sheriff got word later that the Indian told some friends that he had tried several times to get a shot at me, but I always seemed to have several people around me. I have to say it was a big relief to get out of Southport alive.

Judge E. Clay Lewis

Picture from booklet dedicating the bridge on east Beach Drive. Standing: E. Clay Lewis (left), Marion G. "Bubber" Nelson. Photo courtesy of Bay County Public Library

In the late 1950s, we had one bailiff for our court, Uncle Mark Conan. He only worked circuit court with Judge E. Clay Lewis. Since I have seen many judges in the State of Florida and in several different states, I must say Judge Lewis had to be the toughest judge I have ever observed sitting on the bench.

Judge Lewis only knew one sentence and that was the maximum sentence the law allowed if convicted. If the law said one to five years and the man was found guilty, he got five years. Everyone was deathly afraid of Judge Lewis–not only the bad guys but also deputies, policemen, juries, witnesses and any other person who came before him, including lawyers.

Back then there were no court-appointed lawyers, so if you could not afford a lawyer you were on your own.

An 18-year-old white kid who had just graduated from Bay High snatched a bank bag from a lady and ran with it. He was caught in a few minutes. He came from a good family, had no record of ever being in trouble. He pled guilty to robbery and the judge gave him a life sentence.

Even Doc Daffin tried to intervene, but to no avail.

We had a black guy go to trial for aggravated assault on another black person at the Harlem Bar on Cove Boulevard. J. Frank Adams, the State Attorney, picked a jury and just went over the case lightly because he knew the man had no attorney and he sat down.

The judge called the defendant to the stand and told him to tell the jury what happened. The poor guy sat there like he was in a trance or something because he was so afraid to talk. The judge again told him to speak and in his own words tell the jury what happened.

He said, "Yes sir, yes sir. Well, me and my friend girl stopped in the Harlem Bar for a little drink and old Phillip, (the victim) started hitting on my friend girl. I tol' him to leave her alone, but he kep' on. We had a few words and he finally moved out of the way. Me and my friend girl finished our drink and we started to leave. As we walked out the front door old Phillip was standing outside the door and took a swing at me. I ducked and kicked him right in the ass–"

The judge interrupted and scolded him for using that kind of language in his court room and in front of a jury. Judge Lewis said, "If you have to use that descriptive language you use the word rectum instead."

The poor guy just sat there staring at the judge saying, "yes sir, yes sir," over and over. Judge Lewis prompted him to go on and tell the story.

The guy said, "Yes sir," and started all over again. "Well me and my friend girl was in the Harlem Bar to get us a drink and old Phillip came up and started hitting on my friend girl and I told him to leave her alone. We had some words and he moved away. When we finished the drink, we started moving to the door and as we walked out, old Phillip was standing there and took a swing at me. I ducked and I kicked him right in the ..."

There was a long pause. He looked up at the judge and said, "Judge, yo' honor sir, what was it you called that nigger's ass?"

The jury lost it, as well as the State Attorney and all the spectators in the courtroom. Judge Lewis called recess and went to his office. Needless to say the jury found the defendant not guilty.

In a different trial, another black guy was facing a charge of drunk and possession of moonshine whiskey. The jury was in place and State Attorney J. Frank Adams introduced the evidence. The evidence consisted of about two or three ounces of

215

moonshine in the bottom of a half-pint bottle. The defendant was said to be drinking from it when the deputy arrested him for public drunkenness.

The state attorney made a brief statement and let the deputy testify as to the charge. The deputy looked at the bottle and identified it as the one he had taken from the suspect when he arrested him. He handed the bottle back to the attorney, who set it on the edge of the judge's bench.

The defendant was called to the stand and Judge Lewis instructed him to tell his side of the story. As the suspect started to testify, the judge stopped him and called the state attorney to the front of his bench for a conference of some kind. They were in a whispered conversation for several minutes. The prisoner sat in the witness chair looking around the courtroom and noticed the bottle on the corner of the desk. He calmly picked it up, took the lid off and drank down the last two or three swallows, put the lid back on and replaced it on the judge's desk.

The jury exploded in a fit of laughter. Judge Lewis looked up and demanded to know what happened and finally one of the jurors told him. The judge looked totally flustered and glared at the prisoner a moment and then at J. Frank Adams. He said, "Counselor, I believe the prisoner just drank up all the evidence and I will entertain a motion for a directed verdict of not guilty."

The defendant got the not guilty verdict and walked out a free man. I'm not sure he even realized what had happened until it was over and he was leaving.

We started a murder trial one Monday morning and the lawyers started picking a jury. The courtroom was on the third floor and there was no air conditioning. We had to keep all the big windows open facing the street that ran beside the courthouse. Directly across the street from the courthouse was Wilson Funeral Home. Mr. Wilson was having a new roof put on the funeral home and workers were hammering away.

The judge stopped court and sent a deputy across the street with instructions that all work would cease until after his murder trial was over. There was total silence the remainder of the week from the roof of the funeral home.

Bay County Courthouse
Photo Courtesy of Bay County Public Library

Another murder trial was being held and it was so hot everyone had to use hand fans. Judge Lewis stopped the trial and issued an order to be served on the county commission that air conditioning be installed in his courtroom immediately or they must appear before him and show cause why they should not be held in contempt of court.

This was what the bailiff related to the sheriff. As far as I know, that was the first air-conditioning to be installed in the Bay County Courthouse.

We had two guys in jail awaiting sentencing for escape, Connelly and a man by the name of Hendrix. They were what we called career criminals. It was well-known by most law enforcement officers that these two spent every day and night planning an escape.

Connelly had built up about 250 years and Hendrix had over 300 years to serve. I was a jailer while they were in jail and oddly enough we got along great. Connelly was my age and in conversation we found out we had played football against each other while in high school. He went to Pensacola High at the same time I was at Bay High. Both Connelly and Hendrix were greatly feared by jail personnel because of their escape ability.

They had escaped from our jail two times. Each time a prisoner escaped, Doc Daffin fired the jailer. As a result, the jailers steered clear of their cell pod except to feed them and do a head count at the beginning and the end of their shift.

I liked Connelly and we talked a lot when I was on duty. I did small favors, like bring a book and other small things. This was done for most all the inmates except Hendrix and Connelly. Hendrix was always nice to me, but I think that is because Connelly liked me and I never mistreated either of them.

Hendrix was very quiet and generally talked to no one but Connelly. Sometimes he even said a few words to me. On one occasion, Connelly told me they would never escape on my shift and get me fired. He laughed and I didn't know if he was making a joke or not.

I never took any chances around them, but I was still nice to both. Their cell was in maximum security. It consisted of a small cell in the back of a large day cell. At night we had to make them go from the day cell back to the little cell where there were two bunks. The steel door was then rolled shut at the control box out in the hall and the late night shift had to physically go into the cell pod, pull on the small cell door to make sure it locked and look in the small cell to make sure they were both still with us.

One night I went in to check them at 10:00 pm as I was coming on duty. They were both sitting up and I heard Connelly say real low, "No, no, that's Pitts." When I looked in the cell they had guilty looks on their faces. I asked what was going on and they laughed and said nothing just passing the time.

One day the two of them started beating on the bars and yelling about problems and lack of service, etc. The sheriff ordered them taken out of their cell and placed in the tank cell on the first floor. They were to stay there until they learned to be quiet.

That started Connelly singing. He had quite a voice and he sang one Hank Williams song after another. There was no other place to put them, so everyone had to put up with the noise.

This went on all day and most of the night. Each shift change we were required to check the whole jail and count the prisoners. When we checked the jail the following morning, Connelly and Hendrix were gone. They cut through the heavy screen that covered the top of the tank. Then went out a window that led to the outside parking lot right over the sheriff's parking space. They climbed out through a large fan vent and jumped onto the sheriff's new Buick. They went across the 4th Street Bridge and stole a blue Buick at someone's home.

After several months we got word that they were arrested crossing the Mexican border back into the United States. They were brought back to the State of Florida to face the charge of escape. It carried a maximum sentence of ten years, at that time. I came on duty the first night they were back in jail and they shook hands through the bars and seemed glad to see me.

Connelly admitted that before they broke out of the tank, they had gotten a hack saw blade smuggled in and had been sawing the bars on the maximum security cell for many days and nights. To cover the noise, Connelly sang and made a racket while Hendrix sawed. They put soap in the sawed places so the jailer couldn't see the cuts.

They planned to escape when a certain jailer was on duty and to kill him before they left. He said that one jailer gave them a hard time when he was on duty and they had had enough of him. Hendrix had somehow gotten a coat hanger. When the jailer came in to check their cell, they were going to hook him around the neck with the coat hanger. The night they were going to do this, I came in to check them instead of the one they wanted.

I remembered the regular jailer was off sick that night. I had to come in and work a long shift. They did leave on that jailer's shift, but never had another opportunity to kill him. He got fired anyhow because they escaped on his shift.

I asked why they came back to the U.S. when they were safe in Mexico. Connelly said it was not really that safe in Mexico. They were doing fine until one night they were in a pool room playing pool with some Mexicans. Hendrix caught one of them cheating or something and he pulled a knife on Hendrix. Hendrix killed him with his cue stick. That was when they decided it was not safe in Mexico any longer.

When the two were preparing to go before Judge Lewis, Connelly tried to get Hendrix to be nice to the judge. His reasoning was that if they could get the judge to run their sentence concurrently, they might get out someday. Hendrix just laughed.

When they went before Judge Lewis, he asked if Hendrix had anything to say before he passed sentence on him. Hendrix said,

"Yeah, I do. I have a hobby of collecting time and most of all I hate no good SOB's like you."

He called the judge a bald-headed 'blankety-blank' SOB and much more. After running out of all the colorful words he could remember, he stopped talking for a moment and finished by saying, "Give me all the time you can, you old 'so and so' SOB."

Judge Lewis was red-faced and looked like he was going to explode or have a heart attack. He stuttered for a moment or two trying to get his composure. When he did, he said, "Mr. Hendrix, I regret the law does not permit me to give you but 10 years and I do give you that and that sentence will start when you have served the 300 plus years you now have on the books."

Next Connelly walked up and the judge asked if he was collecting time like his friend. He said, "No sir, your honor I have an old mother I would like to see again someday. I would really appreciate it if you could let my sentence run concurrently with what I have on me at this time."

The judge said, "I also regret that I can only give you ten years, but that is your sentence and it will start after you have served the two hundred plus you have on the books."

When they were brought back to jail to await transfer to the state prison, I took them to their cell and Connelly told me what happened. Hendrix was still laughing and said, "Yeah, old Connelly begged and kissed his butt and then got the same ten years I did."

I never heard from the two again except through law enforcement sources. The U.S. Supreme Court made a decision on the Gideon case–that all people would have an attorney appointed to represent them if they had no money. As a result of this ruling thousands of convicted felons, including Connelly and Hendrix, were released from prison.

From what I knew about Hendrix, he was about the meanest man I'd ever met. I don't know how many people he killed, but according to Connelly, Hendrix had a code of honor. Some things he would not do. He wouldn't hurt a woman or child in any way, and he would not rob places where he thought they were uninsured.

He was known by the criminal element as "The Boss." When he was sent to any prison camp in the State of Florida, word went out that The Boss was present and he was immediately in charge. He could have his orders obeyed without hesitation by the inmates.

Knowing the hardened criminal he was makes me appreciate all the more the miracle-working power of Christ. Hendrix accepted Jesus as his Lord and Savior and became a preacher in the closing years of his life. Though I never got to hear him preach, it's interesting to note that he married the widowed sister-in-law of my college roommate, Don York. Don said he made a dynamic preacher.

If God forgave Hendrix for all he ever did, it is certain His forgiveness is vast enough to cover everyone.

Dr. Joe Morris and the Emergency Room

Dr. Morris was one of my favorite doctors. He saved many lives with his skills as a surgeon, including my own.

One night we had a call to a local bar where a knife fight had taken place between two drunks. They were cut all over yet none of the wounds seemed to be life-threatening. We had to take one drunk to the emergency room. I was one of the two deputies it took to hold the injured drunk on the table while Dr. Morris examined him. The drunk was cursing and hollering and making a general nuisance of himself.

The nurse cut off the clothing covering the knife wounds. Dr. Morris got his sewing kit out and ordered the guy to be still, so he could sew him up. The guy demanded the doctor give him some pain killer before he started.

Dr. Morris looked him right in the eyes and said, "Son, that's what's wrong with you now. You've had too much pain killer. Now be still and you two deputies hold him down."

We did. As I recall, Dr. Morris put more than 500 stitches in him.

221

Easter Moonshine Bootlegger Chase

One night, about three days before Easter, I was working the center zone and received a call that the FHP was chasing an older model vehicle suspected of hauling moonshine whiskey on US 231. I, like most law enforcement officers, loved this kind of action, so I headed that direction. I was way out of the area when I got the call, but it was early morning and there was almost no traffic.

When I got to 231 and Cove Boulevard, the trooper and the suspect had entered the black district off Cove Boulevard. The suspect was trying to lose the trooper and zigzagged all over the housing area just off the boulevard.

Somehow, he came back onto 231 with the trooper and me in close pursuit. By this time, a couple of PCPD patrol cars and a state beverage agent had joined in the chase. We headed back north on 231, which was a two lane highway at that time. Each time we tried to get by this guy, he cut us off and ran us off the highway. He was not traveling too terribly fast, 50 or 60, but kept a steady speed.

After we passed through Hiland Park, the trooper had reached his breaking point and started shooting at the tires on the suspect's car. That looked like a good thing to do, so about all the pursuers started doing the same thing.

When we came into Bayou George, all four tires were blasted off and the guy was on four rims. He made a left turn on Cemetery Road, just before the Bayou George Bridge. That road ends way back in the woods near an old cemetery. When he got there, he bailed out and hit the dirt running before the car came to a good stop. In about ten seconds, he was out of sight in the woods.

Apalachicola Correctional Institute was contacted to send bloodhounds to trail the guy. We inspected the abandoned vehicle. The back seat was missing and stacked inside were one-gallon glass jugs of moonshine. We opened the trunk and found it packed full of glass jugs also.

It was unbelievable, that in all that chase and shooting, not one jug had been broken. The moonshine, usually clear, was in a rainbow of colors. The beverage agent advised coloring the shine was a popular thing to do with Easter coming up. There were fifty one-gallon jugs in the vehicle.

The suspect was captured several hours later near Jackson County, about 19 miles from where he abandoned his vehicle. That boy could not only drive and not break the jugs, he could also run.

The beverage agent kept two gallons for evidence. (More than a gallon was needed for a felony charge.) He asked us to help him destroy the other 48. We devised all kinds of ways to break those jugs. We threw some full jugs up in the air and tried to hit them by throwing full jugs at them. That was too hard, so we started taking turns throwing a jug up in the air and shooting at it.

You would be surprised how many times all those officers missed those jugs with their pistols.

This a large delivery of moonshine intercepted in the late 1950s en route to independent distributors in Bay County. Each distributor normally cut the 5 gallons with water to sell in half pints.

223

Domestic Call, Panama City Beach

Let me point out something about domestic calls. There are certain calls an officer goes on that tend to give him a "pucker feeling." (Pucker feeling is when your butt puckers so tight that it will eat a hole in the seat cover.) To me there is no greater pucker feeling than going on a domestic call where the man has beaten up his wife, and she invites you in the home to get him. When you walk into a man's home, you are entering his castle–his domain. Many officers have missed roll call the following day because of entering a home on a domestic complaint.

Unfortunately, our local judge ruled that if either spouse was having a problem with the other and they invited us into their home to resolve the problem, we had the legal right to enter and handle the problem. He also said that if we declined, then we were negligent in our duty. Even though we did not like the judge's ruling, Sheriff Daffin, resolved the dilemma by ordering us to comply with the judge's wishes.

One cold rainy night, I received a call to go to Edgewater Gulf Beach Cottages on the beach and check on a complaint from a woman who claimed her drunken husband had thrown her out. In the wintertime in the early 1960s, almost no one in their right mind was staying on the beaches. This night there were at least two. One of them was a drunk and the other a crying woman standing outside in the rain in her night clothes.

She told me her husband was inside. He was very drunk. He had beaten her up, thrown her outside and wouldn't let her come back inside. The car was locked and the keys were inside the house.

I advised her, that if she invited me in, I could go in and arrest her husband. She was glad to do this. I walked in and was relieved to see that he seemed to be very drunk and not much larger than myself. I asked him to come outside and he advised me to come get him.

He was standing on the far side of the living room backed up against a table. I started walking toward him and just before I got to him he pulled a 38 cal. revolver from behind him, cocked it and leveled it at my head.

I did the sensible thing and stopped. He laughed and said, "I think I will just kill me one cop and be through with it."

I told him that would be a big mistake. My backup would be there any minute, and he'd certainly be killed. He laughed and said, "I don't have anything to live for anyway, so I don't care."

I explained that I had a lot to live for and told him about my family and loved ones and everything else I could think of that might change his mind. (There are a few people who brag about never having been afraid of anything. Let me tell you one thing, the person who says that, is lying.)

My pleading must have sounded really pitiful, along with my knees knocking. Because after a while he laughed again and said, "You are so chicken s_ _ _ I don't need a gun to take care of you. I'll just throw you out myself."

He then turned and laid the gun on the table and as he turned back around I hit him with a flying tackle. Of course I had lied to him about help coming, because I knew there were only two other deputies working and they were on the other side of the county. There was no help coming. So the fight was on.

This guy might have been drunk, but he put up a big fight. We turned over chairs and generally tore the place apart. I don't know how long we fought, but the sheriff's office got a state trooper from town to come to the beach and check on me.

I finally got a chokehold on him and held on until he about passed out and then put the cuffs on him. I sat there a few minutes and got my breath, and silently thanked the Lord for sparing me one more time. I got him by the feet and dragged him out the front door and down the steps. It was still raining.

When I got him out in the yard, Trooper Roddenberry of the Florida Highway Patrol pulled up and helped me load him in the patrol car.

By this time the drunk had revived and was talking bad about me and my ancestors.

On the way to the jail, he started apologizing for not killing me when he could. He promised if he ever had another opportunity he would not fail. I thanked him for not killing me and booked him into the county jail.

Plan 'Trackdown'

Local law enforcement agencies Thursday held a planning session for the final phase of "Operation Truckdown", an intensified effort to reduce accidents in Bay County. Present at the session were (left to right) Ernest Worthington, acting Panama City Police Chief; Capt. K. D. Sconiers, commander, Troop A, Florida Highway Patrol; M. J. (Doc) Daffin, sheriff; Sgt. Jim Roddenberry, FHP; LaVelle Pitts, Springfield Police Chief; Lt. Nathan Sharron, FHP; and C. W. Sassard, sheriff's chief deputy.   (Staff Photo)

Gathered at a planning meeting to reduce car accidents.
Standing: Sgt. Jim Roddenberry; Springfield Police Chief LaVelle Pitts; Lt. Nathan Sharron, FHP; C.W. Sassard, deputy BCSO
Seated: Acting Police Chief Ernest Worthington; Capt. K.D. Sconiers, FHP; Sheriff Doc Daffin

Training Officer Makes a Point

Sheriff Doc Daffin always tried to place a new recruit deputy with a regular officer to learn the ropes and general functions of a deputy. Back in the 1950s and 60s, we had no police standards or requirements to be a deputy sheriff except being 21 years of age and a citizen of the United States. Of course Sheriff Daffin had his own requirements to add, such as: 1. live in Bay County, 2. graduate from Bay High or Rosenwald, 3. have references from one or more very influential citizens in town, 4. be registered Democrat. He also loved to hire those with some military experience. However, in most cases he steered clear of veterans with twenty or more years in the service, saying it was "too hard to teach old dogs new tricks."

New employee, Dennis Pledger, fit into the requirements, did a good job and was well-liked by the other officers. This was a real accomplishment in itself. Most older officers were jealous of new ones and to some degree felt threatened by new guys—especially the young educated officers.

After Dennis had been on the job for quite some time another new guy came on and the sheriff assigned him to ride with Dennis

226

as his training officer. Dennis was a Christian and not bashful about sharing Jesus, especially to a new officer. Some officers didn't like to ride with Dennis, because they didn't want to be preached to all night.

This was true for his new trainee. At the visitor and officer's coffee table in the jail, we usually met and briefed the incoming crew on what happened during our shift. When the new guy was there and Dennis had left, the guys questioned him about how he liked the job and how he was getting along with Dennis. He was very vocal on how Dennis preached to him for eight straight hours. He said he loved the job, but wondered when the preaching would stop. The guys got a real kick out of this because most all had been preached to by Dennis at one time or another.

We were right in the middle of Spring Break, the time when Sodom and Gomorra breaks out on the Panama City Beach. College students arrive and go wild. It would not be unusual for fifty to a hundred arrests to be made each night.

The new guy and Dennis were driving down the Back Beach Road when they noticed a car weaving and running off the road in front of them. Dennis immediately called in the description and tag number of the car and turned on his blue lights. The guy stopped and got out of his car.

When Dennis asked for his driver's license, the subject started cussing and yelling at Dennis. He accused Dennis and his riding partner of trying to make money off out-of-town people. Dennis listened to the guy's tirade as officers are compelled to do. But when he put the subject under arrest for drunk driving and started to place him in the car, the subject became physical, shoved Dennis and resisted. Dennis punched the guy with a hard-thrown, upper-cut to the point of his chin and the guy was down and out.

His trainee was in a state of shock witnessing the "preacher man" take the guy out. They loaded the drunk in the patrol car and were on the way to the jail when Dennis explained, "God doesn't expect us to put up with all that crap."

The trainee had a new appreciation for his preacher-trainer.

227

State of the Art Lie Detector Machine

A fellow deputy sheriff in an adjoining county, built a lie detector machine. I looked at the thing one time and it was so ugly, it was funny. The deputy said he made it with parts from a washing machine, a hose from a vacuum cleaner, an extension cord, light bulb, several items from a lawn mower and a few unidentifiable parts. He assured me it was very effective and offered to demonstrate the machine on me.

I explained that my momma didn't raise "no fool," and declined but asked, "How in the world does this thing work?"

He explained. "Sometimes I have a suspect I'm certain committed a crime. They refuse to admit it and there's not enough physical evidence to take the suspect to court. I take the suspect to an old office in the county jail and sit him in a big wooden chair that resembles "Sparky." (This was the nick name that was given to the Florida electric chair on Death Row.)

"I wrap all these tubes, suction cups and electrical cords around his bare chest, legs, head and arms. Some of the electrical wires are bare and touch the body of the suspect in several places. I explain the lie detector, how accurate it is and tell him I'm going to run a test to prove it. I say, if you answer my questions truthfully, nothing will happen. If you lie, light will pop on and other things will happen to you. Do you understand?"

By this time his suspect was getting a little nervous. He first asked a yes or no question as to the suspect's name, and used his true name. The suspect answered "yes" and nothing happened.

After the first question, he said, "See you told the truth." He next asked the subject two or three questions that were true, like address, live in Florida, etc. He said, "You see you are still telling the truth and the machine can tell."

Then he told the subject to lie on the next question. He asked if his name was John Doe and instructed the subject to say "yes." The deputy was prepared to flip a toggle switch on the side of his desk. This was attached to a cord that was plugged into a 110-volt plug and connected to one of the lines that was attached to the suspect's body.

When the suspect lied about his name, the deputy flipped the switch two or three lights popped on, a buzzer went off, a bell

228

rang and the suspect received a jolt from the current. This was followed by a blood-curdling scream from the suspect who jumped about two feet straight up off the chair.

When he got him back in the chair and settled down, the deputy said, "See, I told you this machine knew when you lied."

The suspect said, "Yes sir, it sure does work." Then he went on to question the suspect about the crime. He said he didn't have an unsolved case since he built the machine. I was impressed, but even as a young officer I wondered about the legality of this contraption.

Not long after this, I had the answer. An FBI agent stopped by our office and asked if we had heard about a homemade lie detector machine being used by a deputy in an adjoining county. He also called the officer's name. We assured him we had never heard of it and he left saying the Justice Department had received several complaints. If they proved to be true, he was going to arrest the deputy.

Someone got on the phone and called the deputy. He was advised of the visitor en route to see him.

I later asked the deputy what happened after he got the phone call and if the agent found the machine. He said the perfect lie detector machine ended up on the bottom of the Apalachicola River.

Marie Bonner

I could write a book on Marie. She was unique and one of the meanest, orneriest women I ever met if you crossed her. She fought in an instant without much urging. She was an excellent cook and bartender. In her later years she was in great demand by some of the big restaurants for her cooking ability.

I had many confrontations with Marie, but we remained friends until her death. I can't recall how many guns, knives and other weapons were taken from her when she hurt or shot someone (or was desperately trying to do so when we intervened).

The only thing that saved Marie from being in jail for murder was that she couldn't shoot worth a toot. When she started shooting, she shot out windows, furniture, the bar, chairs and even vehicles in the parking lot. Like I said, Marie had a reputation and when she got her gun out everyone immediately left the area. Several times people left without their vehicle. It was too risky to take the time to unlock the door and get in and drive away.

Her claim to fame was when she was owner or manager of a juke or honky-tonk. That's when I (along with other law enforcement officers) first got acquainted with Marie. She was married at one time to a guy near Skunk Valley Road in north Bay County. He was about as bad as Marie and how they didn't kill each other I'll never know.

But getting a divorce allowed them to carry on their business interests in two different locations. They both ran jukes. In addition, her ex had a moonshine still and had to spend a lot of time taking care of that business as well.

Marie had a very colorful vocabulary accented by a little speech impediment. She couldn't speak very plainly, especially when she got really mad. But when she got her gun or butcher knife out, she didn't have to speak too much. The weapons spoke volumes.

Marie ran honky-tonks in various places in and around Panama City at various times. Southport was a favorite location, but she handled locations in the City of Panama City, Panama City Beach, Callaway and some unincorporated areas of Bay County.

When she opened a small juke on Airport Road inside the Panama City limits, deputies breathed a sigh of relief, thinking the city police could now contend with her. I don't know how many times they answered calls to her place. I do know that when she made the call herself, she called the sheriff's office, because we continued to answer calls at her place after all.

Late one night, I received a call that a fight was in progress at her bar. I was only a short distance away and went immediately. I got out of the patrol car and didn't hear any gun shots and figured it was all over. I was wrong. When I walked through the door, I saw a guy racing around the bar, which was open at both ends. Marie was right behind him with a large butcher knife. It was a good race and the other drinkers in the bar were backed up around the walls observing the show.

I watched for a moment to make sure Marie and the guy she was chasing were the only dogs in the fight. They seemed to be, so I moved up and as Marie came racing by I caught her arm and took the knife. That stopped the race but not her mouth. She was yelling that he refused to leave when she ordered him out and she decided to throw him out.

I told the guy to get lost and he did not need any encouragement. He was out that door and headed back toward TAFB. I kept Marie's butcher knife to add to the collection of her weapons at the jail that we had confiscated. and let the rest of the patrons continue their partying.

Another of Marie's jukes was on Airport Road and Highway 390. This one had a very large dirt parking area in front and could be accessed from either road. I was working late one night as an investigator for the sheriff's office, and was coming from the beach en route to Lynn Haven. I passed Marie's juke and noticed only a few cars present.

Just after I passed, the dispatcher called for any car in the area near Marie Bonner's juke. I answered and said I had just passed it. The dispatcher said to go back. There was a report of a shooting going on at the present time.

I turned around and was back within one minute. The first thing I saw was a very big cloud of dust in front of the juke. As I pulled in, I almost hit Marie with my vehicle. She was standing in the dust waving one hand, trying to clear the dust from her eyes, and in the other hand she had a pistol. I stopped and got out and immediately took the gun from her.

She was yelling and in her colorful language trying to tell me about two airmen who were causing a disturbance in her place. She ordered them out and they told her they would throw her out instead. That told me these guys were new in town, because no one in their right mind said that to Marie Bonner–not in her place.

Some of the customers verified that this took place and what the two airmen had said. They witnessed Marie drag a big old pistol out from under the bar. The two airmen, who were coming around the end of the bar after Marie, suddenly changed directions and headed for the door with Marie firing the old pistol after them. How she ever kept from killing someone was always a mystery to law enforcement officers. Lord knows she tried on a number of occasions.

I went outside. The dust had settled and I could see two deep tire tracks where the car had taken off. Following the direction they headed, I could see a car in the ditch across Airport Road. It was the car the airmen had been driving.

They left the parking lot so fast, they couldn't make the turn onto Airport Road. The car crossed the road at a high rate of speed and went into the drainage ditch. The two front wheels made it over and stuck on the far side of the ditch and the two rear wheels were on the opposite side of the ditch.

The driver and passenger's doors were open. There was no sign of the airman and I could find no blood, so I assumed they made it safely into the wooded area on the other side of the ditch. Marie was such a bad shot she had even missed the vehicle too.

I kept Marie's gun to add to the collection at the sheriff's office. She came down a few days later, like always, and asked the sheriff for her weapon back. He, like always, declined. I think the sheriff always told her something to the effect that she should stop shooting at these people because some day she might just hit one of them.

And so,…there was a guy from Southport who was part Indian. He was called Junior. (His father was the subject I had to fight in the "Indian, Fire Water and Drunk Driving" story above.)

Junior was a real pain to law enforcement when he started drinking. He sometimes went wild or crazy with rage. When he got in this condition, it didn't matter who confronted him. They had a fight on their hands. I think every deputy at one time or another had a confrontation with Junior.

When Junior and Marie got together, it was like mixing water with hot grease. This happened one night, and Marie finally hit what she was aiming at.

Our officers responded to a shooting at Marie's Place at Airport and Highway 390. The ambulance had picked up one person, Junior, and headed for the hospital. The deputy had arrested Marie and was en route to the jail. I was the on-call investigator and waited for Marie to question her.

I sat across the desk from Marie and figured she would be scared to death, after finally hitting a person, and worried her victim might die. I was wrong. Marie was not scared, but mad as all get out. Before I could advise her of her rights she started telling me what happened.

I finally got her to shut up long enough for me to explain her rights. I emphasized that she had a right to an attorney. I even told her she really needed one before she started talking.

She said she didn't want a lawyer. She wanted to tell me what happened.

She explained that Junior had started trouble with other customers and she finally told him to get out. Junior told her she was not big enough to throw him out and threatened to throw her out. He got up and started for the bar. She drug another old revolver out from behind the bar and fired two or three times at him before he hit the floor.

I had to take a recorded statement, so I tried to help her all I could since she had no attorney. She was so mad I was afraid she would hang herself.

After she told the part where he threatened to throw her out of her own place and started toward the bar, I kind of gave her a leading question. I said, "Is it true that you were in fear of your life when he started toward the bar and you shot him in the leg to stop him?"

She said loudly, "No that's not true. I tried to shoot him between the eyes and missed. I wanted to kill that SOB."

After completing the interview with Marie, I had the matron lock her up and went to check on Junior. When I got downstairs, I found Junior limping in the back door being helped by two deputies.

The officers advised that Junior refused to let the doctors examine him so they brought him to the jail. It seemed that one bullet had hit him in the groin area and he was holding it with both hands and cursing Marie.

He kept saying "That SOB woman has done ruined my sex-orgies." I asked if he wanted to file charges against Marie. He said, "No, he would take care of her himself."

233

I thought about what he said. If I was a betting man, I would put my money on Marie if they ever met again.

I turned Marie out and added one more item to the "Marie Bonner weapon collection."

Chief Kissinger and the White Circle

In the late 1950s, Cedar Grove had a reputation with some of our citizens as being a speed trap. I understand the police chief was originally from up North some place. His uniform was like a New York policeman's, with a big leather belt and a strap on the front of the belt ran around his shoulder and hooked to the belt in the back. We all made fun of him but it didn't faze the chief. He had a good sense of humor and it was really hard to get under his skin.

There was a night club in the middle of Cedar Grove called the White Circle. This was a popular club with dancing, a country music band and some really good free-for-alls at times. From about 9:00 pm until closing, the chief backed his patrol car in beside the White Circle, facing the street. He generally stood just inside the front door of the club. He was a good peace maker, and cracked down on good old boys when they started fighting or got too drunk. He probably came close to making his police department's budget each month at the White Circle. He usually worked alone and seldom called for back-up from the sheriff's office. He was a real big man and could be a tough task master.

The sheriff's office usually had only three cars working the county—the east side, the center and the west side. The shifts ran from 6:00 am to 6:00 pm and 6:00 pm to 6:00 am seven days a week.

We had a new patrol car delivered to the sheriff's office one afternoon and the east side got to drive it. All the emergency equipment had been installed and the car was to be painted the next day. The two east side deputies were warned to treat it with tender care and not get a scratch on it.

Everything was going smoothly because it was a week night and not much activity. The two deputies passed by the White Circle about 2:00 am and noted that most of the customers had left and Chief Kissinger was standing in the door, as usual, talking to the manager.

The deputies drove to Highway 98 in Millville and decided that it was time to get the chief out of the club. Since he hadn't seen the new patrol car, they fired up the big police-interceptor engine and headed back toward U.S. 231 in Hiland Park. When they passed the White Circle, they were doing about 85 or 90 mph. They saw the chief jump from the White Circle entry and head for his car.

The entire parking lot was dirt and they could see, from the street lights, a big cloud of dust as the chief fish-tailed onto East Avenue in pursuit. Being a long way ahead, the deputies turned off their lights and pulled off East Avenue onto Game Farm Road and stopped. The chief zoomed by with his emergency lights flashing and siren blasting. He stopped at the intersection of US 231 and East Avenue for a moment and took off up 231. He came back a short time later, contacted our east side car, and asked their location.

One of the deputies responded, "Parker."

The chief said, "Be on the look out for a new white Ford vehicle. It was running at least 100 mph and about blew Cedar Grove off the map. He then went back to the White Circle.

Just as he got out of his patrol car the deputies came back by the White Circle headed toward Highway 98 in Millville at eighty plus mph. He raced back to his car and the race was on again. He immediately called the east side car and told them that same car had come back by and was flying. He asked them to help stop this car before someone got killed.

So far as I know, every law enforcement officer in the county knew by the following day what had happened—except the chief and Doc Daffin of course. I must admit that even cops play at times.

When working 12-hour shifts with nothing going on, law enforcement officers sometimes invent things to entertain themselves in order to stay awake.

(Speaking of the challenge of staying awake, one particular deputy had a small business shoeing horses and most of the time got little sleep before he had to work a 12-hour shift. His lieutenant wanted to get rid of him because of his sleeping on duty. The sheriff refused to fire him unless he caught him asleep on the job. Determined to catch the deputy asleep, the lieutenant spent a lot of time monitoring him. One day, he spotted him in the early morning hours parked in a grassy area just off Highway 388–head down on his chest and sound asleep. The lieutenant pulled up next to him. As he stopped, the deputy woke up, raised his head and said a loud, "Amen." The lieutenant realized he had lost again and pulled away without saying a word.)

Bully Junior Act 2

Junior grew up and went off to "college"–Raiford State Prison–for a few years on the charge of rape. I grew up and became a deputy sheriff and Junior was back in town. He was married, had two or three children, whipped up on his wife on a regular basis and still lived with his mother–my aunt.

When he got in jail, my aunt came and got him out. I think my aunt and Jesus are the only two in the world who loved Junior unconditionally.

His wife came to see me several times and asked for help after he had beaten her up. I tried to convince her to leave him, but she said she had to have help with the kids and had no place else to go. Since she lived with my aunt, she wouldn't get a warrant for Junior, because my aunt talked her out of it.

I recall wishing I could drive up when Junior was whipping up on his wife and let him know how it felt to be whipped up on. One day she came to my office after I became an investigator, and she had been beaten. She was crying but again refused to prosecute Junior. I told her the next time he came around drinking to get in the car and go to a friend's house until he sobered up.

She said, "I tried, but he runs out of the house and lays down behind the car so I can't back out."

"Run over him the next time he does that."

A couple weeks later, she did.

My aunt called me and yelled on the phone. "That woman backed her car over Junior and broke his leg. She said you told her to do it!"

About six weeks later Junior came limping into my office on crutches with a cast on his leg. He wanted to prosecute his wife, who finally left him. I try not to make light of anyone's misfortune, but my dad always taught me to never hit or mistreat a woman. I reminded him that his wife never prosecuted him, and advised him not to lay down behind a vehicle any more.

He and his wife finally got back together, but to my knowledge he never laid down behind the car again. And my aunt never spoke to me again either.

The Walton Brothers Again

The three Walton brothers were well-known to law enforcement officers and the rowdies who hung around Bay County jukes and bars. They usually traveled together. They were bad dudes in a fight. If you fought one of them, you had to fight all three at the same time. They usually had a friend, Gus, who hung out with them. He was a huge guy and had the same bad disposition as the Walton's. If a police officer was sent out to a disturbance and they knew it was the Walton bunch, the dispatcher tried to find a backup officer to send also. Sometimes it was not possible to get a backup.

This was the case in the City of Springfield when a complaint came into the police station that the Waltons were having a big party at their home in the Sutton quarters section. The chief, George Kittrell, sent his young rookie policeman to check it out and warn them to quiet down.

The rookie, Tommy Likes (alias), had recently been discharged from the U.S. Air Force and had only been working for a few weeks. There was no mandatory training for police during those years. You were just handed a badge, uniform and gun, and told that a supervisor would tell you what to do and how to do it.

Even though the officer was new, he had heard about the Walton brothers. He reportedly said later that when the chief told him to go on this call, he asked who was going to back him up. He was told there was no one on duty but him and the chief. Chief

Kittrell was busy with some people in his office and ordered the officer to just, "Do as I say and handle it." The officer later said he started to turn his badge in and quit, but he had a wife and two little girls, so decided against that.

The officer drove to the Walton house, walked up on the porch and knocked. One of the Waltons answered the door and asked what he wanted.

"The chief sent me to tell you to turn the noise down because of complaints." The Walton boy laughed at him and slammed the door in his face, telling him to get off their property.

The rookie officer was totally crushed, drove back to the police station, and told the chief what happened. The chief was having a bad day. He yelled at the officer and told him, if he wanted to keep this job, he'd better handle the assignment.

Chief Kittrell, telling the story later, said a few minutes after the officer left, he had second thoughts. He jumped in his patrol car and raced to the Walton home. He found the young officer's patrol car with the door open and the front door of the Walton house broken and standing half open.

He pulled his revolver and raced up on the porch. He looked inside and saw all the Walton boys, their family and Gus up against the wall with their hands reaching up as high as they could. The officer stood behind them waving a 12-gauge riot shotgun loaded with double-ought buckshot. He had tears in his eyes, saying, "If any one of you doesn't do what I say, I'll shoot all of you."

The chief calmed the officer down, told him to go back to the office and said he would take it from there.

One of the brothers said, "Chief, that's the first time in my life I was glad to see you. That guy walked up on the porch, kicked the door open and walked in with tears running down his cheeks. He screamed at us to get up against the wall. That boy's crazy."

The chief said two great things came from this situation. First, the rookie didn't kill a half dozen people with his riot gun. Second, from that day on, if the officer got a call to their house, there was no problem. They did exactly as they were told.

 *A valuable lesson was learned that day–don't send a scared rookie officer out alone with orders to handle a dangerous situation.*

Promoted to Investigator (1961- 1963)

This photo depicts Charlie Abbott, center, standing next to Doc Daffin (before the sheriff's indictment).
Photo credit: *Centennial Stories, Celebrating the History of Panama City, 1909-2009*, Marlene Womack.

I started out as a jailer in 1957 at the Bay County Sheriff's Office and moved up to a patrolman. In the early 1960s, Sheriff Daffin was indicted by a federal grand jury and a new man, Charlie Abbott, was appointed sheriff by the governor.

Berwin Williams was a Special Investigator for the Florida Sheriff's Bureau and later with the Florida Department of Law Enforcement. He was sent to Bay County to help Charlie Abbott set up the sheriff's office.

Most of the employees walked out with Sheriff Daffin, because he said everyone who left with him would come back with him. He was confident he would return in two years. I talked to Sheriff Daffin and told him I had been loyal to him, but I had a family to support and needed to stay on with the new sheriff if I could. He replied, "You heard what I said and I meant every word. You leave with me and you come back with me. You stay, then you won't have a job when I return." I felt I had no choice but stay.

The new sheriff and Special Agent Berwin Williams gathered the few who were left at the sheriff's office and asked if anyone had investigative experience. No one raised his hand because our two investigators, Floyd Nixon and Jake Sellers, had left with the sheriff. There was a big 4 X 5 press camera that was used to take pictures of crime scenes. He asked if anyone knew how to use it.

Investigator LaVelle Pitts working under appointed Sheriff, Charlie Abbott, 1961

I raised my hand. He asked if I could develop pictures. I said I could. He said, "You're an investigator."

I thought that was great. I jumped from a deputy to an investigator. You usually had to work for years to be an investigator. I found out rather quickly that the older deputies really resented my promotion, because they had worked as deputies for many years.

I became the chief investigator (the only investigator) and crime scene specialist. The deputies put it on me. Everything that happened, they called me in and turned it over to me. In most cases, I didn't know as much as they did. Special Agent Williams recognized what was happening and brought over two investigators, Emory Williams (no relation to Berwin) and Eddie Boone (who later became Leon County Sheriff) from the Florida Sheriffs' Bureau to give me a crash course in criminal investigation. Special Agent Emory Williams was named acting chief investigator until Berwin felt I was capable of taking over.

My First Murder Case

Before Emory Williams came, we had a murder in Lynn Haven and I was called out. Preliminary investigation revealed that the husband had found out his wife was seeing a car salesman from a local car company. Instead of going to work this particular day, the husband went to C&G Sporting Goods in downtown Panama City and bought a little .25 automatic with a box of ammunition.

He parked near his house and waited. The car salesman, I found out later, was late showing up that morning because of a meeting. The husband gave up on him coming and went to his house to confront his wife. As the husband pulled into his drive, the salesman passed by and saw the husband. He kept going. This saved his life.

The husband accused his wife and they got into a yelling match. He grabbed her by the hair and shot her in the chest and face four times and put the gun in his mouth and fired the last shot. Unfortunately, the children were present and saw everything.

This was the scene I found when I entered the house. The kids were terrified, and so was I. I asked a neighbor woman outside to take the kids home with her. I told the one deputy who came to guard the front door not let anyone in except the medical people. The woman was dead, but somehow the man was still alive. The medics took him to the hospital.

I sat down in a kitchen chair, lit up a cigar and tried to settle down and figure out what I was supposed to do. The deputy brought my camera to the door and asked if I needed it. That reminded me photographs had to be taken, so I was in business now. After taking several pictures, I started drawing a diagram of the crime scene. It took about four hours to complete the work at the crime scene and then I drove to the hospital to check on the husband. He lived several hours before he died. This was the first of many murders I worked during the next twenty plus years.

After this introductory experience to criminal investigation, I was delighted to have Emory Williams take over as acting chief investigator. He taught me a great deal about criminal investigation, which turned out to be very beneficial to my entire career in law enforcement.

Mental Patient in Motel on Beach

While I was chief investigator under Charlie Abbott at the BCSO, we received a call about a person with a shotgun at a motel on the beach. The suspect had run everyone off from the motel and was shut up in a room. He said he would kill anyone who tried to remove him. We checked the name out and found this guy was a mental patient who had somehow escaped from the mental ward at the hospital.

When I got to the motel, there were several patrol cars with armed officers parked in the motel parking lot. The manager of the motel was very upset and demanded we remove this person so his guests could return to their rooms.

I got all the officers together in a high level meeting, away from the public, and asked for suggestions. I have never seen a time when several officers together didn't have a suggestion on how to proceed in a situation. However, this time everyone was quiet. The suspect was known. Everyone there was more or less convinced he would do exactly as he had said–shoot anyone who tried to enter his room.

I don't know who was more concerned about this situation– the motel manager, the guests standing out in the street, or the family members of the suspect who had now arrived. The family members were more fearful of him than anyone else. They assured us he would do just what he said. The sheriff, my boss, was also concerned not only for his men but for votes he could lose if things turned sour.

Since I was the ranking officer, I came up with a plan I hoped would work. We would drive an unmarked car by the front of the room and a deputy would walk along, bent over on the other side of the car. When he passed the motel room door, the officer would race through the door and hope the guy had gone to sleep or would be caught off guard. It had been two or three hours since he had been heard from and the family said he could be asleep.

It was not one of my better ideas, but it was the only one I could come up with at the time. The excitement was building with more and more people gathering to watch the fun.

My idea wasn't very popular, only two or three said it might work. I asked for a volunteer to rush the room and things got real quiet. Officer D.D. Clark volunteered to drive a plain car by the room. All eyes turned to me. It became obvious that I was going to be the one who had to go through the door. It was my idea.

(I've often said I had lots of ideas saved up and no one wanted them. This idea probably explains why.)

I shucked off all excess gear, gun, cuffs, etc. I got ready for a fast trip to the door. I advised the officers that as soon as I entered the room to be right behind me. They eagerly agreed to this.

I trotted along beside the vehicle, bent over in case he peeped out the door which was cracked. When I got even with the door, I made a wild dash, hit the door and burst into the room.

The guy was standing on the opposite side of the bed. The shot gun was leaning against the wall next to him. He turned quickly and grabbed the gun. As he lifted it, I dove across the bed and grabbed him. We hit the floor along with the gun. The guy was big and strong. I knew I was in a heap of trouble if help didn't arrive soon.

About that time, Deputy Clark came flying through the door and ended up on top of both us. We had him cuffed quickly and brought him and the gun out of the room. All the other officers were still behind the patrol cars along with the sightseers.

Be cautious when you present a plan, because you might get put in charge.

Fred Turner

Fred Turner was appointed the lawyer for Clarence Gideon in March, 1963. This landmark case established the public defender system across the nation. Photo courtesy of Bay County Public Library

To get an idea of the kind of lawyer Fred Turner was, I'll start with this story of the man who hauled watermelons for a living.

An elderly man, I'll call him Clem White, lived in an old rundown house with his girlfriend in Fountain, north of Youngstown. He had an old beat-up truck and made a living hauling watermelons for big farms. Sometimes he drank too much after delivering a load of melons.

He was arrested by the Florida Highway Patrol for drunk driving and causing an accident.

When he had his day in court, Judge Bailey called his case. Clem stood up and said, "Here, judge." The judge knew the man and asked him if he had an attorney. He said, "No sir, I can't afford one, judge." (This was before the court had to appoint lawyers for defendants who could not afford a lawyer.)

The judge asked if he still hauled watermelons for a living and he replied, "Yes sir." The judge told him he needed a lawyer, because if the jury found him guilty he would have to take his driver's license. That meant he wouldn't be able to drive for at least a year. "The court will be in recess for 15 minutes while this gentlemen checks around the courthouse and finds an attorney to represent him."

The man walked from the court room and asked a state trooper, standing outside the door, if he knew where he could find a lawyer. The trooper happened to be the one who arrested the man. He smiled and pointed to a man coming down the stairs from another court room. The lawyer was Fred Turner.

The trooper told me later that he knew Fred was a high dollar lawyer and wouldn't take the case, but that was the only lawyer around. Clem ran down the hallway, stopped Mr. Turner and started talking. Mr. Turner started shaking his head and saying, "No, no, no."

Judge J. Bailey
Photo courtesy of Bay County
Public Library

Clem persisted and each time Mr. Turner tried to walk away, Clem got in front of him. Finally, to the trooper's amazement, Mr. Turner turned around and walked back to the court room with the old man. The judge and prosecutor, Dayton Logue, were also surprised.

"Are you going to represent this man?" the judge asked.

Mr. Turner shook his head and said, "I guess so, judge."

The trooper took the stand and stated he was on duty the night in question and was on his way to answer a call on north Highway 231. In Hiland Park, the defendant pulled out of the J.K. Pettis Bar in Hiland Park driving an old truck that appeared to have been wrecked.

The driver was going real slow and as he tried to pass the truck, it crossed over in front of him. (This was before Hwy. 231 was four-laned.) The trooper turned on his blue lights and blew his siren. The driver paid no attention, he just slowed to about two miles per hour and kept moving north on U.S 231. The trooper pulled to the shoulder of the highway, ran to the truck, reached in the window and turned off the truck. After getting the man out of the truck, the trooper said the man was so drunk he could barely walk to the patrol car.

The judge asked Mr. Turner if he had any questions for the witness. He said "No sir, your honor."

The court then called the old man to the stand and Mr. Turner told him to tell the jury what happened. The old fellow said, "Judge, me and my girl-friend had been working all day hauling melons and we stopped by J.K.'s and drank some beer. Well I guess I had too much to drink and me and her got to fussing and she slapped me and I slapped her out of her chair. There were some guys at the bar drinking and they jumped off their stools and beat the crap out of me and threw me out of the bar. I got up and went to my truck and..." he paused and said, "Judge, you know that big old oak tree that sits in J.K.'s parking lot?"

The judge just smiled and nodded his head.

Clem continued, "Well I pulled out of the parking and swiped that old tree and ruined my truck. I got on 231 and started back home. The next thing I knew that patrolman was pulling me out of my truck. That's about it judge."

The judge asked the prosecutor if he had any questions for the defendant. He said, "No, your honor." The judge asked the prosecutor if he would like to address the jury and Mr. Logue said, "No your honor, I think the trooper and the defendant have said all that needs to be said. The judge turned to Mr. Turner and asked if he would like to address the jury and Mr. Turner said, "Yes, your Honor."

He looked over the jury and spoke softly. "Ladies and gentlemen of the jury, I have a few words to say on behalf of my client. First, he has no education. He has worked as a laborer all his life. Yes, he stopped at J.K.'S with his girlfriend. Yes, he had too much to drink that night in question. Yes, he did wreck his only means of support, his truck. Folks, I want to leave you with one thought. On the night in question this man lost his girl-friend, got beat up, and wrecked his truck."

Mr. Turner then held up the old man's driver's license. "Folks this driver's license is all he has left. Are you going to take it too? Mr. Turner turned and walked out of the court room as the jurors walked into the jury room to make their decision.

The jury was out about five minutes and returned to the court room. The judge asked if the jury had come to a decision.

"Yes, your honor," the jury foreman said, "NOT GUILTY."

***

I began my law enforcement career as a jailer at the Bay County Jail. When someone was arrested for DUI, or other miscellaneous charges, the jailer was sometimes required to testify in court and describe the arrested person's condition when he was booked into the jail. I had only been a jailer a short time when I was requested to appear in court as a witness on a Florida Highway Patrol DUI case. Officers warned me that I would be facing a tough lawyer and to be very careful. I was told he even spent one year in prison for refusing to file an income tax return.

When I got on the stand I'll never forget my first look at Attorney Fred Turner. He was dressed in a suit, but wore red socks. I learned this was one of his trademarks, wearing red socks, regardless of his other clothing.

He started questioning me and as he proceeded, he made it sound as if he mistrusted me and hated all law enforcement officers. The longer he questioned me the louder he got. Then he started getting personal in some of his remarks. The judge stopped him at one point and asked if he was questioning the witness's character. Mr. Turner said, "I just might be, Your Honor."

At this point I spoke up and said, "At least I've never been to prison like you." Suddenly, the court room became very quiet. The judge recessed court for fifteen minutes and called me back to his office.

If he had taken his belt off and whipped me, I wouldn't have felt so bad, but he simply explained that a witness could never win an argument with an attorney when he was testifying and what I did was a cardinal sin.

The guy on trial was found guilty and I went back to work at the jail. In a few minutes, I received a phone call from Mr. Turner. He asked me to come to his office, which was near the courthouse. I figured he wanted to have it out with me and I was ready.

When I arrived he was sitting at a large conference table and poured me a cup of coffee. He said he knew I was new on the job

247

and wanted to explain a little about how the court system worked. He said he knew he represented many people who were guilty, but it was his responsibility to do everything in his power to make sure this person got a fair trial and if possible get him exonerated.

He went on to say that one of the first things a lawyer did was try to get the jury's mind off the defendant and on the officer who arrested the poor soul. His technique was to try the officer before the jury. He said there was nothing personal meant by it and after the trial, no matter the verdict, he'd go have a cup of coffee with the officer. I said, "No sir, not me."

***

The next time I had a confrontation with Mr. Turner was after I became an investigator and got information a guy was selling drugs out of his new Cadillac on Panama City Beach.

Our State Attorney lived in Blountstown and wasn't available so I found an old case file with a search warrant and drew one up myself to search the car. It took several hours to work on the wording and properly format the three page affidavit. I got it signed, and searched the car. I seized drugs, the car with an expensive set of golf clubs, and made one arrest. This was the first big drug arrest ever made in Bay County and it appeared on the front page of the News Herald. I was a big hero until I got to court and it took Attorney Fred Turner about fifteen minutes to get my search warrant thrown out and his defendant released with his new Cadillac and golf clubs.

After court, I went to Fred's office, handed him the search warrant and said, "What's wrong with this?"

He laughed and said, "All of it. Never put a lot of words in an affidavit because the more you put in, the more I have to expound on in order to get it thrown out. Yours should have been one paragraph but you had three pages."

He went on to say your State Attorney should draw these up for you or go over it before you take it to the judge.

"That is hard to do with the State Attorney living in another city."

"Okay, if you ever have to do another important search warrant and have a problem, come see me or call me and I'll advise you."

Later when I worked a double murder, I took him up on his offer.

***

Executed on the Last Day

Grocer Slayer Executed At Raiford Prison

Convicted shotgun slayer Emmett Clark Blake, sentenced June 22, 1962 to die in the electric chair for the slaying of Brannonville grocer Johnny Beverly, died Tuesday when he was executed at Raiford State Prison.

Blake, who was also charged with the slaying of another man in the store, John T. Holt, has been asking to be put to death since shortly after he was sentenced. His request was finally granted.

In a recent letter to Gov. Farris Bryant, Blake asked him to proceed with the signing of the death warrant. He claimed that his rights were being disregarded and that he wanted to die and demanded speedy execution.

Panama City News Herald article (5-13-1964). Emmett Blake died in the electric chair on the last day of executions before the death penalty was suspended. Executions resumed in Florida in 1979. Article courtesy Bay County Public Library

I was working the night shift and was out on the beach when I received a call from the dispatcher to get to Brannonville, a small community located just east of Panama City city limits. I was told to go to a little store on Highway 231 where a shooting had been reported. I requested a marked unit go and secure the scene until I arrived. I put the blue light on the dash of my unmarked car, turned on the siren and headed out. When I arrived, a deputy was standing in the door. He said, "LaVelle, we've got two dead people here."

Both were shot with a shotgun. The cash register drawer was standing open with no money in it except change. I requested road blocks be put up on all entries and exits

249

to Bay County, and to look for anything suspicious A deputy outside the store came to me and said to call the office right away. The sheriff's office had received a call from J.K. Pettis, who ran a bar and lounge in Hiland Park. He said he had a couple of guys in his bar acting real suspicious. When the car with blue light and siren went by (which would have been me), they got in their car and left quickly headed toward the beach.

He didn't know who they were. He gave us a car description and said he thought it was a Texas tag. The information was given to all units and in a short time I received a call that a car answering the description was stopped by deputies on the west end of the beach. Two men inside seemed to be nervous and said they were on their way back to Texas.

I gave instructions for one officer to drive their car back to the jail and the other officer to bring the suspects back in handcuffs in the patrol car. This was when Charlie Abbott was in office and I was the only investigator. I had to work the crime scene, gather all the evidence and do all the witness interviews.

I interviewed a few people around who didn't know anything. There were no eye witnesses. I took photos of the crime scene where a spent shotgun shell was on the floor. I left a deputy there to secure the area, then went to the jail.

The suspects weren't talking. I felt we might have the right people and wanted to make sure no mistakes were made with a search, since Fred Turner had taught me a hard lesson in how easily he could get a search warrant thrown out. He later explained how I should keep search warrants very simple, and offered his help any time.

So I had the suspects placed in separate cells and drove to Lynn Haven where Fred Turner lived. Mr. Turner was probably one of the smartest lawyers I ever knew and he could "eat your lunch" on the witness stand. I knocked on his door in the early morning.

Turner Home

After about the third knock, Mr. Turner with blood shot eyes and wearing a nightgown, cracked the door open.

He said, "Pitts, what's wrong, what's happened?"

"Remember you telling me if I needed help drawing up a search warrant that you would advise me?"

He looked at his watch and said, "Yeah I remember, but at two o'clock in the morning?"

"I'm sorry, but I can't pick my times."

"Well, I'm awake now. You ruined my night's sleep. Come on in."

I went in and explained the situation. He gave me a brief outline of what to put in the search warrant, explaining that the mistake law enforcement often made was including wording that was not needed. "Give a short probable cause and that gives a lawyer very little to attack. When you write up a three or four page outline, I can generally get it thrown out."

And he had proven that to me in the past. Armed with his suggestions, I went back to the office and drew up a very simple search warrant.

Then I went and woke up Judge Bailey in the Cove. He signed it. I returned to the sheriff's office and the deputies who stopped the suspects and I searched the vehicle. Behind the back seat, we found a saw-off single barrel 12- gauge shotgun which turned out to be the murder weapon. (The crime lab later confirmed that the empty casing found in front of the cash register was identical to the firing pin on the shotgun.)

251

Only one of the suspects, Emmett Blake, talked. I got him in my office, advised him of his constitutional rights and he said, "I don't need a lawyer. I'll talk to you."

I told him we had his weapon and felt certain the lab would show it was used in the crime. After I told him what we had, I asked if he wanted to talk about it. Blake said, "Sure, I'll talk about it." Every question I asked him, he either admitted or denied. I finally asked him to just tell me his story. It was one of the most thorough confessions I've ever received.

He hadn't been out of the Army very long and he and his buddy wanted to see the beach. They were drinking at a little bar in Hiland Park when they got into town and ran out of money. They remembered passing a small grocery story on Highway 231.

They drove back to the store, got out and went in. Blake took his shotgun. There were two older guys sitting behind the counter. One stood and asked if he could help him. Blake told him, "Yeah, sit back down and keep your mouth shut. I just want your money."

The man sat back down. Blake opened the register and took all the cash out, which wasn't very much. As he put the money in a bag, the old man who had stood up before, stood again. Blake turned and shot him. He opened the gun, took out the empty shell, replaced it with another round from his pocket. By the time he had reloaded the other man had jumped up, so he shot him too.

I asked why he shot them.

He said, "Because I told them to stay seated and they didn't."

They were arraigned and jailed and when the trial came up, Fred Turner was appointed to represent Blake. During the trial, Turner raked me over the coals along with everyone else who testified as he normally did, but one thing he couldn't attack was the search warrant. Turner finished his argument without putting Blake on the stand.

After the jury went out, it was customary to wait in the courtroom until the jury returned with a verdict. I approached Mr. Turner and asked, "Why didn't you let Blake testify?"

"I couldn't do that."

"Why?"

"Because he would have told the truth and gotten a sure guilty verdict."

252

"Well, he is guilty."

Turner said, "No, you don't get it, I'm trying to save the man's life. I shouldn't have given you advice on how to prepare a search warrant."

(He did give me good instruction. Since that time, to the end of my law enforcement career, I never had another search warrant thrown out of court.)

The jury came back with a verdict of guilty as charged. The judge sentenced Blake to die in the electric chair. His friend pled guilty for a life sentence and the appeals process started.

Prior to the trial, an expert criminal psychologist was hired by the State to examine Blake in the event his attorney tried to plead insanity. This is a common process in a capital case. Two psychiatrists came from Pensacola and spent several hours examining Emmett Blake. Upon completion of their questioning and testing they gave a report. I was present along with the sheriff and state attorney.

They said there was nothing wrong with Blake's mind, except he was a killer, and it didn't seem to bother him to kill. They administered a test used to help judge a person's IQ. The test consisted of twenty-six areas of human knowledge, such as, physics, language, math, etc. He said the highest he'd ever had anyone make on it was two or three correct. Blake got all twenty-six right and complained the test was simple. One psychiatrist said, "The guy is a genius. I've never seen one with an IQ like his."

While Blake was held in solitary confinement, Alex Stewart, one of our dispatchers, had to pass by Blake's small cell to go from the communication room downstairs. He liked to stop and talk to Blake a minute or two whenever he went for a coffee break.

Blake asked Stewart if he had anything to read. Stewart had a copy of *War and Peace*, a very long book, and gave it to Blake. At the coffee table, Stewart told us about giving him the book. "That should give him something to keep him busy for a few weeks."

The following morning, Stewart stopped by Blake's cell and asked if he had started the book yet. Blake handed the book to Stewart through the bars and said, "I finished it."

Stewart laughed and said, "No way. It took me several months to read that book. You're telling me you read it in one day?"

Blake said, "Open the book and ask me a question."

Stewart came downstairs, book in hand, in shock. "You're not going to believe this. That guy read this book in one day." He related that he could cite a page number to Blake, ask a question about the story and he could answer his question and also tell him what was written before or after on the page.

I talked to Blake several times after he was convicted. He was interesting to talk to and we got along well. I asked if taking a person's life bothered him. He said it didn't bother him to kill a person, but he loved animals, especially dogs. "I'd hurt someone for messing with a dog. Dogs are great. You can depend on them and they love you unconditionally."

He went on to say, "People just want to get something from you, to beat you or make something off of you. I never completed school. I quit because it was so easy, but I read anything I could get my hands on, all the time. I learned that if you want something, you take it, so I stayed in trouble all the time."

"I finally got drafted and went in the Army. They taught me how to kill, and I was good at it. I received a bunch of decorations." (His family sent records on his military duty and he had received every award given by the Army except the Congressional Medal of Honor and had been nominated for that.) "But then they brought me back home and what they taught me to do, they don't want me to do anymore. It was all right when I killed who they wanted me to kill. It doesn't make sense."

Blake always wanted to talk about Twigs, the BCSO's bloodhound. Just before he was to leave for death row at Raiford State Prison, he asked for a favor. I said, "What's that?"

"Would you bring that bloodhound up and put him in the cell with me and let me pet him?"

"The sheriff will have to approve. I doubt he will."

"I'd really appreciate it."

I asked the sheriff. He said, "You know better than that. That guy might kill that dog."

"He might kill anyone and everyone in this jail, but that dog won't be harmed."

"Are you sure of that?"

"As sure as I've ever been,"

"All right, you can do it, but if something happens to that dog, it's on your head."

I got Twigs, brought him to Blake's cell and let him in. Twigs loved to be petted. Blake got down on his knees and hugged that dog like he was a long lost friend. Twigs licked him and wagged his big tail.

Every little while, I checked on them. Blake said, "We're all right." He had that dog stretched out on his bunk and Blake sat on the concrete floor beside him. He rubbed the dog's back, petted him, and scratched behind his ears. Old Twigs was sound asleep, just enjoying it. Twigs stayed in the maximum security cell almost all afternoon and I finally went up and got him and took him back to his pen.

Blake said, "I can never thank you enough. That was the nicest thing that happened to me in a long time. The next morning a special-built prison transport van, deemed "the black Mariah," arrived from Raiford.

Jailers put leg irons around Blake's ankles, a chain around his waist with handcuffs attached to the chain. He had to be helped out because he could only take small steps. When he was about to get in the van, a lot of the staff was standing around knowing this was the last time they'd see him. He looked at me standing nearby and started to hop toward me. The guys escorting him started to stop him. I said, "No, leave him alone."

He hopped over to me and opened his hand and I shook it. He said, "Look, I know you feel bad about me going to be executed, but don't feel bad. I'm getting exactly what I deserve. I'm guilty and you did not lie the first time. You told the truth when you testified. If the lawyer had let me testify, I'd have told it the same way you did. Don't worry about it, you did the right thing." Then he got on the van.

There was a big write up in the paper. Later the governor got a letter from Blake's brother in Texas, who was a wealthy oil man as I recall. He asked the governor to change the sentence to life in prison instead of the death penalty. He pointed out that that there could be great benefit to humanity by utilizing a person with his IQ. The governor was apparently considering his plea, but Blake wrote the governor, quoted State law, and requested the governor do his sworn duty. The governor did sign the death warrant and Blake was executed on May 12, 1964, the last day executions were performed in Florida before the U.S. Supreme Court struck down the death penalty in the Furman vs. Georgia ruling.

Florida's original electric chair was made by inmates from oak in 1923 after the Florida legislature designated electrocution as the official mode of execution. (Prior to that, executions were carried out by counties, usually by hanging.)

Florida law was rewritten and the death penalty reinstated in 1976, with the first execution resumed in 1979. During the span after Blake was executed until the law was reinstated, the death sentences of 95 men and one woman were commuted. I received an invitation to attend the execution of Blake, but turned it down.

Emmett Blake was probably the most unforgettable character I met during my law enforcement career. And a great irony was that Fred Turner, the man who advised me on how to draw up a good search warrant, was Blake's court-appointed attorney.

Clarence Gideon

Clarence Gideon was street smart. He had very little formal education but had "studied" extensively in various jails with those known as "jailhouse lawyers." He was arrested numerous times for various offenses from public drunkenness to burglary and his response each time was, "Prove it," and then he'd say nothing else. That tactic alone got him off of various crimes.

On one occasion, we received word from Louisiana that he was caught coming out of a pawn shop window with a sack of guns. When the officer placed him under arrest for burglary and grand theft, Gideon just said, "Prove it." The court later released him, how and why we don't know, but we do know he had no attorney. This was the track record he brought to Bay County.

Clarence Gideon

> **Top of the Decade**
>
> ➤ In *Baker v. Carr*, the Supreme Court paves the way for reapportionment of electoral districts across the nation, 1962.
>
> ➤ In *Gideon v. Wainwright*, the Supreme Court guarantees indigents a lawyer for trials involving serious crimes, 1963.
>
> ➤ Martin Luther King's jailing in Birmingham, Ala., which gave new respectability to the strategy of disobedience to unjust laws, 1963.

The Bay Harbor Bar was located just outside the entrance to the International Paper Company. Everitt Avenue separates the City of Springfield from the City of Panama City and the Bay Harbor Bar was on the Panama City side. This was one rough place to be when the natives started serious drinking and shooting pool. And it was this bar that had its share of national attention after Attorney Fred Turner represented Gideon in his retrial when the Supreme Court ruled he was entitled to an attorney.

Gideon was caught with stolen goods in hand from the bar by a detective friend of mine from the Panama City Police Department. Gideon did not have money to hire an attorney and was convicted and sentenced to prison. The United States Supreme Court ruled in favor of Gideon's petition for a right to counsel. Fred Turner argued his case citing conflicts in witness testimony and Gideon was acquitted. As a result of the Supreme Court ruling, 976 in Florida alone were released from prison, and an additional 500 given retrials. (Among those released were Connelly and Hendrix, serving in excess of 350 years each, for numerous crimes. See their story under Judge E. Clay Lewis.)

Fred Turner, finally got the position he always wanted, Circuit Judge of the 14th Judicial Circuit for the State of Florida. I was privileged to know and work with him.

Becoming Springfield Chief of Police (1963-65)

While Charlie Abbott was the appointed sheriff, Doc was preparing for trial. Federal investigators had found two witnesses who admitted paying Doc so they could make and sell moonshine. The Federal Grand Jury indicted Doc and that is when the governor fired him. When the federal trial date arrived, Doc and his attorney showed up, but the two witnesses could not be found. The case was dropped.

Doc ran again, got re-elected and true to his word, let it be known that he was going to fire all those who had stayed and worked under Charlie Abbott. So I resigned about a week before he took office. They interviewed Doc on TV and asked what he thought about me quitting. He said, "He can't quit. He's got to wait 'til Monday so I can fire him." That was the only funny thing about it. I quit, so he didn't get to fire me.

I went out to see Mr. J.E. Churchwell, owner of most of Long Beach. I knew each year he hired extra men to police his Hang Out and various other businesses. He was a good friend and agreed to take me on.

Daffin Outlines Stand On Pitts Controversy

By BILL JOHNSON
State Editor

Sheriff M. J. (Doc) Daffin today pointed out that the Sheriff's Department radio system is the "life line" to investigations and to have "an undesirable, or unreliable person listening in could sabotage, or at best hinder, successful investigations."

Sheriff Daffin, commenting on the decision to sever the Springfield Police Department's radio system from his network following hiring by Springfield City commissioners of a former deputy sheriff as chief of police Monday night, said: "I reserve the right to determine who should listen in on investigations.

my carrying out the job the people of Bay County have elected me to do," he added.

"The voters have elected me to be sheriff, and I'm going to do this to the best of my ability," Daffin continued. "The voters of Springfield have elected commissioners to run their government, and I'm sure they will do that to the best of their ability, but my first obligation is to the efficient operation of the Sheriff's Department, and I intend to carry this out."

Daffin explained that the Sheriff's Department operates on a

(See DAFFIN, Page 2)

259

I thought my biggest problem was over until the following morning when Mr. Churchwell called. He apologized and said Sheriff Daffin had called him and told him not to put me to work. He said, "You know I have to get along with the sheriff." I told him I understood.

Then I applied for the job as Chief of Police in Springfield. There were only two cars in the department and the radios in them belonged to the sheriff's office. The radios were on BCSO frequency. The sheriff's office answered the Springfield complaint calls and sent a Springfield police car to answer them. If a Springfield car was not available, the sheriff's office handled the call. Springfield also used the county jail.

Doc told the Springfield Commission that if they hired me, he'd take his radios out of the cars, plus he'd cut them off from the jail and they'd have no place to put prisoners.

I called the mayor and told him I didn't want to cause him any problems, so I decided not to pursue anything else in Bay County and left for Louisiana to possibly find a job in the oil fields. I was really bitter at that time.

I called my mother from Yazoo City, Mississippi, to let her know where I was.

She said, "The mayor called from Springfield and wants you to call him right away."

"What have I done now?"

Mom said she didn't know, but she encouraged me to call Mayor Barton. "He really wants you to call him. He said to call him collect."

I called him.

He said, "Look, that old man is not going to tell us how to run our city. We decided to build our own jail cell over here, and we'll buy radios and we want you to come back as our chief."

I said, "Mayor, are you sure? That's going to cause you a lot of problems and cost a lot of money."

He said, "I don't care, he's not going to push us around like this. How soon can you get here?"

"Probably 24 hours."

He said, "Be at work. It's civil service, so we'll have to start you as a patrolman. When you take the exam for chief, we'll put you in as chief."

When I got back, the only policeman there was the former rookie officer I wrote about earlier in the Walton brothers incident. The chief had quit and gone to work for Doc. So I started as a patrolman until my position was official and the former rookie was acting police chief. I started at sixty-five dollars a week.

I was to see Betty Powell, the civil service secretary. The mayor had talked to her and I was to take the civil service test in her office. I went down and she said it was set up for Monday night. (This was the weekend.) I asked if she had any idea what was on it.

She said she did, helped me review for it and told me, "We want you to pass this sucker."

I passed. I became chief and the rookie was moved

Pitts Is Hired In Springfield Despite Threat From Daffin

In spite of a threat by Sheriff M. J. (Doc) Daffin that he would remove the radios from the police cars, the Springfield Commission Monday night employed Lavelle Pitts as police chief of the city.

Pitts, a deputy for four years under Daffin and most recently chief investigator under Sheriff Abbott, was objected to by Daffin as the man for the post.

Springfield Commissioners at the special meeting, voted unanimously to hire Pitts, who was recommended highly by Civil Service Chairman Will Brogdon. Pitts assumed the post immedi-

their own radio equipment (Barton said he would put up the first $100 to make the purchase). The department could also apply for a tie-in with the Panama City Police radio system, or Springfield could operate without radio equipment.

Commissioner Champ Clark said, "I am not in favor of anyone telling us what to do in Springfield — let us get our own radios. I am not in favor of knuckling down to any one man," he added.

to the fire department. I got a new patrolman who got involved in a poker game with one of the local good old boys and ended up in the Bay County Jail.

My next patrolman was a retired Coast Guard Chief, JJ Gallagher. JJ was one of the finest men I ever worked with. The next officer we hired was Pat Pearson, a retired Air Police Officer from TAFB. He too was an outstanding officer. Later we hired Tommy Smith. Tommy had worked at the sheriff's office. He was a good friend who had no fear of any man. If anyone wanted to fight, he was always ready.

Springfield Police Chief, 1963-65

The mayor was true to his word. The city had a building constructed for commission meetings and it included some jail cells in the back. They also purchased new radios for our patrol cars with a frequency of our own. We hired our own radio dispatchers and the citizens really got behind the commission and the police department. In a short time everything was running smoothly.

There were eight cities in Bay County and Springfield was the only one that had no contact with the sheriff's office or the county jail. I was fortunate to have investigative experience, so I handled all the major investigations and my officers took care of the misdemeanor type cases. The city hired a local attorney, James Hansford, as city judge and he held court one day a week in the city commission room to handle our city cases.

Lady, the K-9

A German Shepherd K-9 from Tyndall Air Force Base named Lady was given to the police department because the dog's handler was retiring and no one else could manage her. Her handler was a resident in Springfield and asked if I would take the dog if he gave me pointers on how to work with her. It took a while for her to accept me as boss, but after she did, she became a good friend and protector.

My family fell in love with her and she with them. I heard her whining one night and checked on her. My two-year-old, Susan, was sitting on top of Lady and trying to pull her tongue out. Lady never growled or offered to bite her. But when she went to work she could become a very dangerous and vicious weapon.

Lady rode in my patrol car and got a lot of attention. She generally rode in the back seat. When I got a call to one of our honky-tonks, I'd got out and left her in the car with the windows down, in case I needed her, and checked the situation. Lady jumped in the front seat and watch attentively with her ears perked up.

If there were a lot of rowdy people I walked to the door, clapped my hands one time and Lady flew out of the car window and came to my side. With Lady at my side, it was amazing how the crowd quieted down. If anyone got too close to me, she growled and bared her teeth and the person backed off.

I left her in our dispatch office most nights, because our female dispatchers were there alone. Sometimes a person stopped by looking for a police officer or wanting to file a complaint.

I received a call one night from a night dispatcher to come to the office. When I arrived, Lady, who was on a leash held by the dispatcher, had a very irate City Commissioner penned up against the wall. The Commissioner yelled that the dog had to go because she tried to attack him.

The dispatcher said, "The dog did nothing until you tried to put your hands on me, and I yelled at you."

She later explained that the Commissioner kept trying to touch her and she kept trying to get out of his way. When he backed her into a corner, she yelled at him to stop and Lady came off the floor from another corner and went after him. The dispatcher was able to grab her leash or she might have done serious damage to the Commissioner.

At the close of the next commission meeting, after the citizens had left, the Commissioner who had the problem with the dog said, "Gentlemen, we have to get rid of that dog the chief has before she bites a citizen and we get sued." I happened to be in the back of the room and heard the remark. I joined the group and suggested the Commissioner tell the others the real reason he wanted to get rid of the dog.

He didn't, so I did. That brought some smiles and laughter from the Mayor and other Commissioners. The subject never came up again.

Caught in the Act

While serving as Chief of Police for the Springfield Police Department, I received a call to go to Bay Harbor. There was a report of a shooting at a large rooming house.

Bay Harbor, during that particular time period, was a rough place made up of a pool hall, a bar and lounge, a grocery store and a large frame rooming house. The boundary of the city limits was in the middle of Everitt Avenue, which ran north and south. The bar and poolroom were on the Panama City side. Hill's Grocery Store and the rooming house were on Springfield's side.

Usually when a police officer responded, the culprits raced across the street to the other city to avoid arrest. By the time we could call the other police department the suspects were long gone.

On this day I received a call from dispatch that shots were being fired at the rooming house in Bay Harbor near the main gate of the paper mill. I arrived at the scene, parked my vehicle and started walking toward the house.

I saw a man race around one corner of the rooming house. I recognized him as Louie, a guy I grew up with in Holmes County. He and his family lived on a farm adjoining ours. Louie stopped at the other corner of the house and looked in both directions. Suddenly a man appeared at the corner Louie had left, with a gun in his hand. As he fired, Louie took off toward the next corner. Each time the man got to a corner, he fired at the spot Louie just vacated.

I never knew old Louie could run that fast. He was a little on the fat side with a large belly, but he was winning the race from corner to corner. I almost didn't recognize him. He was white as a sheet and his long hair flew in the wind as he ran. The last time I had seen Louie was about six years before, when I arrested him for extortion. He had been sentenced to five years in the state penitentiary and couldn't have been out very long.

I got to an unoccupied corner of the building, and when Louie got there I made him go to the other corner and wait. As the suspect rounded the corner, I stood there with my weapon in my hand and told him to drop his. He dropped his gun and immediately started explaining how he had caught Louie in bed with his wife. He said he had five kids, had just gotten back in town and found that man had moved in with his wife.

I cuffed him and placed him in my patrol car. By that time, Louie, the man's wife, and a crowd had gathered. Louie wanted to make sure I was going to take the irate husband to jail.

I told Louie I should turn the man loose and give him his gun back. Louie said, "You wouldn't do that would you?"

The man's wife spoke up and said, "You can't turn him loose; he's a fugitive." I got on the radio and it was true. He was an escapee from the State of Texas. There went my good intentions of turning him loose. As I drove away, Louie and the woman went back into the building arm and arm.

Sometimes the scales of justice seem to tilt the wrong way. I had to remind myself that I only enforced the laws, I did not make them.

But as it turned out, Louie was arrested a few weeks later for stealing hogs from Tyndall Air Force Base and sent to the federal penitentiary. The woman he was with that day, ended up marrying Louie's older brother, and they became my next door neighbors in Springfield.

Louie's brother helped raise those children and supplied all their needs including a good education. As far as I know, the kids turned out well, especially considering what they went through. One of the girls baby-sat for me. When I saw her again years later, she and her husband owned and operated a restaurant where we had Full Gospel Businessmen's meetings.

God can take bad situations into His own hands and turn them into something good.

Bully Junior Act 3

My cousin, Junior, kept popping up in my life. He lived in Millville, about a mile outside Springfield, where I was chief of police.

In Springfield, we had a little one-room frame shack about 6x6 feet in size. This building sat on a big lot near the intersection of U.S. Highway 98 and SR 22, next to Tot's Bar. The man who owned it used it for a cabstand and had two or three old cabs that worked out of it. There was a table inside with an operator who took requests for and dispatched the cabs.

About one or two times a month a group of riffraff got together late at night, met at the cab stand and had a big poker or dice game. The man who ran the game was Junior.

One of the group always sat or stood by an open window in the shack to watch for the law. It was impossible to slip up on them because there was a large vacant lot to cross before getting to the shack.

As a result of complaints from wives whose husbands had lost their grocery money in the games, I intended to put an end to their gambling. (Up to that time, I heard that a little game was going on but thought it was low stakes and didn't pay much attention to it.) When it was reported that some guys were losing their entire week's pay, it put a different light on the matter.

When I found out that Junior was running the game, I put myself on night duty until we worked out a plan to bust him and his cohorts.

One night I parked my patrol car and walked up as close as I could get and stood in the dark trying to come up with a plan. The lookout was distracted by the game. The game was getting exciting and he was paying more attention to the game than the outside area.

Finally, I took advantage of his interest in the game and slipped up to the door and stepped inside. There were about six guys in the game. They had their money on the table in front of them. Junior had the dice in his hand about to roll them when he looked up and saw me. He immediately put the dice in his mouth and swallowed them. My evidence was gone.

I couldn't believe my eyes. I don't know how he was able to get those big dice down. I had two choices: (1) I could arrest Junior and the others, put them in jail and wait for a bowel movement and hope for the best. If I did that, and had to take Junior to the hospital, it would cost the city a lot of money. I took choice (2) and asked the players which of them had money on the table.

They all quickly denied ownership of any of the money, so I seized the money and turned it in to the fine and forfeit account, walked out and told Junior I hoped he died.

I guess that wasn't a very charitable remark, but he didn't die and they probably used the same dice again. At least they changed locations and moved out of my city.

Tot's Bar and Lounge

On the weekend there was usually a very large crowd attending Tot's Bar and Lounge. One night I was sitting across the highway at the Springfield Plaza and noticed movement in the wooded area behind and to the right of the bar. I continued to watch and determined it was a person standing behind a tree. I pulled my patrol car over, got out and confronted a very upset woman holding a shot gun. She explained her husband was in the bar with another woman and when they came out she was going to kill them.

I calmed her down and talked to her about her responsibility to the three children she said were at home. I told her if she killed him, which he probably deserved, then I would have to arrest her and that meant someone else would have to raise her children. I convinced her to go home and let me handle her problem.

Officer Gallagher took her home and I went into the bar. It was filled with people, mostly couples. It got real quiet when I entered. I walked up the front of the bar and ordered a cup of coffee. I then turned to face the bar's patrons and made an announcement.

"There's a lady concealed in the woods outside with a gun and she's waiting for her husband to come out with his girlfriend so she can shoot both of them. I told her she hasn't done anything yet to violate the law, but if she does shoot her husband and his girlfriend, I'd have to arrest her. I don't think she'll do anything while I'm inside the bar, but when I leave I can't promise you what will happen."

There were a few moments of silence and then two or three couples started leaving followed by a mad exodus like school letting out in the afternoon. I wondered how many men were there with someone other than their wife.

Challenge to a Duel by a Student

While serving as Springfield Chief of Police, I received a call about a student on the campus of Everitt Jr. High School who was armed with a pistol.

When I arrived at the school, there were a large number of students gathered on the old football practice field behind the school. The students started moving away as I walked across the field. There, standing alone with a pistol in his hand, was a kid who I had experienced problems with on a number of occasions. On this occasion, he not only had a .38 caliber revolver with a 4-inch barrel in his hand, but he was drunk.

He yelled that he had waited for this day and stuck the pistol inside his belt, inviting me to draw any time I was ready. Many things ran through my mind. I could easily draw my weapon and shoot him, but could imagine the headlines the following day about a police officer who over-reacted and killed a youngster. I could turn and run, but it was 50 or 75 yards to the nearest shelter. If he started shooting, he could hit me and any number of kids who were standing there watching. Of all the scenarios I thought of, none seemed to make me a sure winner.

I agreed to draw on him, but told him we were too far apart and needed to get closer.

He said, "Okay, just draw when you're ready."

I started walking toward him and talking as I walked. When I was about five steps away, he realized he had made a mistake and grabbed his pistol.

I rushed him. The thing that saved the day was that the hammer of the pistol got caught in his shirt. I grabbed the gun before he could get it loose. After cuffing him, I checked the gun and it was fully loaded. As I escorted the boy to my patrol car I thought how lucky I was.

As I look back, I believe this was another God intervention.

Doc and I Cross Swords Again

While I was Springfield Chief of Police, Doc instructed his deputies to patrol Springfield and take all the calls that were usually referred to the city. He also instructed his deputies that they were not to converse with me or my department.

The fire chief for the City of Springfield had been in the position only a few weeks and lived a few blocks from my home in Springfield.

One night Officer Gallagher knocked on my door about midnight, waking me up. He said, "I hate to wake you, but the fire chief's wife shot him and the sheriff's office is working the case. I quickly got dressed and went to the home of our fire chief and found deputies and investigators all over.

I was advised by an officer at the door that the sheriff had told them to work the case and not to let anyone else in the house until they finished their investigation. I gently pushed him aside after advising him that this was my city and I was working the case. I went in and found they had taken the wife to the sheriff's office to be interviewed.

I took photographs of the crime scene and drew a crime scene diagram. The next morning the News Herald reported that Sheriff Daffin had released the wife after his investigators looked into the shooting and determined the shooting was justified. I got on my patrol car, drove down the street and arrested the fire chief's wife. I put her in the Springfield jail and charged her with murder.

The woman was never convicted. Back then, that was no big surprise. During my 32 years of law enforcement I never witnessed a conviction of a woman murdering her husband. I still believe I was right in arresting the woman, however, in order to let the justice system determine guilt or innocence rather than the sheriff's office. I showed the sheriff I was still around, but he got the last laugh.

Getting Even

I was the only chief of police in the county that the sheriff could not control and it really bothered him. The deputies did not dare stop and talk to me or any of my officers. An old friend I had worked with a long time apologized and said Sheriff Daffin had threatened to fire anyone who was caught working with or talking to me.

I still had friends with the State Beverage Department and with other state agencies who knew of my problems with the sheriff, and quietly helped me when they could.

I was still sore about how I had to leave the sheriff's office and as chief I suppose I did some things that caused the sheriff a lot of heart burn. I had the opportunity to make a raid on a house that had been selling moonshine and Bolita tickets. In addition to a little moonshine, we seized a trunk (footlocker) with more than 5200 Bolita tickets. It was "get-even" time and I made a big release showing the tickets which reflected on Doc. (That was part of the reason he was removed from office, for allowing the Bolita dealers to operate.) Of course, this just further fueled the feud between the two of us. Doc held a news conference and screamed and shouted that there were no Bolita rackets in Bay County and these were old tickets and "the police chief knows it."

Not many people believed the sheriff because I produced thousands of tickets we had seized with a search warrant. I loved every minute of it because I knew he must be peeling the paint off the sheriff's office walls with his "colorful" language.

JJ Gallagher, LaVelle Pitts, Bill McCraw; SPD Bolita ticket raid

State Attorney, J. Frank Adams called me the afternoon the story hit the News Herald and said, "You, Doc and I need to have a meeting." Doc and I refused to meet at either the BCSO or SPD so Adams suggested a neutral office in the courthouse. We agreed.

Mr. Adams began, "Gentlemen, we need to declare a truce in this war between you two."

I said, "The sheriff started the war, I am only defending myself."

The sheriff lit up the room with some expletives and said some awful things about me and my family tree.

I started laughing at him and that really set him off.

The State Attorney tried to arbitrate but made no progress and had to adjourn the meeting. The war continued.

Not long after this meeting my Assistant Police Chief Bill McCraw, unknown to me, attended a local low-stakes poker game each week that eventually became high stakes. He became indebted to a shady character for several hundred dollars. I found out later, this guy offered my officer a deal. If he acted as lookout at Tot's Bar after it closed one night, he would break in, get the petty cash and cancel the officer's debt.

My officer agreed, but it was a set up. Doc had the place staked out and when the entry was made his deputies arrested both

271

the officer and the guy inside the bar. Doc thought I would be involved and was disappointed when I didn't show up. I found out when Officer Gallagher knocked on my door, woke me up and told me what happened.

This made big headlines in the newspaper and the lead story on Channel 7. Doc took the opportunity to berate me and my department. I was furious, but I knew my assistant chief was wrong. Doc was one up on me.

Ending the War

The war between Doc Daffin and me had waged for two years. It was election time in 1964 and Doc had two opponents. Of course I was encouraging people to vote for one of the opponents.

About two weeks before the election, Officer J.J. Gallagher stopped one of Doc's off-duty deputies on School Avenue in Springfield with fifty gallons of moonshine whiskey in his personal vehicle. He was attempting to make a delivery to a moonshine retailer we had been watching for some time.

I knew the deputy and was disappointed that a law enforcement officer was involved in this activity. On the other hand, I realized this was a tailor-made opportunity to do a number on Doc Daffin. I thought about how much the television and newspaper would love the story. It was very temping.

But then I recalled Uncle Custer's words about putting myself in the place of the person I was about to arrest and realized that but for the grace of God this man could be holding my fate in his hand. I thought of the embarrassment, not only to the deputy's family but to everyone who wore a badge.

Even though I wanted to get even with Doc, I knew he had nothing to do with this whiskey delivery. With this in mind, I called the dispatcher and advised her to call Doc Daffin's chief deputy, Gerald Bass, and ask him to meet me near Rutherford High School on School Avenue right away.

Gerald Bass arrived and I showed him what we had. He was shocked and just walked around and looked up and down the street. I knew he was looking for the news media.

"What do you intend to do?" he asked.

"I know what I'd like to do but I decided to turn the deputy and the whiskey over to you on one condition.

"What's that?"

"Tell the sheriff that if I was as sorry a SOB as he was, I'd make a case and call all the media.

"Are you serious?"

I nodded.

He smiled. "I'll tell him exactly what you said."

I sent Gallagher to help take the vehicle and whiskey to the Bay County Jail and Gerald took the deputy.

Later Gerald told me what transpired with the sheriff after he delivered my message.

The sheriff responded, "Is that what Pitts said?"

"Yes sir, that's exactly what he said."

The sheriff turned and walked away. He fired the deputy and destroyed the whiskey.

There was no oral agreement or formal truce. Neither the sheriff nor I ever mentioned it from that day on.

Doc won that election. The following day my office called on my patrol car and said the sheriff wanted to see me at the jail. I hoped he was not going to start our war again because I was tired of fighting.

I walked in the back of the jail which was full of his cohorts and deputies celebrating the sheriff's reelection. He hollered, "Come on back here boy." I didn't know what to expect.

I walked to the coffee table. Sheriff Daffin stood, walked over and put his arm around my shoulders and said, "Folks let me tell you something. This boy and me have had a little war going on for the past two years but it's over. He is part of our family. Son, do you want your job back?"

I was shocked and finally I said, "Thank you sheriff, but I have a job."

He said, "Okay. If you change your mind, just come on back and go to work anytime you want." He looked at the crowd who had gathered and said, "If this boy ever comes here and needs anything, he is to have it. If he doesn't get it, I'll fire the man who doesn't give it to him. Now, boy, sit down and have some coffee."

I was back at the coffee table. I knew then the war was finally over and silently thanked the Lord.

 *Showing kindness can make a friend out of an enemy. My Dad was fond of quoting, Romans 12:20: "If your enemies are hungry, give them something to eat. And if they are thirsty, give them something to drink. This will be the same as piling burning coals on their heads."*

More about Sheriff M.J. Doc Daffin

Election Stories

When the next election approached, a very wealthy business man talked to me about running against Doc Daffin. He said he would come up with all the money I needed and he thought I could win. I thanked him and told him that first I was not a politician, and second I didn't fall off the last watermelon truck that passed through Bay County. I had watched Doc in too many

Sheriff M.J. "Doc" Daffin

campaigns and the people loved him. I didn't think there was anyone in Bay County who could beat Doc. If he was still alive and wanted the job today, I believe he would still be sheriff.

Senator Dempsey Barron, was running for re-election and wanted me to help him in the black section of Springfield. He was concerned about his opponent, popular local attorney Leo Jones, who had Doc's backing. I told him my help would be of no use. If Doc put out the word to vote for his opponent, then every black voter in Springfield would vote for his opponent.

He said he had a plan and showed me a large grocery bag full of small bills. He was going to go house to house and spend every dollar to beat his opponent in the black area. I assured him that they would be more than happy to take his money, but still vote the way Doc Daffin wanted. Dempsey gave out a lot of money and when the votes were counted his opponent got all but three votes in the black precincts.

One of the deputies told me later that some of Doc's friends were kidding Doc about the three votes for the other man. Doc laughed and said, "That's okay. Those three voters must have accidently pulled the wrong lever."

Senator Barron still won the election by a few votes, but got no help from the black vote. Actually, there was a reason Doc's candidate probably lost the overall vote. A couple of days before the election, a chitterling supper political rally was held. In addition to the chitterlings, there was booze being passed around. Leo had a few drinks, and fell off the speaker's platform into the crowd.

In another election, there were two people running against Doc. Both had lots of money. They each had large campaign signs with their photographs on them and put out hundreds all over the county. Back then there was a pistol range located at the current location of the Panama City Police Department on 15th Street. Various clubs and other organizations used this location for cookouts, reunions, political rallies and large gatherings. The Ku Klux Klan was active at this time. One Saturday, just prior to the election, the Klan sponsored a cookout and put up a big sign at the entrance to the pistol range inviting the public to attend.

I was at the jail on the Friday night before the KKK cookout the following afternoon. Doc came in with a stack of his opponents' campaign signs. He told the operator to have all three black deputies come to the jail and see him. When they arrived, he handed each of them a bundle of the campaign signs with instructions to nail them up on all the posts leading into the pistol range and around the speaker's stand. They were to go in their personal vehicles and wear plain clothes. If any of his signs were in the area, they were to take them down. He then advised them to go all over the county and pick up all the black preachers and other black leaders they knew and drive them by the pistol range to see the signs. They did as they were told.

On election day those two opponents got less than 50 black votes out of several thousand who voted. Again he laughed and said he forgave those 50 or so who voted against him. "I'm sure they meant well, but accidently pulled the wrong lever."

Campaigning Doc Daffin Style

Doc Daffin was the only elected official I ever knew who really looked forward to having an opponent and campaigning. I think he would have been broken-hearted if no one ran against him.

During campaign season, Doc walked down one side of Harrison Avenue starting near Bay High, proceeded to the marina, crossed the street and walked all the way back. He shook every hand of those he met along the way.

All the big stores were on Harrison Avenue. There were no shopping centers so Bay Countians ended up on Harrison Avenue most every week. He probably covered Harrison two or three times a week.

He took babies out of strollers or mothers' arms and fussed over and kissed them. Woodrow Gainer, local bail bondsman and uncle of my good friend George Gainer, was kidding Doc one day at the jail.

"It's ridiculous to hug and kiss those youngsters, they're too young to vote."

Doc replied, "That's okay. They will be someday, and I'll still be running."

Downtown Harrison Avenue, 1950s.
Photo courtesy Bay County Public Library

Many townspeople made an effort to meet and shake hands with Doc Daffin during his "Harrison Avenue hand-shaking, women-hugging, baby-kissing campaign walks."

Doc had a remarkable memory. Many times I saw him talk to a complete stranger and when he found out the person grew up in Bay County, he asked about his mother and father. It amazed me how he almost, without fail, knew one of the parents and usually their grandparents. Sometimes he said, "Boy, I dated your mom (or your grandma). You know you might have been my son."

One day when he was shaking hands, he picked up a little girl and her mom said "Honey, do you know who that man is holding you?" The little girl said, "Mommy, dishes Doc Daffin." The sheriff was elated and from that day on he always introduced himself when speaking at a rally or on television as, "Dishes yo' Sheriff, M. J. Doc Daffin." (Doc's real name was Mitchell Jacoby Daffin. I named my first son, David Mitchell, after Doc. I wonder if that influenced Mitchell's decision to make a career of law enforcement?)

I found out that Doc had supporters all over the county who called or went to see him if they saw any of his deputies speeding, talking to a girl or anything they thought was wrong. I also learned, like all the other guys, that when he called you in his office and questioned you, it was best you told him the truth. In the first place, we didn't know what he knew and second we knew

277

that if we lied and he did know the truth, we would be fired on the spot. If you told him the truth, most of the time he chewed you out and told you not to let that happen again.

At election time he instructed his employees: "The election is coming up and none of you will politic for anyone but me. If anyone asks you who you are supporting for county commissioner, you say, Doc Daffin. If they ask about the governor's race, you say Doc Daffin. If they mention School Superintendent, you say, Doc Daffin. It's not good to mix your politics. If you say who you want in another race, they'll go away and tell everyone the sheriff is supporting that person because his deputy is. Then I'll hear about it. And you better hope the person you're supporting in another race wins and will give you a job, because you won't have a job as a deputy anymore."

In a political rally in the City of Parker, I observed the sheriff and three opponents speak to a large crowd. Each candidate got up and talked bad about Doc Daffin and his drinking, his women, and allowing illegal things to go on in Bay County.

When Doc got up to speak he smiled and said, "Dishes yo' Sheriff M. J. Doc Daffin. These boys up here running are good old boys, but this ain't no place for a boy. This is a man's job. And besides there's no opening. The job is filled. These boys have promised you all kinds of things. I only promise you one thing—that I will take care of all the women folk, and I really don't give a damn what happens to the men folk."

The crowd went wild with applause as Doc turned and shook hands with the three running against him.

The following morning at the coffee table I told the sheriff I was surprised at his speech the night before. He looked at me with his dead-pan look and asked why? I said, "Those other guys called you everything under the sun and you didn't defend yourself."

He said, "Son there is something you need to learn. We each had only five minutes to speak. My three opponents spent their five minutes talking about me. I spent my five minutes talking about me. So I figure every one there got 20 minutes hearing about Doc Daffin. Now who do you think those people went home thinking about last night?"

"No Visitors"

Doc was known to drink in excess sometimes. When he went on a drunk, Doc might be out of the office for two or three weeks. Usually Marvin Freeman found him and took him to Adams Hospital. Dr. Adams checked him into the hospital, put a "No Visitors" sign on the door and didn't allow anyone to see him until he got straight and on his feet again.

When he sobered up, he was grumpy as an old bear coming out of hibernation. A "busy body" who worked in the front office filled him in on everything that happened while he was gone. Sometimes one or two people lost their jobs after the informant's report.

Marvin Freeman told me that two or three times the governor got a complaint and sent investigators over to catch Doc drunk, so he could fire him. Marvin said he had spent many hours hauling Doc from one area to another keeping him away from the governor's investigators. They never caught him.

From Sheriff Doc Daffin I learned and observed many things:

- *When a person comes to you with a problem, it is important to solve that problem or make sure that person leaves thinking you did or at least would try to resolve their dilemma.*

- *You do not do as the boss does but as the boss says to do.*

- *Doc's office was always open for anyone to walk in and talk to him. That went for a deputy, jailer, radio dispatcher, office worker, a big wig in the community or a rum-head looking for a hand out. I never saw him try to duck out from seeing anyone who wanted to talk to him.*

- *He believed in having a listed phone at his home. He stated that the citizens of Bay County employed him and they had a right to call and talk to him any time they wished. If he was home and you called him, any hour day or night, that phone rang one time. He picked up and said, "All right" Not only that, if he was on his vehicle and someone called the sheriff's office to speak to the sheriff, the dispatcher had instructions to get the person's phone number and call him on the police radio in his car. The sheriff returned that call as soon as he could find a phone or phone booth. (This was in the days before cell phones or car phones.) He also required all his employees to have a listed number for the reason listed above and because I agreed with his philosophy, I have always had my home phone listed and still do.*

• *I never heard of him getting mad about getting a late night phone call. I made some of them to him myself. I even stopped by and knocked on his door several times late at night or in early morning hours. He opened the door right away and said, "What's up, boy?"*

A True Friend

I was invited to a fishing trip and cook out on the Apalachicola River. There were ten or fifteen law enforcement officers present and we were staying in a big lodge on the river in Liberty County. About 2:30 am, someone beat on the door and said, "This is the Sheriff of Liberty County. Is LaVelle Pitts in there?"

I hollered back, "Yes," and went to the door. Sure enough it was the Liberty County Sheriff and he did not seem real happy to being there. He said, "Doc Daffin called me and asked me to come out here and get you to call him tonight." I asked if he knew what for and he said he had no idea.

I went out to Highway 20, found a phone booth, and called the sheriff. He said "Boy, do you want to be a Deputy U.S. Marshal? Bob Sikes called and said there was an opening and wanted me to name one. I told him I had one in mind, but had to call him first. I wanted to give you first shot at it."

I told him, "I appreciate the offer, but I wouldn't like a job where the most I ever did was serve civil papers and haul federal prisoners to federal court."

He said, "I wouldn't either, but I wanted you to have first choice." I thanked him again and went back to the lodge. When Doc said the war was over between us, it was over.

Another time after Doc and I made peace with each other, I was contacted and offered a job as a Deputy Fire Marshal. This was a great position with a big pay increase. I had not applied for it and was surprised when it was offered. (Actually, the only jobs I ever filled out applications for were when I first went on with Doc, and when I applied to work on the beach for J E Churchwell, and Doc told him not to hire me.)

I quickly accepted the Deputy State Fire Marshal job which began a new direction with my life. I learned later that Sheriff Daffin had recommended me for the job.

Deputy State Fire Marshal (1965)

As a Deputy Fire Marshal, my office was located in the Bay County Courthouse and I covered eight counties. My job was to respond to requests for assistance on suspicious fires in my area. Most requests came from volunteer fire departments, and there were many.

Most local communities had volunteer fire departments manned with unpaid volunteers. They were good at responding to fires and putting them out, but when it came to investigating anything suspicious about the fire, they always called the Fire Marshal's Office. I stayed on the road most of the time.

I had experience investigating crimes but very little where arson was suspected. The first thing I did was try to visit as many Volunteer Fire Departments as possible and meet the men who did all the work. I found them to be great people who appreciated any and all help they could get. These men might not be investigators but they knew the people in their community and usually had some good ideas about who might have started a fire.

With a few visits and a lot of coffee drinking these guys supplied me information that solved many arson cases. I received much credit from Tallahassee, but had to let the Tallahassee office

281

know that it was the volunteer fire fighters who were owed the credit.

Due to the large number of fire investigations and the large number of small Volunteer Fire Departments in counties like Walton, Holmes, Santa Rosa and Jackson, Tallahassee decided to put an office in Ft. Walton. My new job as Deputy State Fire Marshal required me to drive my own vehicle. The State paid me mileage. This resulted in my

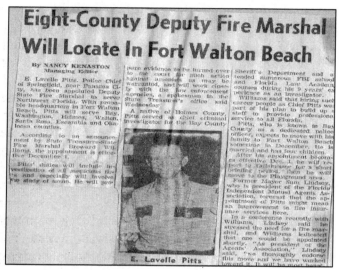

Eight-County Deputy Fire Marshal Will Locate In Fort Walton Beach

By NANCY KENASTON
Managing Editor

E. Lavelle Pitts, Police Chief of Springfield, near Panama City, has been appointed Deputy State Fire Marshal to serve Northwest Florida. With probable headquarters in Fort Walton Beach, Pitts will serve Bay, Washington, Holmes, Walton, Santa Rosa, Escambia and Okaloosa counties.

According to an announcement by State Treasurer-State Fire Marshal Broward Williams, the appointment is effective December 1.

Pitts' duties will include investigation of all suspicious fires and especially will involve the study of arson. He will pro-

pare evidence to be turned over to the court for such action against arsonists as may be warranted, and will work closely with the law enforcement agencies, a spokesman in the State Treasurer's office said Wednesday.

A native of Holmes County, Pitts served as chief criminal investigator for the Bay County

Sheriff's Department and attended numerous FBI school and Florida Law Academy courses during his 9 years' experience as an investigator.

Williams said that hiring such career people as Chief Pitts was part of his plan to build up and to provide professional service to all Florida.

Pitts, who is known in Bay County as a dedicated police officer, expects to move with his family to Fort Walton Beach sometime in December. He is married and has four children. After his appointment becomes effective Dec. 1, he will be commuting between their he will move to the Playground area.

Former Mayor Sam Lindsey, who is president of the Florida Independent Mutual Agents Association, forecast that the appointment of Pitts might mean an improvement in fire insurance services here.

In a conference recently with Williams, Lindsey said he stressed the need for a fire marshal, and Williams indicated that one would be appointed shortly. "As president of the Agents' Association," Lindsey said, "we thoroughly endorse this move and we have worked toward it. It will be most bene-

E. Lavelle Pitts

purchasing a new Mustang from Cook-Whitehead Ford in Panama City.

I had the new car for only a few days when I was ordered to check out the area for a new office and home. This was to be another life-changing day for me and my family as Sarah and I set out for Ft Walton.

Shortly after entering Walton County on U.S. Highway 98, a car meeting me had stopped with his left turn signal on, waiting for me to go by. The speed limit was 65 mph at that time and that was my speed when a Cadillac pulled out to pass the stopped vehicle. There was no place to go or a way to stop. The Cadillac met us head on.

Florida did not have the seat belt law at that time, but Sarah and I had ours on. The doctor said that is what saved us.

I recall locking my arms on the steering wheel just before impact. I saw something like a flash of a light and everything went dark and quiet.

When I came to, everything was very quiet. My wife was bent forward over the dash and bleeding from the face. Blood was all over my lap and our seat belts held us erect. I tried to open my door and had to bang it several times with my shoulder before it came open. I fell part way out of the car and my seat belt held me. I reached back and unlatched the seat belt and fell out of the car onto the grass.

I noticed a car with several people drive by real slow and continue on. Two or three other cars slowed down and drove on. I tried to get up and get Sarah out but I couldn't stand up.

A vehicle finally stopped and a man got out and told me he was a deputy sheriff from Arizona in Florida to pick up a prisoner. He asked what he could do. I asked him to get my wife out of the front seat and call an ambulance.

I looked at the Cadillac. It was a short distance away and it appeared the driver was leaning over the dash and not moving. The passenger, a lady, was hanging out the passenger window and not moving. (I found out later they died on impact. According to the State Trooper who worked the accident, the two people in the other car were an elderly couple. The man had poor eyesight and wasn't supposed to drive, but did sometimes. His wife had to tell him when he could pass a vehicle on the highway.)

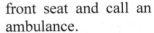

Ex-Springfield Couple Injured

The Florida Highway Patrol arrived on the scene and then an ambulance came from Ft. Walton. The next thing I remember was waking up in the emergency room in Ft. Walton and my dad was there. He was talking to a doctor who said I was in shock and with rest I would be okay.

I told my dad that I was not in shock, and I wanted to go to Bay Memorial in Panama City. He went to the phone and called

Southerland. (Funeral homes used to provide service to pick up the injured, there was no emergency ambulance service at that time.) They came over, and even though the doctor objected, I was loaded in the ambulance and taken to Panama City

We arrived at the hospital emergency entrance where I had worked so many cases. I saw Dr. Joe Morris standing outside with some other medical staff. As they were pulling me out, he asked if I had a seat belt on at the time of the accident, and I told him I did. He advised the people to take me straight to surgery.

A day or two later I woke up and found myself in a room with flowers all over the place. I thought I was dead and was seeing my own funeral. Then I noticed my mom sitting in a chair near my bed and she was asleep. I called to her and she jumped up and ran to me. She said they had taken Sarah to Pensacola and thought she was going to be okay.

There was a "no visitor" sign on my door, but Chief Deputy Gerald Bass eased in and brought me up to date on what had happened. He said the television and radio stations broadcasted that I needed blood. He went with several deputies to give blood. When he got to the hospital, he said he was surprised at the long line waiting to give blood. Several of the donors included people from the black community. There was even a black guy in line in front of him that I had arrested before. Gerald said the TV and radio stations finally had to thank people for coming in and asked them to please stop. They had enough blood.

Dr. Morris arrived and explained my condition. He said wearing the seat belts had saved our lives. However, the seat belt restraint caused a lot of damage to the stomach area and internal bleeding. If I had not arrived at BMH when I did, he said I would have been dead in about 45 minutes or less. My stomach was so full of blood, I was about to drown in my own blood. If dad had let the Ft. Walton doctor keep me overnight like he wanted, I would have died. Looking back, I believe God had other plans for me.

While recuperating from the accident, the children and I stayed with my mom and dad at their house in Hiland Park. When Sarah was released from the Pensacola hospital, she also moved in the house with my parents until we were well enough to move back into our house in Springfield.

Unknown to me at that time, Senator Dempsey Barron, Doc Daffin and Berwin Williams recommended me and I was hired as a new agent for the Florida Sheriff's Bureau which is now the Florida Department of Law Enforcement.

Florida Sheriff's Bureau (1966)

When Ed Yarbourough took over as Executive Director of the Florida Sheriff's Bureau, he needed an agent in north Florida and hired me based on recommendations. Though I had some experience as an investigator, I had never really been trained in the finer points of criminal investigations and putting together case files for criminal prosecution.

Prior to leaving on my first big job investigating cases all over the state, I stopped and had a cup of coffee with my friend, Attorney Fred Turner. I confided in him that I was a little concerned about my new job and working all over the state where I knew no one.

He said don't worry you will do great. You are a good investigator; you will make friends and have no problem. I said what if I get into trouble in Miami or even get in jail, what will I do? He said, no problem, call me and I'll grab two or three witnesses and we'll be right down there and get you out.

My first assignment was at Tallahassee headquarters where I underwent intensive training. When I was schooled enough in ballistics to please the head of the crime lab, Special Agent in Charge (SAIC) Jim Halligan, then I moved to the fingerprint section where I was instructed on how to find, lift and preserve latent fingerprints. After this, I went to the document section where SAIC Kelly taught me technical things regarding handwriting and forgery. This training continued, including crime scene search, preservation of evidence, photography and preparation of case material for the prosecutor to use in court.

The bureau was operated under the auspices of all the sheriffs in the State of Florida. When a sheriff called for help on a big case, a special agent from the Florida Sheriff's Bureau was sent. If you didn't get along with the sheriff requesting help, you just might find yourself looking for another job.

I had very little experience writing reports. So during the several weeks I was in Tallahassee, I took advantage of some of the best investigators in the country employed by the FSB, by picking their brains and taking notes. We had former FBI Agents, Army Criminal Investigation Division (CID) agents, and top investigators from departments in Miami, Tampa, and Jacksonville, and technicians from the FBI Lab in Washington.

I spent hours at night studying case files from special agents all over the state. When I found a well-prepared file, I copied it and kept it to refer to when I was in the field. I'd stay up late studying files on every felony-type crime and read about the procedures taken. When I wrote my reports, I used these as guidelines..

They issued me an old Galaxy 500 Ford. The tools they gave me were a manual Royal typewriter, a box full of paper and a lot of carbon paper. (This was before computers, spell check, printers and copy machines.) I had to type my own reports and make a copy for myself, Tallahassee, the state attorney where I was working, and the sheriff who asked FSB for help. So there was an original and four copies to make. By the time I corrected all the copies, put a paper behind the error and erased it, the papers were a mess.

I wasn't totally dumb. I went to various judges' offices, made friends with their secretaries and was not too proud to ask for help with my typing. They felt sorry for me, I guess, and helped me type my cases. My reports started looking pretty good.

Burglary in Defuniak Springs

I was called to Defuniak Springs by Sheriff Anderson. There had been a burglary at the big Farmer's Coop outside the city. The safe had been opened and several thousand dollars in cash taken. The pressure was on me to solve that case. Apparently a number of burglaries had taken place over a period of several weeks and brought a lot of pressure on the sheriff from the press and the people.

I arrived and checked into a small, cheap motel on U.S. 90. That night I pulled out my copies of burglary cases I kept stored in the trunk of my car, and read them from cover to cover.

The following morning, I went to the building, did my inspection, and listened to the manager explain what had happened. The burglar entered the building through a window. Inside, the intruder got a sledge hammer. Using the sledge hammer, a big hole was made in the concrete vault where money and important records were kept. The tools were left there. I dusted them, but there was nothing but smudges. I noticed that one of the chips, from busting the concrete, flew up and broke a light bulb. It would have been totally dark without the light in there. I saw that the burglar had taken the broken bulb out and replaced it with another one. A tag for gloves was found on the floor in front of a glove display, so it was obvious gloves were used.

I reasoned it would be awfully hard to screw a bulb in a socket with a heavy pair of work gloves on. I got on a ladder and very carefully took that bulb out using a pair of light weight cotton gloves issued to work crime scenes, dropped it in a paper bag and stapled it up.

After I got all this done, I obtained a set of finger prints from all employees and sent them to Tallahassee. One fingerprint on the light bulb came back matching an employee's who no longer worked at the Coop. I turned the report over to the sheriff, and picked up the former employee.

Solving that case got me a lot of prestige in Tallahassee, and Sheriff Anderson was elated.

This was a case of using common sense, as I'd witnessed from my dad, to be successful in my job.

The Sims Murders (October 22, 1966)

I was working as a State Investigator and Special Agent, Florida Sheriff's Bureau, with a home office in Panama City. I received a call to pack my suitcase and report to the Tallahassee office without delay. The Special Agent in Charge said a college professor, his wife, and 12-year-old daughter had been murdered, and it could be a lengthy assignment.

Arriving in Tallahassee, I was directed to report to the Leon County Sheriff's Office. That office was being utilized as overall command post for the investigation. As I recall, there were law enforcement officers from most of the state agencies, as well as the Tallahassee Police Department, involved.

I was assigned to work with a young deputy by the name of

LaVelle & Larry Campbell

Larry Campbell. He was a graduate of FSU and a very intelligent young man. (Intelligent was not something I would have admitted to his face, however.)

At the time we were assigned to work this case, I was a new agent with the FSB and had worked a few local murder cases in the Bay County area—nothing of the magnitude of the case Larry and I were getting into.

Larry had never worked a murder case that I know of. Neither of us could be looked upon as real Sherlock Holmes types. Larry did know the Tallahassee area, and I didn't.

Our first assignment was to question the two older daughters of the murdered family. They were baby-sitting at the time of the murder and arrived home to find their parents and 12-year-old sister dead.

The two sisters were 16 years of age with ten months difference between them. Along with questioning the girls, we

288

were to escort them everywhere they went. They were never to be left alone. At the end of the day, we were to deliver them to a safe house and pick them up the following morning.

After a period of time, we were relieved of the escort duty and assigned to start canvassing the neighborhood. We were instructed to take statements from anyone who may have seen something suspicious on the day and night of the murders, including the days leading up to that fateful night.

We used the old rock in the pool method. If you throw a rock in a pool it makes a ripple and spreads out to gradually cover the entire pool. In this case it covered the entire neighborhood. So we started with next door neighbors of the victims' home and worked outward.

The night before we started the interviews, I dropped Campbell off at his vehicle as we were securing for the night. On the way to my motel, I drove back by the Sims house. It was close to 10:00 pm and the house was dark with only night lights on inside. Crime scene tape completely surrounded the yard, and keep out signs were posted.

Sometimes when I work a murder case, I like to go back to the scene at about the same time the crime occurred. I try to think like the villain might have been thinking and why he might have done what he did. When you have no leads, you'll try most anything to come up with something that makes sense.

I parked my unmarked state car on the street and made my way through the crime scene tape. I unlocked the garage and eased inside the house. It is a scary feeling going into a house where someone has been brutally murdered.

I sat down on the edge of the bed where the bodies were found and tried to think like

SIMS HOME — The home of Robert Sims, remains unsolved. This State Department of Education executive in the weeks immedi who was murdered, along with his wife triple murder. Althou

Sims Home

the murderer might have thought. There were blood stains all over the floor and the room was totally torn apart by our crime scene specialist. The bedroom was in the very back of the large brick home. The estimated time of the deaths was between 9:30 pm and 10:00 pm which made it close to the half time of the FSU and Mississippi State football game being played the night of the murders.

As I sat there thinking, I heard the front door opening very slowly. I reached for my weapon and remembered I had locked it in my car. The first thing I thought was the killer had returned to the scene of his crime. Scared doesn't describe the feeling I had. Terrified was more like it.

Whoever had committed the crime left very little physical evidence at the scene. If I was about to die, I intended to leave plenty of physical evidence behind for the guys to work with.

I eased into the bedroom closet and pulled the door almost closed. I could hear this person slowly walking down the hallway. I got my pocket knife out and opened it up. The intruder stopped now and then, stood quietly for a moment and then took another step or two. I was sure whoever it was could hear my heart thumping, because I could hear it plainly. This person finally reached the bedroom door and stopped. There was a dim night light on and I could hear his breathing or maybe it was mine.

As he stepped into the room, I leaped out of the closet grabbed him and yelled, "Police!" He screamed louder than me, turned to face me and I found I had two arms full of a uniformed Tallahassee police officer. He was just as scared as I was.

When we both finally got our hearts beating normally, we walked out of the house. He said he noticed a strange vehicle out front and thought he should have a look. We both agreed that it was doubtful either of us would be checking this house again any time in the near future.

Each investigator on the case interviewed many people during the weeks following the murder—some we pursued vigorously.

There were two students, male and female about 20 years of age, who lived in a neighborhood near the murder scene. The girl was a student at a junior college in an adjoining county. Investigation revealed that she and her boyfriend were lovers and bragged about having sex in cemeteries while laying on the tombstones. Further questioning of people at the junior college, revealed that the girl lived in a room for two in the campus dormitory, but no one would live with her.

One of her former roommates said this girl had placed a casket on top of her bed and at night she slept inside the casket. She had a sign over her dorm door that read "A tisket a tasket come sleep in my casket," and bragged about going into funeral homes at night with her boyfriend and molesting dead people.

We brought the female subject in and had some interesting interviews. Most of her interviews were conducted by Campbell. Many of the things we had heard, she admitted and laughed about. She was eliminated as a suspect but some of us felt she was certainly capable of the murders.

The people heading up the investigation called me in one day and said that due to some of the strange leads that had been coming in, they wanted me to travel to Chicago and spend some time with Special Agent McLaughlin of the FBI. He was recognized as the foremost expert in the field of sex-related crimes. Arrangements were made to meet with him at an office he occupied in the Chicago Police Headquarters. He spent a few days with me, went over our case and gave us the benefit of his thinking. This trip resulted in one of the most informative sessions I've ever had.

The FBI is like most law enforcement agencies. They have good guys and bad guys. You have to judge each one individually. Many of the federal law enforcement officers are great lawmen and will go out of their way to help another lawman. But there's that ten percent who think they are anointed instead of appointed and aren't helpful.

McLaughlin was definitely a good cop. He went over our case carefully and pulled files with similarities that might help our investigation. This agent had been a part of many investigations of nation-wide notoriety. I thought I knew what a weirdo was, but McLaughlin really knew the meaning of that word in the many hundreds of cases in which he had been associated.

After that Chicago visit, the task force developed a suspect who was the minister of a large church in Tallahassee. He was acquainted with the Sims family. A lady came forward who was a member of this minister's church. She had gone to the pastor for counseling and claimed he had sexually assaulted her after placing her under hypnosis. This apparently had happened more than one time. The last trip she went in for counseling, she came out of the hypnotic trance and realized this guy had been having sex with her and she had not been aware of it.

She went home and told her husband and the two of them went straight to the state attorney's office. The husband felt that the pastor could have been involved in the murder of the Sims family.

This hypnotizing thing did not go over very well with the task force, especially the state attorney. Not one of us believed you could be hypnotized against your will. This lady and her husband would not be put off and demanded we look into this. Someone made the suggestion that we talk to a master hypnotist and get a final opinion to satisfy the lady and her husband.

It was determined that the University of Miami had a professor who was known as a master hypnotist. An appointment was made and Sam, one of our polygraph experts and former U.S. Army Criminal Investigative Division officer, was selected to go. Sam didn't want to waste money flying to Miami because he said, "Everyone knows you can't be hypnotized unless you want to be." Needless to say, Sam lost the argument and was on a plane for Miami.

Sam returned two days later and addressed the task force members. He advised in substance as follows:

He arrived at the University of Miami campus and was directed to the professor's office. The professor greeted Sam and invited him to have a seat in front of his large executive desk. The professor then asked Sam to brief him on what the lady had said and everything he knew about the minister. Sam did and the professor sat quietly for a moment and said Sam you need to understand there are hypnotists and there are hypnotists. There are very few master hypnotists who work in the public domain. It surely sounds like this young lady has or could have been in the presence of a master hypnotist if she is being truthful with you.

Sam asked the professor if he really believed a person could be hypnotized against their will or without knowing what was going on. The professor replied, "Most certainly, if this person is a master hypnotist he can place you in an hypnotic state and then bring you out of it and you will never know he has done this."

Sam carried on a conversation for a few minutes, got up, thanked the professor and headed for the door. The professor smiled as he rose from behind his desk and said, "Obviously you don't believe what I have told you about a master hypnotist do you?"

Sam said, "With all due respect, sir, no I really don't. But I do thank you for your time."

The professor smiled and said, "I could tell you felt that way when you came in, so to prove a point I relieved you of your I.D. and badge holder as well as your billfold." He opened his desk drawer and handed Sam his ID with his badge and his wallet. Sam quickly slapped his breast pocket and hip pocket and both were empty.

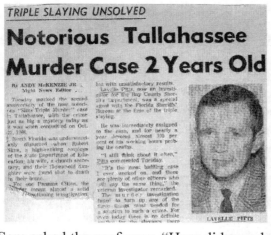

TRIPLE SLAYING UNSOLVED

Notorious Tallahassee Murder Case 2 Years Old

By ANDY McKENZIE JR.
Night News Editor

LAVELLE PITTS

Sam asked the professor, "How did you do that?"

The professor said, "Sam, I hypnotized you to prove a point." The professor escorted Sam out and told him to have a nice day.

Sam was still in shock when he talked to the group and said he was amazed that the guy could have done that. He never saw the professor get up from behind his desk until he started to leave.

So much for some of Florida's most brilliant investigators and their opinions and knowledge of hypnotism.

Campbell later became the Sheriff of Leon County and could go into a much more detailed account of this case, especially if he speaks about the prime suspect–the minister that reportedly could hypnotize you. This case got nation-wide press and I was amazed at the number of weirdoes that came out of the woodwork as suspects. It has never been officially solved.

The Case of the Murdered Millionaire Rancher (Von Maxcy, 1966)

As a Special Agent for the Florida Sheriff's Bureau, it was not unusual to be assigned to different areas of Florida on serious crimes. We only had eight agents to cover the entire state. I probably had the largest area in square miles–Perry to Pensacola– but fewer sensational type cases.

I received a call from my SAIC in Tallahassee to pack a bag and head to Sebring, Florida, to investigate the murder of a millionaire rancher.

I arrived at the local sheriff's office and met with four or five other special agents from various districts in Florida as well as several FSB crime scene specialists from Tallahassee. We went out to the crime scene which was located some distance from town in a very large ranch house. It was in the middle of a cattle ranch and orange groves.

We were instructed to walk through the house and point out to the crime scene specialists items of special interest to be photographed or fingerprinted that might give us a clue as to what happened.

One of the young crime scene specialists was from Graceville. He was walking around and couldn't help being in awe of this home. It even had an Olympic-size swimming pool inside the house. While looking up at the sky lights he stepped off into the pool and went out of sight. Everyone thought it was funny except the special agent in charge.

After fishing the crime scene guy out of the pool, the SAIC gave him a quick tongue-lashing as to the seriousness of the investigation and told him to keep his mind on business.

The Special Agent in Sebring area gave us his summation of what the evidence thus far led him to believe. He stated that the victim was shopping with his wife in downtown Sebring. He went home to take a shower and was to go back to town and meet his wife for lunch.

He arrived at his ranch home and parked his new Lincoln in the driveway. He went into the house, then into a large bathroom where his closet, shower, tub and other bath accessories were located. It appeared that while he was getting undressed, someone, who had been hiding behind the shower curtain, suddenly came out of the tub, threw the shower curtain over the victim's head and started stabbing him in the back. After the victim fell to the floor, the suspect fled the scene. The victim appeared to have gotten up from the floor of the bathroom, staggered to the dresser in the bedroom where he fell to the floor and died.

The suspect apparently took the victim's Lincoln, drove back through town and on to the airport where he parked the vehicle and probably left on a plane.

The autopsy found that the rancher died from multiple stab wounds in the back. The crime scene investigator found a bullet in the far corner of the bedroom. This was sent back to the Tallahassee crime lab.

There were no bullet wounds in the body, so it caused us concern as to where the bullet fit into the crime. We wondered if the rancher shot the intruder and he might have been wounded. But no gun was found in the house.

The agent from Miami advised that their medical examiner, Dr. Joe Davis, was the best in the nation and he could call him about the bullet we found. Dr. Davis, on a conference call, was filled in on all the details of the case and about the bullet found in the far corner of the bedroom.

After a slight pause, he asked if the body had been buried yet. He was told the funeral was that day and was probably going on right then.

He said, "Go to the grave side and after everyone leaves stop the burial. Open the casket and have one of your investigators open the rancher's eyes with his fingers. You should find a bullet hole in one of his eyes."

He theorized the suspect probably thought the victim was dead and when he was leaving, looked back and saw him staggering out of the bathroom. He could have pulled a gun and fired one shot into the head. The bullet could have entered the eye, glanced off the skull, and exited out one of the stab wounds in the back going into the far part of the room. The eye would have immediately closed concealing the bullet wound.

295

The officers did what the doctor said—opened the casket and pried open the rancher's eyes. One of the eyes had a perfectly round bullet hole dead center of the eye ball.

The agents working the case formed teams. I went out with Eddie Boone. We were assigned to interview everyone who knew the victim, and all the people who did business with him or his family. This included everyone along the route from town to his ranch and back to the airport.

We found two or three people who had met the Lincoln coming from the ranch and had waved, thinking it was the rancher, and the driver waved back at them. This had to have been the murder suspect. We believed we were dealing with a professional hit man.

Someone must have dropped the suspect off at the ranch. He appeared to know the victim would be coming home alone and could drive the victim's car back to the airport after the murder.

The victim's wife was interviewed and stated she was shopping and her husband had gone home to take a bath and change clothes and was to come back for a lunch date.

The victim's family was interviewed and immediately stated that they believed the wife was involved in his murder. They said she was nothing but a bar hop, and he had met her, fallen in love, and married her not long after they first met.

Several hundred man hours went into the interviewing of friends, neighbors and anyone else who had done business or associated with the victim or his wife. All possible leads were checked and rechecked. Everyone spoke highly of the victim; no one we talked to cared for his wife. Finally most of the agents were sent back to their home areas and a small crew, including me, was left to continue the investigation.

Meanwhile the widow was selling cattle, equipment, and other items from the ranch as fast as she could. The family of the rancher was upset and put pressure on the law enforcement people to stop her.

Sometimes, when all avenues have been tried, you need to improvise. We determined that the bar and lounge, where the widow used to work, was run by a shady character.

A few calls were made, and a good-looking hooker who agreed to work as an informant arrived from Miami and checked into a local motel. She went to the local bar where the old boyfriend of the widow worked and had no trouble garnering attention, especially from the bar owner. He took over for the bartender and served the young lady himself. By the second drink he was sitting on the stool next to her. She talked to him and left shortly thereafter.

For several nights the hooker informant went to the bar for two or three drinks and returned to her motel. Talk of this new girl in town spread and got back to the widow. This led to a phone call to the old boyfriend, also her former boss. She questioned him about the new girl in town.

He brushed her off and told her it was none of her business. She got mad and told him he better break it off with this new girl or she would talk to the police. He hung up on her after a few more hard words.

About ten minutes later the widow heard her door bell ring. When she went to the door, she found a friendly FSB Agent outside who had been privy to her conversation with her old boyfriend by way of a court-ordered tap on her phone line. She invited him in and said, "I need to talk to you."

The state attorney granted her immunity which covered only the actual murder of her husband. She opened up and there was our case. The widow had to be granted immunity for her connection with the murder of her husband, but her testimony was enough to indict her current boyfriend the bar owner. The hooker who had played her part well, left for Miami the day after the arrest.

It was discovered that the bar owner had contacted some old friend with organized crime and paid him a sum of money to come in with another friend and kill the rancher. One rented a vehicle and carried the other to the ranch and dropped him off with the key he had been furnished by the rancher's wife. The hit man walked right in, knew what time the rancher would come home, and exactly what he would do when he arrived home. All this was prearranged by the wife and the bar owner.

Phone calls were made to Boston. They were familiar with the crime family these two were from and put out a pick-up on the suspects. A couple of our special agents flew to Boston with murder warrants to bring the two gunmen to Florida.

Arriving in Boston, the police told the agents they had just received a call from an unknown source who gave the location of a car where the two suspects could be found. The agents accompanied the Boston police and went across town to an alley where they found the car. No one was in the vehicle but the keys were in the front seat.

One of the officers took the keys and opened the trunk. There, bound and gagged and shot in the head, were the two suspects they were looking for. The local police were not surprised. They explained this is what usually happened when someone went outside the crime family to do a job and the family found out about it.

The case came to trial and the bar owner was convicted of murder. The wife had immunity for murder, but not perjury. During the trial she not only testified against her ex-boyfriend/bar owner, but perjured herself. She was convicted of perjury and sent to prison as well.

Bear

As a Special Agent for the Florida Sheriff's Bureau, I had been working only a few months when I received a call from my director to pack a bag and head to the sheriff's office in Bradenton, Florida. I was briefed by a team of investigators upon arrival.

I left late in the afternoon and arrived in Bradenton around midnight. I was briefed by a couple of agents who looked as though they had not had much sleep. They explained their case as follows:

In the past several months the Central Florida area had been plagued with robberies, assaults and murder. The two suspects were black males. Most of their victims were ranchers.

The day before I arrived, they had picked up a suspect they believed was one of the two involved. This man was a huge black male known as "Bear." They had questioned him continually for about 20 hours trying to break him. Bear was very cooperative up to the point of admitting he had anything to do with the robberies and murder. He had not asked for a lawyer and they intended to keep questioning him until he did. They said they were about worn out and needed another officer to interview him for a while to give them a break.

Without further ado, I was taken upstairs to the interrogation room and introduced to Bear. He was very big and ugly. He shook hands with me and sat back down. I couldn't remember ever being thrown into the fire as quickly as on this case. I sat down and we looked at each other for a moment.

I started off by asking him where he was from. He said he grew up on a small farm in the Panhandle of Florida. I advised him I grew up on a farm in Bonifay, Florida. I told him about some of the things I did–plowing a mule and chores I had to do. He started telling me some things he did.

I think he was relieved to be off the subject of crime for a change. We talked about 30 minutes and I told him about mom making me go to church every Sunday and Wednesday night. He said the same thing happened to him.

I said, "I bet your mom was a praying mom, was she not?"

He said, "She sure was."

I then asked if she would approve of the things he had been doing and he dropped his head and said, "No, she didn't raise me that way."

After a few minutes of this kind of talk, I asked him if he would like to come clean and clear up all the things he had done and start a new life. He sat there a moment and said, "Yeah, I think I would."

He started talking.

After listening for some time, I said, "Wait just a moment. Do you mind if I have someone write all this down?" He said he didn't mind.

I went downstairs and told the agents that whoever had all the details on the cases should go up with a recorder and take a statement.

They looked at me a minute and one of them said, "Look, we're tired and beat and don't need anyone trying to be funny."

When I finally convinced them I was serious, one of the agents grabbed his recorder and case file and took off upstairs. The other guys sat me down and demanded to know what I did to the guy to get him to talk.

I had been sent into the room to give the other agents a break, and keep the man occupied for an hour or so. I had no case file of details or much knowledge of the cases they were working. That old counseling from Uncle Custer Russ came back to mind. Treat a person like you wanted him to treat you if you were in his situation. Bear not only gave them all the details the officers needed, he also furnished the name of his associate.

Over more than 30 years of law enforcement, I am amazed at the number of hard-core criminals who became tame as little kittens and admitted wrongdoing when asked if their mother or grandmother told them to tell the truth or took them to church.

(With the Christian foundation of our country under attack, and the removal of prayer and the Bible from our schools, I believe this line of questioning is less likely to work and a major reason for increases in crime.)

Pussy Cat Go-Go Club

While employed as a Special Agent with the State of Florida, I was en route to Milton from Tallahassee and made the mistake of stopping by the Bay County Jail for a cup of coffee. I thought it would be nice to see my old comrades at shift change–about 6:00pm. Everyone was crowded around the jail kitchen table drinking coffee, including Sheriff Doc Daffin.

After all the handshaking and hoopla, Sheriff Daffin said, "Boy, you came along at just the right time. We are going to raid the Pussy Cat Go-Go Club and their big poker game."

Knowing the club he was talking about, I said, "Sheriff, you've got more than enough here to handle the problem."

300

He said, "No, they have a lookout on the front porch and he will advise them if we pull in. I want you to take about five of these deputies and go around through the woods and sneak up and hit the back door. When you go through the back door the other officers will hit the front."

I told him they'd probably have the back door locked and he said to kick it down.

By this time I knew there was no way out, so I agreed. Knowing the reputation of the Pussy Cat Go Go Club, it should be an interesting night. I had no idea just how interesting it would turn out to be.

Five uniformed deputies and I, in plain clothes, drove out to the area. We went down a dirt road and left our cars. We walked as close as we thought we could, without being seen. It was very dark and we had a little trouble finding the fire trail we knew was there.

When we found it, I instructed everyone to get down on all fours and crawl until we got within a few feet of the back door. The signal to rush the door would be when I stood up.

There were at least three issues that could cause us problems. (There are always problems that pop up and things never go as planned.)

The intelligence information did not say if there was one, two or three back doors. This we should have known before the raid. We knew there was a small back porch on the back side of the building and that there was at least one door located on this porch.

This was in the summer time and there were thousands of people on the Panama City beaches. That was bad for a raid.

There was no moon and we could barely see the trail. This was also good, in a way, because they could not see us—or so we thought.

We had one more problem we weren't aware of. They had posted a guard, not only in front of the place, but in the woods behind the place. Their guard was on the very fire trail we were crawling up on our hands and knees.

Just as we were getting close to the jumping up place, this large shadow suddenly stood right up in front of me and said, "Any of you SOB's move, I'll shoot."

301

I could just make out the man standing there and it appeared he had a gun in his hand. All I could hear behind me was the little clicks as the deputies were unsnapping their holstered weapons. I had to make a quick management decision. First, I knew most of the deputies who were with me and had been on the firing range with most of them. Not one could shoot good enough to write home about. I knew if one of them fired, they would all start firing and they stood as good or better chance of hitting me as they did the bad guy. I also knew if they missed both of us, the bad guy would shoot and he couldn't miss me. I was only three or four feet from where he stood.

Odds were if I jumped the guy he would shoot me, and if I sat tight and stayed on my hands and knees one of my guys would start shooting. He might kill two or three of us. Either way I couldn't see myself as coming out of this situation a winner.

So I came up off the ground and made a diving tackle at the bad guy. He fired and I thought I heard the bullet pass by my ear. The power flash almost blinded me. He and I hit the ground and the deputy behind me, Jimmy Cauley, said, "I got him, you go ahead."

I rolled off the man and ran toward the back porch with the other deputies close behind. As I neared the porch, a big German Shepherd came flying off the porch and I could see his white teeth shining. This was definitely not going to be a good night.

As the dog lunged off the porch, he was stopped in mid-air by a chain attached to his neck. I made a left turn and raced to the front of the building and through the front door. I continued on back to the gambling room. The lookout was so interested in watching the game through a partially open door, that he never saw us coming.

We charged into the room and the poker game was still in progress. There was so much noise in the lounge and bar, they hadn't heard all the ruckus in back.

We arrested the entire group, the owners of the club and closed the place down.

Back outside, I noticed two deputies guiding the lookout, who shot at us, to a patrol car. He had a bloody, messed up face. I asked what happened. Cauley said he tried to run away and ran into a tree. I didn't pursue the matter. There are some things that I just didn't need to know.

The group that was delegated to enter the front door wanted to know why we "jumped the gun" and hit the place before the designated time. They were miffed about missing all the action. I told them it was a long story and we decided to change the plans at the last minute. After hearing the details, Sheriff Daffin concurred.

This incident brings to mind Psalm 46–God is our refuge and strength, a very present help in trouble.

Sheriff of Jefferson County (1967)
I received a call to report to the Director Yarborough's office in Tallahassee while working as a FSB Special Agent. This caused a little heartburn wondering what I had done or not done to get a call from the director. Normally all my instructions came from the Special Agent in Charge Emory Williams, also located in the Tallahassee headquarters.

Mr. Yarborough was a former sheriff and appointed by the governor to his present position. He had a good reputation throughout the State and was well-liked by his agents and staff.

I was escorted into his office by SAIC Williams and Director Yarborough got right to the point.

"Governor Kirk just fired the Sheriff of Jefferson County after he was indicted by a grand jury. He appointed a wildlife officer from Jefferson County to be sheriff until the next regular election. The governor called me and asked that I send one of my agents, with sheriff's office experience, to help the newly appointed sheriff until he feels comfortable in handling the office alone."

This was my new assignment, hopefully for only a few days. The following morning I met with the former game warden and new sheriff in the Jefferson County Sheriff's Office and Jail.

303

Jefferson County Sheriff's Office

The new sheriff was very nervous. I was not in much better shape myself. I started giving him a Doc Daffin crash course in how to be a sheriff and run a county jail. I was uncomfortable, especially knowing the grand jury had just indicted the former sheriff and his deputies. We had no one to show us around or answer questions.

We started by taking an inventory and found several guns were missing. I called my SAIC, asked for and received two agents to assist us in locating and recovering the weapons. Fortunately, there weren't many complaint calls in the county during that time. When a call did come in, I left the new sheriff in the office and responded to the person in trouble or addressed the problem.

After about five days of non-stop day and night trying to survive and make a sheriff out of a game warden, I was very tired and down in the dumps. The new sheriff told me he had to run to his old office in Tallahassee for some unfinished business and would be back in a couple of hours. I settled in to answer the phone and sent my two bureau agents out on calls.

Three or four hours later, I received a call from someone who advised he was the administrative assistant to Governor Kirk. He said the appointed sheriff had come in and resigned and the governor had appointed me to be sheriff for about five days until he could find another replacement. I knew this had to be a practical joke from some of my sheriff's bureau buddies and laughed at him.

"Look, do you really expect me to believe this? I'm a Democrat and he's a Republican, so I know you're pulling my leg."

He sounded kind of ticked off. "The governor doesn't appoint according to party, but the best qualified person for the job." He assured me he was not kidding and said a telegram would be delivered the next morning to confirm the appointment. He added that if I didn't believe it, I could drive to Tallahassee and go by the telegraph office on Monroe Street and pick up the telegram myself. He hung up.

I thought to myself–surely those guys don't think that I am that stupid as to drive all the way to Tallahassee to the telegraph office just to give them a big laugh.

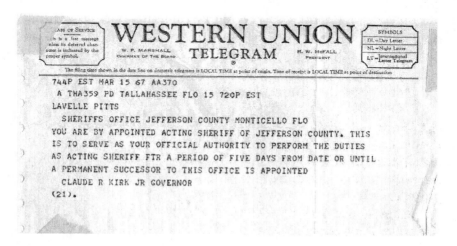

```
744P EST MAR 15 67 AA370
  A THA359 PD TALLAHASSEE FLO 15 720P EST
LAVELLE PITTS
  SHERIFFS OFFICE JEFFERSON COUNTY MONTICELLO FLO
YOU ARE BY APPOINTED ACTING SHERIFF OF JEFFERSON COUNTY. THIS
IS TO SERVE AS YOUR OFFICIAL AUTHORITY TO PERFORM THE DUTIES
AS ACTING SHERIFF FTR A PERIOD OF FIVE DAYS FROM DATE OR UNTIL
A PERMANENT SUCCESSOR TO THIS OFFICE IS APPOINTED
  CLAUDE R KIRK JR GOVERNOR
  (21).
```

However, it did start to bother me. Since the appointed sheriff hadn't returned or called, I reluctantly got on my car and drove to Tallahassee. I circled the Western Union block several times and couldn't see any of the Bureau's unmarked cars.

Finally I stopped and went in, expecting the FSB guys to step out from behind the counter laughing. I asked the clerk if he had a message for me. After showing him my ID he handed me a telegram that read I had indeed been appointed Sheriff of Jefferson County and it was signed by the governor.

I drove the twenty miles back to Jefferson County in a daze. A month ago I had never even stopped in Jefferson County and now I was sheriff–a scary feeling.

Staffing the JCSO

The following morning I called the Bay County Sheriff's Office and told them my dilemma and asked if they knew of any officer who wanted to be a deputy in Jefferson County for a week or two.

That same day I received a call from Pee Wee Preston, who said he would like to come and work for me. I told him it was fairly certain that the next sheriff to be appointed would let him go after he took over, but he said he still wanted to come. He'd been out of the Air Force a short period of time and had a wife and small child.

In the meantime, the governor's office called and the same administrator, after chiding me a little for not believing him about the appointment, passed on directives. Governor Kirk planned to wait on appointing a new sheriff until I had an opportunity to close down the gambling operations and the illegal whiskey sales in Jefferson County. He also agreed to furnish state law enforcement and undercover officers to make buys and gather intelligence information that would help bring down the big operators.

Don Bragg, agent on loan to work with me from Florida Sheriff's Bureau.

I was quick to accept the undercover people and met each one outside Tallahassee and briefed them on their assignments. I wanted to start making buys from the whiskey dealers and Bolita houses. When we knew all the people involved, then we could bring in a large group of officers for a big roundup with search warrants.

Pee Wee arrived with his wife and child in a couple of days, and I put him in charge of the jail. He moved his family into the living quarters of the jail. Pee Wee did a fine job taking care of the jail and his wife handled the women prisoners. Pee Wee also helped answer emergency calls at night.

I received a call from Tommy Smith from Bay County, who volunteered to come work with me. I explained it was a short-term job, but he was having marital problems and said he wanted to come. I had mixed feelings about Tommy. He was a huge man, could whip his weight in wildcats and was considered bad, bad, bad. I don't mean that he was a bad person, but when challenged he was very bold and accepted the challenge regardless of the other person's sex, age, build, reputation, position or the number of persons involved. He was 6 feet 4 inches, weighed well over 270 pounds and was every inch muscle. (An incident involving Tommy is related under Marvin Freeman and the Early Events at the Bay County Sheriff's Office–1957-61.)

Tommy arrived and became my road deputy. He rambled all over Jefferson County and responded to the calls that Pee Wee or I sent him on.

How to Serve a Warrant in Less than 30 Minutes

The morning after Tommy started work, I went to the downtown barber shop. This was supposed to be the place to find out what was going on, had been going on or was planned for the future. While I was getting my hair cut, the barber brought up the new deputy, as I knew he probably would.

I gave him and the others in the shop a little background on Tommy, including the football player from Auburn. Needless to say the word went out. The last thing I wanted was for some of the good old boys to challenge Tommy, so I laid it on thick.

Before and after I hired Tommy, I talked to him about our position in Jefferson County. I wanted him to be very careful about a confrontation with any person. He assured me he understood and nothing would happen.

Tommy visited all the businesses and hangouts in the county getting acquainted with people, and most had heard of him before they met him. I received a warrant for a black person and had no idea what he looked like only that he hung out at the large black bar in town. The population of Jefferson County was over 51 percent black. I gave the warrant to Tommy with the only information we had and told him to handle it with care because this guy had a bad reputation.

Tommy went straight to the black bar and lounge, walked in the door and with a loud voice said. "Let me have your attention. I have a warrant for (calling the person's name). I want him to walk over to the bar where I am standing, NOW!"

According to the guys at the barber shop, things got really quiet for a moment and slowly this one black dude made his way through the crowd and walked over to Tommy and said, "I'm the one you're looking for."

Tommy cuffed him and brought him to the jail. I could hardly believe my eyes. Tommy had been gone for less than 30 minutes.

Tommy Arrests a Store Owner

A lady came in my office one afternoon who seemed to be really upset. She explained that her teenage son had gone into a store located in the south end of Jefferson County and got into an argument with the owner about something and the store owner had beaten her son and thrown him out.

She explained this had happened to other people, also. She said the law never did much, and most people were afraid of the man and would not prosecute him. I assured her we would arrest the man and prosecute him if she agreed to sign an affidavit for a warrant. She did and the people in the judge's office warned me that the man probably would resist. I called Tommy in and explained the whole situation to him and noticed he had started grinning when I told him how bad this guy was. I emphasized that he was to be nice to the store owner unless he resisted. If he did, use as little force as possible and bring him to jail.

A person in the store later told me what happened when Tommy came in to arrest the store owner. He said the marked patrol car came racing up and slid up to a stop in front of the store. A big deputy jumped out and walked in quickly and announced in a loud voice that he was looking for (named the owner), who had beat up a kid. He said he had a warrant for his arrest. Things got real quiet and the owner finally said in a low voice, "That must be me."

Tommy told him to go get in the patrol car. The owner asked if he could close his store up before he left and Tommy told him to make it fast. When they arrived at the jail Tommy booked him and turned the warrant in to me. He was disappointed the guy didn't give him any trouble at all. The only ones happy were the kid's mother and me.

Tommy Finds Some Wild Turkeys

One afternoon, Tommy came to the office real excited and said, "LaVelle, I found a bunch of wild turkeys today down near the river on the north side of the county. I got two or three shots at them with my riot shot gun, but after they flew away I checked the shells and found they were number 8 shot. I need some buck shot, in case I see them again."

LaVelle, Sheriff of Jefferson County

I explained he was not to hunt while on duty and told him we didn't have any buck shot.

The following morning an older black man, dressed in overalls and carrying a straw hat in his hand, came to my office. He said, "Sheriff, sir, could I talk to you a little?"

I told him sure and asked what he had on his mind.

He said, "I don't mean to complain, but I's a farmer on the north side of the county and yesterday one of your deputies came by my farm and, sheriff, he shot hell out of my turkeys. Could you please ask him not to do that again?"

I assured him that would not happen again and offered to pay for his turkeys.

He declined and said they were not hurt very bad but he sure didn't want him shooting them again. After he left, I called Tommy in. He was red-faced and embarrassed when he left my office.

(Tommy once asked me if I had heard the old saying that no matter how good a fighter you were, there was always someone better. I assured him that I had heard that all my life. He said he had too, but had never found that person. He didn't say it like he was bragging, but was just being factual. However, he did meet

309

his match one day. After working with me in Jefferson County, he returned to Bay County as Springfield Chief of Police. He was shot in the back and killed with his own .357 magnum by his wife.)

Meeting the Golf Pro

I tried to mix in with the locals and get to know as many as possible. I found the people were very friendly and helpful. Each Thursday afternoon everything closed down and most went to the local golf course and played golf. I was invited.

I went down, rented a set of clubs, bought a dozen balls. and went to the course early. I had caddied in high school, but never played. I did fairly good until the first water hole and ended up hitting all 12 of my balls into the pond. I didn't want to lose those balls, so I pulled off my shoes, rolled up my pants legs, waded out and started looking for my golf balls.

After finding two or three and throwing them out on dry ground, a guy on a golf cart came racing up (as fast as a golf cart races) and yelled at me.

"What the hell do you think you're doing?"

"Retrieving my golf balls."

"No way. Any ball goes in the water is the property of the country club."

I continued looking for my golf balls.

He became flustered and said, "I'll have you know I'm the golf pro of this club and I'll call the sheriff if you don't get out of that pond right now. Just who the hell do you think you are anyway?"

I stopped, looked him over and said, "I *am* the sheriff."

He sat there in shock for a few moments then said, "The one just appointed by the governor?"

I answered in the affirmative.

He got out of his golf cart and pulled off his shoes and said, "Here let me help you." We became good friends and he let me use a set of clubs each Thursday and play with his group so he could coach me.

"I Make My Living Selling Numbers."

The second week as sheriff, I was alone in my office going over some paperwork when an elderly black man knocked on the door. I told him to come in.

He was very courteous, gave his name and stood there, hat in hand. "Sheriff, sir," he began, "I believe in being truthful and coming right to the point, if that's all right."

I told him, "Fine. Tell me what's on your mind."

He said, "Sheriff, I make my living selling numbers and the last sheriff and me had a good understanding. I knew how much it was going to cost me to do business, and I came by every week and paid my dues. I took care of my business and he took care of his. We never had any problems. I was wondering if we could continue doing the same. If I'm not paying enough I could maybe pay a little more."

I told him I really appreciated him coming in and being up front with me. I respected him for that. I said, "I'm not going to charge you anything to do business in Jefferson County. But if we catch you, and we will, that's when you will have to pay up."

He stood there a moment, smiled and stuck his hand out and shook mine. He said "I do appreciate you telling me how it is and not beating around the bush."

Working the Rackets

I knew I needed a black undercover officer to really get into the numbers racket in Jefferson County. After the conversation with the old gentleman, I could see there were some shrewd individuals involved in the numbers racket and most, if not all, were black.

I called a friend, Andy Anderson, who was Sheriff of Walton County, and asked if I could borrow one of his black deputies. I had one in mind I had worked with who had proven to be very bright and knowledgeable of Florida law. After I agreed to pay the officer's salary and all expenses, the sheriff put him on a bus to Tallahassee with his suitcase.

I picked him up and briefed him on what was going on. We shopped around and bought an old car with a Georgia tag on it and he drifted into Jefferson County looking for work. No one knew his identity but me.

Things were very quiet for a few weeks. The racketeers were expecting big raids and arrests. When that didn't happen, things settled down. I suppose the bad guys thought I was just marking time until the new sheriff took over, so they gradually got back in business. Our undercover people, sent by Governor Kirk from the Beverage Department, started picking up a buy of whiskey here and there. The Bolita tickets started showing up again and my undercover black guy worked right in with the bar bunch and some of the number runners (salesmen).

Barber Shop "Sheriffing"

I learned from our undercover people that a big poker game was held one night each week in a local men's clubhouse. This was late at night and only a few very carefully chosen people were invited. Most were businessmen in town, including the local police chief, who had been chief for many years. He was a likeable fellow and old.

After determining the game was not just a nickel and dime game, I knew it had to be stopped. I made it a point to make a trip to the barber shop and get a haircut when I saw the chief was there.

As usual the shop was full of locals and some businessmen. They were full of questions about the goings on at the sheriff's office. I told them things were very quiet, and I was looking forward to a new appointee being named by the governor so I could get back to my old job.

The barber behind my chair asked me if I knew some of the history of Jefferson County's past sheriffs. I replied that I did not. He explained that at least one or two sheriffs had been murdered while in office for putting certain people in jail. He said, "You're putting some big name people in jail every now and then. Aren't you worried you could be killed?"

I replied, "No, I don't worry about that because I'm expendable and not that important. If that happened, the governor would appoint a really good sheriff to come in and really clean house in Jefferson County." This brought some laughter from some of the customers in the shop.

I said, "One thing that does bother me, is the rumor I've heard about a local high stakes poker game involving businessmen in town. I don't know that there's anything to it, but we're checking it out. I really hope that it's not true because I have met some of the people that are rumored to be involved in the game, and they are really nice people. This time there was no laughing. The only sound was the buzzing of electric clippers.

Our guys checked the clubhouse on poker night that week. It was closed up tight and remained that way until I left Jefferson County.

Breaking up the Whiskey and Bolita Business

The whiskey business was very profitable in Jefferson County because it was a dry county. That means that no one could buy or sell bonded whiskey in the county. Twenty miles away in Tallahassee, you could legally purchase all you wanted, as long as you were of age and stayed within the state and federal law.

Enterprising people bought large quantities of legal whiskey in Tallahassee, brought it to Jefferson County, and sold it out of their home or from a secret location known to prospective buyers. The really bad thing was the seller jacked the price up and sold to any person who had the money including those who were underage.

On information received from the undercover officers, I drove out a few times at night and was amazed at the number of people who were buying whiskey off the back porch of farm houses and homes around Jefferson County. Sometimes there was a long line of mostly teenage customers on football weekends.

The day finally arrived when we had enough undercover purchases of whiskey and Bolita tickets to put on affidavits for search warrants. The workers in the judge's office and other courthouse employees were either related to, or friends with, some of the people we were getting search warrants for. I realized one phone call could jeopardize the entire operation, so we initiated a plan.

I had all the task force gather in the proximity of the intended searches. I took Tommy Smith with me to the courthouse and laid all the search warrants on the county judge's desk for his signature. He seemed to be shocked. He started reading the warrants and commenting on first one and then another, surprised the people named on the warrants would do such a thing.

He finally signed all the warrants and started to get up. I asked if I could go over a few questions with him and handed Tommy the stack of warrants. I told Tommy I would get with him at the jail and talk about how to serve the warrants. When Tommy left, I started asking the judge questions about search and seizure and various other questions about some of the people we had made buys from.

In the meantime, Tommy was racing from point to point and handing out search warrants to state officers waiting to move on serving the warrants. I left the judge's office about 25 minutes after Tommy left with the signed warrants. I hoped we had beaten the warning phone calls most likely being made from inside the courthouse.

When I got back to the jail, cars were coming in with cases of bonded whiskey and prisoners. The prisoners were being booked and the whiskey stacked in large cells we used as evidence lockers.

One vehicle came in with a load of office equipment, typewriters, checkbooks, files, records and other miscellaneous equipment used in a Bolita bank house. Along with the equipment, they brought in the black man who had visited me and offered to pay me to do business.

He smiled, walked over, and shook hands with me and said, "Well, sheriff, you got me and like you said it's time to pay up. I likes a man who keeps his word."

This was by far the most congenial arrest we made. The whiskey sellers were not so good-natured. We seized enough bonded whiskey to fill two cell blocks and made many arrests.

This broke up and put a big hurt on the whiskey and numbers racket in Jefferson County. I am sure it did not last long, but it did leave the governor free to appoint a real sheriff for the good people of Jefferson County.

Leaving Jefferson County

I left some very good friends in Jefferson County. Some of the greatest people I have ever known helped me and took care of me and my officers. Some I really appreciated were Pee Wee, his wife, Tommy Smith, the golf pro, the county judge, the barber and many others, including the Bay County Sheriff's Office, The Walton County Sheriff's Office and their black deputy and the many beverage agents and Florida Sheriff's Bureau agents who helped out and especially Governor Claude Kirk. The Bolita king even came to me when he heard I was leaving and tried to talk me into staying and running for sheriff. "I can't believe you want me to stay after I put you in jail."

He laughed and said, "That's alright. You put me in jail, but you also put a bunch of those white boys in jail too. I have no complaints."

What was to be five days turned into seven months in Jefferson County. In the meantime the Florida Sheriff's Bureau was changed to the Florida Department of Law Enforcement and they appointed a new director. The new guidelines required a criminology degree to be an agent. I didn't have a degree. After I finished in Jefferson County, I had no position to return to, so I went back to Bay County. I probably could have gone to Governor Kirk and been grandfathered in, but I had my feelings hurt.

(In fact several years later, I had an opportunity to meet and talk over old times with Governor Kirk. He was surprised that my old job had been abolished and said that if I had contacted him, he could and would have ordered the new agency to put me back to work.)

Anyhow, I went back to Panama City and a good friend, Herb Hinson, wanted me to help him sell insurance because I knew so many people.

Back to BCSO (1968)

While trying to sell insurance, I still went by the sheriff's office to have coffee with the deputies every chance I got. One morning, Sheriff Daffin was present and asked what I was doing. He laughed when I told him I was selling insurance and said he needed me to help his investigators identify a body they had found in Deer Point Lake.

The body was a white male and had no clothes on. He obviously had been tortured and after dying was dumped in the lake. Tullis Easterling, retired FBI agent, was Doc's chief investigator at that time.

I was briefed by Mr. Easterling and then compiled all the information we had and sent bulletins out to law enforcement agencies nationwide. The following morning, I received an inquiry from the Atlanta Police Department advising they thought the victim might be from Atlanta. They advised they had a detective en route to Bay County with photographs to try to identify the subject.

The following day the victim was identified by the detective as a person, according to their information, who had been having an affair with a married woman and was caught by the husband. We were advised later that the husband was arrested and charged with murder.

What was supposed to be a one day case, ended up being four days. I was finishing the paperwork when Sheriff Daffin walked by my borrowed office and asked how I was doing. I advised I was finishing up my reports for Mr. Easterling and would be out of his hair. He laughed and tossed a leather case on my desk and walked off.

I opened it to find a badge and credentials for me as Bay County Deputy Sheriff and Investigator, signed by the sheriff. I didn't think long before accepting the offer. Fortunately, my insurance salesman days were over. This was another case of Sheriff Daffin helping me along in my law enforcement career.

I had been back with the BCSO a short time when I received a call from my old friend, Larry Campbell, who was a captain and chief of detectives with the Leon County Sheriff's Office in Tallahassee. Larry advised he was taking a new position as Special Agent in Charge of the FDLE Office in Tampa and had recommended me to Sheriff Hamlin as his successor at the LCSO.

I had mixed emotions about leaving Bay County, but it was a $3,000 a year pay raise.

I went to Sheriff Daffin and explained my dilemma. Without hesitation the sheriff said, "Take the job. You have worked hard for an opportunity like this and they can pay much more than we can." He went on to say he hated to lose me, but was glad to see me advance in law enforcement.

I drove to Tallahassee and after a short interview with Sheriff Hamlin, I became the new captain and chief of detectives for the Leon County Sheriff's Office in the State Capitol. Doc made a big news release. He used me as an example of losing investigators he had trained because the county commission wouldn't budget him enough money to compete with higher paying law enforcement agencies. When I went to Tallahassee, my salary jumped from $5,200 to $8,500 a year.

Pitts Joins Leon Sheriff's Force

Capt. Larry Campbell, chief of detectives for the Leon County Sheriff's Department, has resigned to accept a position with the Florida Department of Law Enforcement.

Sheriff Raymond Hamlin announced his successor as Lavelle Pitts, a 35-year-old detective with the Bay County Sheriff's Office who once worked homicides around the state with Campbell when the wife, Cathy, to accept the position of special agent.

Campbell has worked in almost all positions in the sheriff's department since he came there in 1964. He began as a jailer, then became a radio operator, bailiff, deputy, and then a detective from 1966 until February, 1967.

He then joined the Florida Sheriff's Bureau as agent in charge of Duval and 11 surrounding counties until Oct., 1967 when he was named an

Pitts   Campbell
detective, chief of the uniformed division and later

months, he resigned and rejoined the Bureau. When the Bureau was reorganized, Pitts decided to go back to the Bay County Sheriff's Office as a detective where he has remained since that time.

In 1967, while with the Bureau, Pitts was assigned to assist Campbell in investigation of the Sims murder case and ran down leads covering 24 states. Both men have worked numerous homicides in Florida.

Chief of Detectives, Leon County Sheriff's Office (1970)

I inherited several excellent detectives from Campbell–all with criminology degrees, except me. The biggest problem I had to start with was getting them on a Doc Daffin schedule of getting to work early. The first day on the job they started straggling in between 8:30 and 9:30 am.

We immediately had a staff meeting. I advised normal work hours began at 6:00 am, but as I was new on the job I would give them a break and they could come in at 7:00 am. They were horrified and said they'd never come in that early unless called out on a serious crime.

The new hours worked fairly well for most, with the exception of Jim White. Jim had been working in warrants and wanted to be an investigator more than anything in the world. So,

I asked the sheriff to let me borrow him to work undercover. He didn't look like a policeman. He was a fat boy that looked younger than he was.

The sheriff told me, "You don't want that boy. He's snake bit. Everything he does turns out bad."

I said, "He seems pretty smart. He has a criminology degree."

"He has a great IQ, but he's dangerous."

"I'd still like to try him."

"All right. But if he screws up, it's going to be on you."

This was how Jim became a detective. Jim was the youngest detective and it seemed he could never make the office by 7:00 am. I called him into my office for the third time.

He explained he had tried. He bought an alarm clock but that didn't help. Then he bought a couple more, still no luck. "But I have a new plan. I'm going to get a number two aluminum washtub, put all my Big Ben alarm clocks in the center and set them to go off at the same time."

I told him his plan better work or I was going to transfer him back to his old job as a radio dispatcher. He got to work on time for a while but one day he overslept. Jim was resourceful. He got one of the detectives to take his coat and hang it in Jim's office so it looked like he'd been there and just stepped out if I checked his office.

I found out what he did, but never got onto Jim because he was one of the most likeable guys I had ever worked with. He was smart, but things seemed to go wrong when Jim was involved. When he related things that happened to him, he kept us in stitches.

One time, I overheard all of the detectives in the coffee room, next door to my office, laughing and talking about the worst whipping they ever got while growing up. I was about to go in and break up the conference when Jim spoke up.

He said, "None of you guys can touch the whipping I got from my dad. When I was growing up, my dad took me duck hunting on the Choctawhatchee River. We had a large bateau boat with a 50-horse Johnson motor. I always wanted to run the boat, but dad said I was too young. I asked how old I needed to be, and he said twelve years old.

318

The day I turned twelve, duck season opened and it was freezing cold. Dad said, 'Son, we're going duck hunting tomorrow, and I will let you drive the boat.'

That was the happiest day of my life. We left the boat launching ramp and I got down next to that big motor. Dad sat in front of the boat in a heavy coat with his new 12-guage Remington shotgun, he got for Christmas, lying across his lap. It was quite a long way down the river to the duck hunting area, so I let the boat go wide open.

I thought I had died and gone to heaven. Dad just leaned over, hiding his face from the cold as best as he could. I was looking all over the river at everything and feeling like I had finally become a man. We had been running about ten or fifteen minutes when I looked to my right and found I had gotten too close to the bank of the river. We were fast approaching a big tree with a huge limb hanging low out over the water.

I knew I couldn't stop soon enough and yelled as loud as I could, 'DUCK!' My dad leaped to his feet and said, 'Where, where?' The limb caught him and swept him right out of the boat into the freezing water, shotgun and all. Dad, about frozen, made it to the bank without his shotgun, which was somewhere on the river bottom. We both watched his hat floating down the river, then he started pulling his belt off. That, guys, was a real whippin'." Jim might not have been a seasoned detective but he kept us entertained.

The Half-Way House in Tallahassee

After arriving in Tallahassee, I received several complaints about a house on Pensacola Street. It was supposed to be a half-way house where students who had a drug problem could get free counseling. Word was the house served as a front for selling drugs.

I called Jim to help work it and he was elated. I went over details on how to make a controlled buy. Two of the detectives would take him out to the place, search him and make sure he had nothing on him, give him a twenty dollar bill, watch him go in the place, watch him come out. He was to go straight back to the car with his marijuana purchase and be searched again to prove he just received the drugs. That's what we needed to get a search warrant.

All the other detectives were kind of miffed at me for putting him out there, because they were all scared to death of him. They said if you sent him to get a bucket of water, he'd spill it before he got back. He just couldn't do anything right. He tried, but always managed to screw up.

I talked to him and cautioned, "Whatever you do, don't mess up. I stuck my neck out for you and I want you to succeed, so be real careful."

He made a buy right off. He was so proud he didn't know what to do. The other guys didn't have much to say. They still didn't have much confidence in him.

The heat was on. The sheriff wanted the half-way house busted.

We got a search warrant drawn up and got ready to go. We knew the house would be full of students. I had three detectives with me. There were two doors to cover, front and back. Jim begged, "Can I serve the warrant? Can I serve the warrant?"

Geiger, my lieutenant, said, "No, no, no. You'll screw it up. I'll do it."

I said, "No. He's got to learn. Let him serve it."

I instructed him to knock on the door and say, "Sheriff's office, search warrant." If they didn't open the door immediately, to push the door open and go in.

I could tell Jim was nervous. I went over the search procedure one more time and told him to calm down and just do his job. I would be right behind him.

There were students in the yard around the house and several cars parked outside. Everything went according to plan until we got about four steps from the entrance. Jim forgot about knocking on the door and announcing his identity. He suddenly yelled, "Sheriff's office, search warrant," and hit the door with his shoulder while running full speed ahead.

The door was not locked and flew open. Jim fell flat on his stomach and started sliding across the waxed oak floor through the living room into the kitchen. There were probably 20 or more students standing around smoking pot. Jim slid across the floor holding the search warrant in one hand and repeating over and over, "Sheriff's Office, search warrant."

Jim slid past the two detectives coming in the back door. The Lieutenant couldn't resist. He bent over, like a home plate umpire, and yelled, "Safe."

The three of us got everything kind of under control and ordered the subjects to stand still and not move.

About this time Jim got up and asked me what he should do. I advised him to read the search warrant to the occupants, which he did.

It became very quiet and you could hear little plinks and plops all across the room as the students dropped drug paraphernalia from their pockets. Several drug arrests were made and the sheriff was happy that the place was closed. I was happy to get Jim through his first drug raid without getting one of us or them killed.

Sgt. Willie Meggs, and Captain LaVelle Pitts, made capture.

Nine Shot Six Shooter

While working as chief of detectives for the Leon County Sheriff's Office, a 14-year-old girl, her father and young brother were kidnapped from an all night coin laundry in downtown Tallahassee. We quickly learned the suspect was an escaped convict armed and dangerous.

An APB (all points bulletin) was put out on the victim's car the suspect was traveling in. We received a call from the FHP that a trooper chased the vehicle into a wooded area in Liberty County. He abandoned the vehicle and ran into the woods holding onto the girl. The trooper gave up the chase after the suspect started shooting at him, and called for help and back-up assistance.

I left the office, taking one of my detectives, Willie Meggs, with me. We found the trooper. The suspect had gotten the stolen vehicle stuck, left the father and his son with the vehicle and took off through the woods with the girl and a pistol.

The Sheriff of Liberty County and one of his deputies were also at the scene. We spread out. The Liberty County Deputy, Willie and myself went in the direction the convict and girl had gone. We had not gone very far when we spotted them a good distance away.

They saw us about the same time and the convict started firing. We hurriedly sought cover. I found myself and the Liberty County Deputy behind the same log. This deputy was very big—about 275 pounds. How we both got behind the same log and completely concealed ourselves, I'll never know. You can do all kinds of impossible things when you are being shot at. Willie was a short distance away, also behind cover.

The convict stopped firing for a short time. He was probably reloading, and when he started shooting again I heard the deputy counting, "One, two, three, four."

I asked, "What are you doing?"

He said, "I'm counting his shots. When he shoots the sixth one, we can rush him before he can reload." He then said, "Five. Are you ready Captain?"

I asked him if he ever heard of a pistol that shot more than six shots. He said, "No that's a six-shooter. Are you going with me?"

I said, "No, you go ahead. This is your county and I'll just let you take the lead."

At this time the guy fired again and the deputy said, "Six. I'm going after him."

Just as he was starting to get up the guy fired two more rounds. The deputy said, "I be damned. It does shoot more than six shots." He got back behind the log.

We couldn't shoot back for fear of hitting the girl, so we waited. The guy shot for a while and then moved on. He held the girl with one hand and his pistol in the other.

I asked Willie, who was a good athlete and former Seminole football player, if he could run back through the woods, circle around and get in front of the convict and girl to intercept him. He said he believed he could and took off.

About an hour later, after moving several more times and shooting several more shots, he got up and started to move again and suddenly Willie stood up from behind some bushes with a shotgun leveled at the convict. He told him to drop his weapon. He did because Willie was only a few feet from him.

The convict had sexually assaulted the girl but otherwise she was in good shape. The sheriff from Liberty County arrived, carrying a shotgun. He walked up to the prisoner and broke the handle out of his shotgun over the prisoner's head. The convict fell to the ground and before he could hit him again, Willie Meggs got between them and said "That's enough, sheriff. He's my prisoner and I am taking him back to Tallahassee."

The sheriff was unhappy but backed off. Willie handcuffed the revived convict and took him out of the woods and to the Leon County Jail.

(I can't say enough about Detective Willie Meggs. He is a fine Christian man and one of the hardest workers I have ever been around. In addition to his police work he and a friend had a paint striping business for parking lots. They worked nights and off days to make extra money for their family and to pay for Willie's continuing education at FSU. Meggs later went to law school at FSU, worked as Assistant State Attorney and then was elected State Attorney.)

I picked up the weapon the convict had and showed it to the deputy. It was a nine shot .22 caliber revolver. He said, "Boy, I learned something new today."

President Nixon (1970)

I was a captain and chief of detectives, LCSO, in Tallahassee, Florida, when President Nixon was running for his second term. He was popular at that time, but the Viet Nam war was not. He decided to come to the Florida capitol, and make a speech at the airport.

Crowd control during Nixon visit, Lavelle is on the far right, October, 1970

Radical students at FSU and FAMU were geared up to harass him at the airport. The Secret Service arranged a meeting with the sheriff and ranking police officers to set up his protection.

Through our sources on the college campuses we learned that several thousand students were going to attend the rally and get as close to the speaker's stand as possible. When the President started to speak they planned to disrupt the event. The Secret Service told us we needed to do everything we could to make sure this did not happen.

We decided to rope off several areas and separate the sheep from the goats, so to speak, as they arrived. We knew most of the radicals or the leaders so this was the plan. The sheriff's deputies, Tallahassee police and reserves would man the roped off areas and we hoped we could get all the separation done quickly so there would be no problem near the President.

Next we brought in several paddy wagons, manned by my good friend Capt. C.C. Skidmore of the Florida Marine Patrol, and placed them in strategic areas so they could be reached quickly, but concealed from the goat area so they didn't get suspicious.

As the President arrived, the students came in by the hundreds and they were coming in fast to get a front row seat. The rope separation worked real well for a while, but some of those college students caught on. They started coming out of the roped area. As they came out, we escorted them to the nearest paddy wagon and loaded them. The others got the idea and decided it might be better to stay in the goat area rather than run the risk of riding the paddy wagon to jail.

I am proud to say this was one day the federal, state, county and city agencies worked together and we received a glowing report from the President through his Secret Service. He even sent each officer a gold tie pin with the seal of the President of the United States as his thanks. I was also given a small gold secret service pen to put on my lapel.

The many radicals we had housed in the paddy wagons were punished enough by missing the speech, so we opened the doors and sent them back to school.

Jim White and the LSD Caper

I decided to let Jim make another buy. I was trying to keep him in investigations doing enough good things, so the sheriff would let me keep him. That's what Jim was begging for. The detectives as well as the sheriff questioned why I bothered trying to help him become an investigator. Jim had a great personality, a way of getting along with people and super intelligent. I saw a lot of potential in him.

There was a house out on the edge of town that supposedly was selling LSD for ten dollars a tab. My detectives said the drug dealers were suspicious of undercover buys. As a result, the dealer sometimes made the buyer swallow the tab before he left.

Based on this information, I instructed the detectives to teach their buyers to put the tab under their tongue, simulate swallowing, and then let the dealer see it was gone. Then the buyer was to leave the establishment quickly and take the tab to the detective working the case.

We showed Jim how to do that. In preparation for the buy, we went by to check this place out. There was big irrigation ditch that ran around the house which had a big yard.

Jim had an undercover person, who was a student, prepared to make the drug buy (because Jim got burned on a buy he made earlier). Jim was instructed on how to search his buyer before and after the buy and on how to preserve the evidence for a search warrant.

Jim prepped the guy and showed him how to put it under his tongue. He told him when he came out to go across the yard, walk down the road a little ways and he'd pick him up like he was hitchhiking.

Everything went fine. Jim's undercover informant made the buy and he came running back. Jim was down the road a little ways. The guy came running across the yard just as hard as he could run. When he got to the irrigation ditch, instead of running through it, he tried to jump it. He only made it about half way across before crashing into the bottom of the ditch. He crawled out of the ditch and went and got in Jim's car.

Jim took off. He asked the student if he made the buy, and he said, "Yeah, man. No problem, got it."

Jim said, "Let me have it."

The boy looked at him and said, "I can't. When I fell in that ditch, I swallowed it."

I asked Jim what he did after that and he said, "Captain, I was thinking the kid would go berserk any minute so I took him home."

"You wasted ten dollars of our money and we have no evidence?"

"Captain, he swallowed it, I didn't know what to do."

The other detectives were quick to point out that they had told me he'd screw it up.

Undercover with the Radicals

The sheriff was about to put Jim back serving papers. I approached the sheriff about using Jim as an undercover student to keep us informed about radical students on the FSU campus who were marching and demonstrating in opposition to the Viet Nam War.

These students were giving us fits. They had already taken over a building or two on campus which we had to take back. Everybody was issued riot helmets.

I convinced the sheriff to let Jim get involved in it. He looked like a student anyway. We needed pictures of the people, so Jim started wearing his camera around his neck everywhere he went.

The radicals took him right in. (Dave McGee, a student who later became a top prosecutor in the United States Attorney's Office was one of the members in the radical group at the time.) Jim got to be a member of this outlaw group as their official photographer.

They gave up marching on the campus and started marching on the state buildings. He got pictures of them marching on the courthouse and the capitol. We had to go and lock the capitol doors to keep them from going in there.

Jim came to me and said he had information that the group was going to try to take over the Ft. Benning Army base in Columbus, Georgia on the upcoming Armed Forces Day. The plan was to filter in a few students at a time and when they got enough inside the base, they were going to take over the operations center and embarrass the government.

I contacted the Provost Marshal and told him what information we had. He got really shook up. I said, "Maybe we can help you on this thing."

I had Jim develop all his pictures. There were over 200 photos that had shots of most everyone in the organization. We made copies and sent them to the Provost Marshal.

The day of the big military show there were lots of people (regular citizens along with these radical students) all lined up at the gate to come on base. Every entrance to the base had copies of Jim's photographs. When a radical entered, he or she was pulled out. They lost their opportunity to take over and came back to Tallahassee. They never knew that Jim did it. The command personnel were ecstatic in their appreciation of the Leon County Sheriff's Office. This helped save Jim's job as an investigator.

Defining Dumb

Another time Jim walked in my office and just as serious as could be said, "Captain, do you think I'm dumb?" I laughed and said, "No, Jim, I think you are very smart–just lacking a little common sense, at times.

He said, "Could you come here a minute and I'll prove to you how dumb I am."

I walked into the coffee room and he pointed to all the detectives' diplomas hanging on the walls.

"Do you see any difference in these diplomas?" he asked.

"No, only the dates and the names."

Sheriff's Department Makes $60,000 Marijuana Catch In City
Gene Geiger, Willie Meggs, Sheriff Hamlin, Lavelle Pitts look at haul

Trunkload of Marijuana Diverted at Bus Depot

An all-night vigil by two sheriff's detectives here last night resulted in the confiscation of more than 50 pounds and $60,000 worth of marijuana.

bottles in the trunk, "apparently to neutralize the smell of marijuana." The sheriff said investigation is continuing into the source of the marijuana.

Gene Geiger, Willie Meggs, Sheriff Hamlin, & LaVelle Pitts

He pointed to Gene's diploma and said, "Gene and I went to FSU, took classes together and graduated the same year. Gene never studied. He partied all the time. All those others were about like Gene, except maybe Willie Meggs. I busted my butt day and night to make good grades. Gene paid someone to take most of his tests or bought the answers from someone who had taken the test. Gene partied and got drunk and had a ball and ended up with a diploma exactly like mine. Now doesn't that prove I'm a real dumb ass?"

I said, "No, Jim it might not show on paper but someday you'll have reason to be proud of your effort."

(After I left the Leon County Sheriff's Office, Jim went on to law school and became a lawyer. He was a legal advisor to Florida Governor Bob Graham and later a professor at Florida State University.)

The Case that Changed My Life

When I assumed the position as the Leon County Chief of Detectives, my first marriage had ended a couple of years earlier, and a second marriage had recently ended in divorce. At this point I didn't care to be around women, except maybe to put them in jail.

One morning in 1970, I was on my way back to my office from the FSU campus and received a call from dispatch that the Tallahassee Police Department wished to see me at their office. I was only about a block away so I pulled in and went directly to the criminal division. Entering the office of the chief of detectives, I saw the captain and lieutenant sitting at their conference table with a white female on the far side of the table.

I couldn't tell much about her. She looked like a whipped puppy, appeared to have been crying and seemed as if she had lost her last friend. The captain advised the lady had been kidnapped from the FSU campus, taken out in the county and assaulted. Since the incident took place in the county, they were going to turn the case over to the sheriff's office.

I drove the subject to the hospital for a physical examination. From there I delivered her to her car so she could get cleaned up and change clothes. I gave her directions to the Leon Sheriff's Office located in the courthouse on Monroe Street across from the Capitol Building.

I went down to meet her in the parking garage underneath the courthouse. As I was walking from the elevator, I saw the victim walking through the basement entrance of the parking garage. She was wearing a red mini-dress and had medium-length brown hair. As I watched her approach, the words came to me–*This is the kind of woman I could love and marry*. I immediately rebuked myself and couldn't believe I even thought that.

I opened the elevator with my key and we rode up to the 2nd floor without talking. I got off the elevator and took her to the office of one of my detectives so he could take her complaint and get a statement. I found all the detective offices were empty.

Capt. Pitts and victim at crime scene

I asked my secretary where everyone was and she advised everyone was out to lunch. I looked at my watch and it was a little after 12:00 noon. I asked the victim to come to my office so I could take the report.

I filled out the report and took a statement from her. She advised she was getting out of her car, going to class when this black male grabbed her and put a knife to her throat and forced her to drive to a wooded area in the northern part of Leon County where he sexually assaulted her. During the assault he cut her hand with his knife. He then forced her to drive back and drop him off just outside the city.

After the interview, we returned to the scene of the crime. I assured her we would find the attacker and arrest him. I then delivered her vehicle to FDLE Special Agent Danny Hasty for processing. Danny, I believe, was the best crime scene specialist the State of Florida had at that time.

I called one of our department's black deputies to my office. He was an excellent officer and very good at coming up with information. I explained the case to him and the description of the

330

suspect she gave us. I also requested he make contact with all his sources and encouraged him to put special emphasis on assisting us in finding the suspect on this case.

The victim was a wreck both physically and mentally. She had no family in Tallahassee, so I encouraged her to call me any time day or night if she had any questions or needed updating on the investigation. She did call. She was terrified this person would look her up again. There was a restaurant near her home and we met there for coffee and conversation which seemed to calm her.

I received a call from Agent Hasty advising he had latent fingerprints that he believed were from the suspect. All he needed now was a set of known prints from the suspect.

A few days later, our black deputy called me and advised he had picked up a black male he believed could be the one we were looking for. I met him at the jail and saw that the suspect matched the physical description the victim had furnished us. Major case prints were taken which consisted of hands, palms, and sides of palms and tips of fingers. These were rushed to Agent Hasty for possible identification. The victim was called and asked to come to the county jail and view a line-up. To be admissible in court, the line up had to be made up of several persons similar in appearance.

The victim arrived and was very nervous. We explained that she would not be seen by the suspect. She would be viewing him through a one-way glass. It takes a lot of preparation to set up a suspect line-up and often the victim cannot identify the person or says it looks a little like number so & so, but can't be sure. While we were organizing the line-up, Agent Hasty called and advised he had matched the suspect's prints we sent to him, to those found in the victim's vehicle.

We knew that if the victim couldn't identify the suspect, we still didn't have a really tight case. He could say he had broken into her car to steal something, but never attacked her.

The victim went into the dark room and when the curtain was pulled back from the one-way window she looked at the subjects for a moment and walked out. I said, "Well what do you think?" She called out a number but said she could only be sure if she could hear his voice.

331

The suspect she picked was placed in an office and questioned while the victim stood just outside the door and listened to his voice. She then made a positive ID. The one she selected was the one Agent Hasty had just identified. At this point we had a good case in the making. We assured her that the one she identified was the guilty one and the fingerprints also identified him.

I had the suspect brought into my office. After advising him of his rights, which he said he understood, I started questioning him about his whereabouts on the day and time of the sexual assault. He had it all worked out where he was and whom he was with and did not seem nervous. After listening to him for a period of time, I let him know we knew he was lying and had identified him by his prints and the victim had identified him in the lineup.

Suddenly he was very nervous and sat with his head down for a few minutes and finally said, "You have me. I did it."

I took a sworn statement from him and then did something that, up to that time no one (according to the State Attorney, Bill Hopkins) had ever done and had it introduced into court. I asked the suspect if he would ride with officers and re-enact the crime from FSU to the wooded area and back to where he got out of the victim's car.

He agreed and Detective Jim White videotaped the re-enactment of the area from where he forced the victim back into her car at knife point and the wooded area where the assault took place and back to the dirt road where he got out of her car.

After reviewing the evidence, the attorney for the suspect agreed to a plea of guilty for a life in prison sentence. If he had gone to trial he could have been sentenced to die in the Florida electric chair. At that time, the crime of rape carried a maximum penalty of death.

The victim did recover from all the fear and trauma and graduated from FSU with honors and a master's degree. I returned to Bay County as chief deputy for the Bay County Sheriff's Office and made a lovely lady victim my wife. I convinced her that I would continue to protect her as long as I lived.

We were married at Woodlawn Methodist Church on Panama City Beach in a small wedding with my long time friends, George

Gainer and Sgt.CC Skidmore, as my best men. Also in attendance were Sheriff Easterling and his wife, Carolyn. George took us to Captain Anderson's Restaurant and paid for a big seafood dinner, arranged for a nice motel located on the beautiful Gulf of Mexico and also gave us the use of a new Lincoln car to go to Leesburg later to break the news to my new wife's parents.

I grew up a simple farm boy, average I guess with other boys my age. Like other kids I dreamed of many goals I wanted in life. I wanted her to be good-looking, have a good personality, and be smart. God answered my prayers by wrapping my desires into one person, Sally Jo Landphair. Another blessing is that my first wife, Sarah, lives near us, and we all get along well. I have been blessed with six children–four with Sarah and two with Sally Jo.

I thank God for my salvation and the family He placed in my life.

Back to BCSO Again (1971)

Sheriff Doc Daffin died in early 1971. Tullis Easterling was appointed sheriff and I was asked to return as chief deputy. The position was also referred to as undersheriff or administrative assistant.

**LaVelle, Chief Deputy,
BCSO, 1971**

During this time I was fortunate to gain more experience in drug and narcotics investigations.

Florida Marine Patrol Anti-Drug Smuggling Unit (1973-1980)

In 1973, Harmon Shields, head of the Department of Natural Resources as well as the Florida Marine Patrol, interviewed me about coming to work with the Florida Marine Patrol. He advised he was starting a special drug task force and investigative unit to combat drug importation into the State of Florida by water and air.

SHERIFF'S ADMINISTRATIVE ASSISTANT LAVELLE PITTS (LEFT) AND BAY COUNTY SHERIFF TULLIS EASTERLING reveal part of one $4,500 cache of narcotics taken in a raid recently. It included three "gardens" of growing marijuana, sheets of plain paper dotted with blue spots of LSD and a large quantity of amphetamine capsules. The four arrested in this particular raid were released on $1,000 bond each.

**LaVelle and Sheriff Tullis Easterling, displaying
narcotics contraband.**

News clips from some of the many smuggling cases
worked in the 1970s.

Apalachicola River Detail
Governor Bob Graham, white slacks, Lowell Russ in plain clothes behind him, LaVelle to the right with other FMP officers on one of the governor's work details.

This idea came from Sgt. C.C. Skidmore. Skidmore was a close friend of Mr. Shields and made him aware of the tons of drugs being shipped into Florida by shrimp boats. Very little was being done to stop them and the Coast Guard could only do so much. The program was encouraged and supported by Governor Graham.

Mr. Shields requested that I select a group of officers and train them to work the entire coast around Florida and work with other law enforcement agencies to curtail these large drug shipments. I accepted this position with the rank of Major and immediately started interviewing officers around the state for my team.

I finally chose a team of seven investigators scattered out around the entire coast of Florida. We had some of the finest boats and aircraft available. Each officer had a high speed unmarked boat and an unmarked vehicle. We had access to a twin engine airplane with a pilot.

My first mission was to meet with other law enforcement agencies and gain their cooperation. I visited DEA in Jacksonville and later in Washington and Miami. They were elated and assured me of their full cooperation. The U.S. Customs Offices were visited in Miami and New Orleans, and then Washington D.C. FDLE as well as sheriffs and police chiefs from around the State were asked to join us in a united drug fighting force. DEA and Customs Patrol were eager to get involved because of our manpower and equipment along the entire coast of the State of Florida.

This new Florida Marine Patrol Team along with U.S. Customs, Customs Patrol, DEA and local sheriffs, police officers and IRS Investigators were responsible for seizing the largest shipments of drugs ever seized in the USA up to that time. Hundreds of tons of marijuana and other drugs, vehicles, boats, aircraft, guns, buses, motor homes, and U.S. currency were intercepted while this task force was in place.

United Press International

Raid gets cash, drugs

A tip from a motel clerk led to the seizure of more than $1 million in cash and seven pounds of cocaine Monday night in what police say wa

Working Drug Smuggling

Based on information, received by Marine Patrol investigators there was a shrimp boat loaded with marijuana en route from

Columbia, South America to St. George Island. This island is located near Apalachicola, Florida. I contacted Franklin County Sheriff Taylor as well as my regular working buddies in DEA and Customs Patrol.

We set up a meeting at the sheriff's beach cottage on St. George Island. This meeting was to organize a joint task force to intercept the load when it reached its destination. This was a meeting similar to the many we were now organizing with DEA, Customs Patrol, and local law enforcement agencies that happened to be in the area where a load was expected to off-load.

LaVelle working a detail with investigators and officers.

The Special Agents in Charge of DEA and Customs Patrol, the sheriff or police chief of the jurisdiction we were in and I, as chief of the Marine Patrol Drug unit, stayed together with hand-held radios so we could speak to our investigators. We were all on different radio frequencies. With the officers in charge staying together, all the agents got the same orders and we knew the people around them were "singing out of the same hymn book."

Together, we made a formidable group that gave a lot of smugglers a welcoming party when they arrived in Florida from Columbia, Jamaica and Mexico. Most of our drugs were coming from these three locations.

Another thing U.S. Customs Patrol occasionally did was swear in all the Florida Marine Patrol Officers as U.S. Customs Patrol Officers so we were covered by the federal government for arrest and injury purposes.

Sheriff Taylor was known as a great host, and he suggested we have a cookout at his beach cottage. It was two days before the load was due. We were able to use this time to get to know all the strange faces from the various agencies involved in the operation. We had a good time in spite of our DEA friends from Louisiana who insisted on making the seafood gumbo Cajun style. I watched those guys throw all kinds of sea-going varmints into a large pot along with crabs. They ribbed me a little but after seeing eyeballs floating around in the boiling water, there was no way I could eat it.

After socializing, we got to work on a game plan. Department heads were to stay out of sight in the sheriff's cottage. Three unmarked FMP boats, each manned with a Marine Patrol officer and a Customs or DEA officer, drifted around the island. They had rods and reels with a metal nut or spark plug weight on the end of the line but no hook, so they could pretend to fish. Another unmarked patrol boat slowly moved around the area trolling in the event the drug vessel came in at a different location on the island or anchored in deep water and then offloaded. There were other marked patrol boats concealed with uniformed officers in locations where they could respond rapidly when called.

Our information was that the off-loading crew would not go out until the drug vessel came in as close to the island as possible and dropped anchor. Usually mullet flat bottom boats were used by the off-load crew because they could haul several hundred pounds of marijuana and travel in real shallow water almost to the shore.

They normally off-loaded at a location as near the bank as possible so the transport vehicles could get loaded quickly. Each vehicle picked up a quantity that was prearranged and pulled out.

340

The next truck pulled in and went through the same process. This continued until the vessel had off-loaded its shipment of compacted baled marijuana.

Typical off-loading procedure—Here officers off-load an intercepted marijuana drop near Vero Beach

This was the procedure used at most off-load sites. From experience, we had developed a system for intercepting large loads of marijuana especially if our prior information was good. But the best of plans go awry occasionally, even with good information. This load was no exception.

The large shrimp boat arrived as scheduled, several mullet skiffs gathered, but no trucks showed up on the island. It dawned on us the mullet skiffs were going to deliver their loads to various locations along the coast line and not the island. We had to make a quick decision. We decided to intercept the off-load boats as they left the mother ship rather than chance losing some of them going off in different directions. With this in mind, we radioed each patrol boat to intercept the mullet skiffs after they left the mother ship and moved quite a distance from the off-loading site. They

341

were to board, arrest, cuff, and escort their seizure to a location where uniformed officers waited on patrol cars.

The problems started when the mullet skiffs refused to stop and headed for the shallow water of the island. They made it to shore and our patrol boats with the large motors were stranded on the sand bars. As soon as the dopers hit the island they jumped out of the boats and started running across the sand dunes. All the officers in the command post immediately moved out and started chasing the dopers on foot. Some we caught and some got away.

We did get the mother ship and several tons of marijuana. I tracked someone running across the sand dunes. About 300 yards from where they came ashore, I ran up on a wire cage with two beautiful parrots inside. I guess the doper decided he could make better time without these little prizes in his arms. I rescued the parrots and brought them home. We named them Mary Jane and Reefer (slang terms or marijuana).

Often the law violators involved in these shipments were fishermen who stopped fishing and started hauling dope. Marine Patrol officers visited marinas around the state as a routine. Any shrimp boats with rusted cables and winches became suspect, since their equipment wasn't being used to haul in shrimp.

Seeing new trucks and other vehicles parked near the boat was another clue. Sometimes they checked out the boat owner's house and found him living in a new brick home with a new Mercedes sport car in the driveway. This was a good indication that this person was living far above his means of fishing for a living. A photograph was taken of the shrimp boat and sent to my office at Marine Patrol headquarters. I made flyers of suspected drug boats and owners and sent them to DEA, US Customs Patrol and all of the FMP officers throughout the state.

The majority of the people in the finance end of smuggling marijuana and other drugs were business-types. Most of the smuggling organizers had contacts with local businessmen and women, lawyers, doctors and some law enforcement. Getting into smuggling could be an attractive temptation to those who saw they could double and triple their investment in 30 to 60 days.

Once the money people were lined up, owners of commercial fishing boats were contacted. Fishermen were often barely earning a living and they could make $50,000 for each trip. A trip usually took two to four weeks. A shrimp boat captain told me that one trip made him more money than he had made in all his years of fishing.

The organizer, after he had his financing arranged, made contact with his source in South America and obtained a LORAN reading for the exact location to pick up the drugs. In most cases the captain was given three or four different locations to deliver his load. As he got within radio contact with the financer, he was told which site to steer to. Sometimes they changed locations two or three times before the load made shore.

One load was to be dropped near Port St. Joe, Florida and was changed to a location near Daytona Beach on the East Coast. Just hours before landing near Daytona Beach, they changed again to a large Georgia plantation several miles past Jacksonville, Florida. This load was well-organized and well-scouted by sources known only to DEA.

We had a small aircraft following the progress of the ship. We moved a lot of officers each time the aircraft advised us they were passing up another suspected off-load site. One of the sites was St. Augustine. The agency heads set up a command post at a motel there and it was so cold, there was a rare snow. When we received notice that they were passing up the St. Augustine offload site, we had to race to our cars to move out again. The steps were so icy I fell down a flight of stairs into the snow. The snow had covered our vehicles, so we had to run around the parking lot scraping snow off the license tags to identify our cars before we could leave.

When we left Florida we lost all the local officers and U.S. Customs quickly swore all my Florida Marine Patrol officers in as U.S. Customs Patrol officers and we continued into Georgia.

We arrived about midnight, during the offloading of the mother ship. All the bad guys ran leaving the marijuana behind and the boat still running. A Marine Patrol officer and DEA agent ran to secure the boat which was left in gear and gradually started moving out to sea while they were searching it. Fortunately for us and the DEA agent and Marine Patrol officer knew how to bring the boat back in to shore.

343

Special Agent Ginley notified Georgia authorities and requested help in securing the plantation. We decided not to send anyone into the swamps for fear of them getting lost and/or freezing to death. We tried to build a big fire by piling up all the wood we could find in the area, but it wouldn't start because the wood was wet. There were several gas cans sitting by the dock, and one of the guys picked up a can and brought it back to start the fire.

He spread fuel all over the wood and walked several yards away and set the gas can next to several other gas cans near our patrol cars. A match was put to the wood and a huge fire ignited, but immediately spread on a trail headed toward the gas can that apparently leaked. Everyone rushed to move their vehicles and I headed for the gas can. I made it just before the fire did and threw it into a safe area. Disaster averted.

The decision Ginley made to hold our troops out of the swamp, turned out to be a good choice. With our warm fire burning brightly, the boat crew and off-loaders started drifting out of the swamp. They decided they would rather face jail than to freeze to death in the cold, dark swamp.

To our amazement, two of those who came out of the swamp claimed to be Harvard professors. They disclaimed being a part of the drug operation and tried to convince us that they were supporters of President Jimmy Carter and trying to find his farm. One of the DEA officers spoke up and said that alone was enough to put them in jail. It turned out they were a part of the off-loading crew and it was later discovered they really were Harvard professors.

These are examples of typical drug operations we worked all over our state. There were several drug-related millionaires in Georgia and Florida who were less than 30 years of age. Most were college graduates. One guy had large horse farms in north Florida and south Georgia. He was 26 years old.

There were a number of commercial fishermen who obtained great wealth in drug importation and distributions that we identified. Where we sometimes failed to obtain enough evidence to tie them directly to a load, we could always depend on the IRS to move in and lend a helping hand.

Working with task force loading a seizure made in Old
Rose Harbor, Key West, 1974

In one case that was brought to federal court, the judge forfeited all the convicted doper's property. His wife's two vehicles, his farm, cattle, horses, tractor and other equipment all became the property of the U.S. Government. The man and his wife, who were standing in front of the judge's bench complained. The man said, "Judge, the only thing you have left my wife and me is the ring on her finger. The judge looked over at the U.S. Marshal in the court and instructed him to remove the ring from her finger. He did.

The different agencies worked well together but we did learn from experience to be very careful when sharing information. On one occasion we wasted several weeks on surveillance and stake-outs sharing our information with a local sheriff. We found out later he was passing on this information to the smuggling group we were trying to bust. We finally resolved that situation by busting the group and DEA arrested the sheriff and charged and convicted him in federal court.

DC-3 Aircraft and Drug Smuggling

DC3 seized in Franklin County, 1978

We discovered that many of the smugglers were going to Arizona and purchasing old surplus DC-3 military aircraft. This was a twin engine aircraft that had a lot of empty space for drugs. The aircraft were relatively cheap and with little effort could be flown to Columbia, Mexico and other small countries to pick up a load of marijuana, coke or Quaaludes. The aircraft was flown back to the U.S. and came into Florida very low to get under the radar. The plane was landed at some deserted airstrip in the Panhandle or in a marshy area like the Everglades.

An off-load crew was ready, removed the load and the plane could be gone in minutes. If the plane landed in the Everglades, air boats picked up the shipment and the plane was simply left behind. Every so often we got a report from one of our pilots that another DC-3 was down in the Glades. We knew another load had made it in.

After Georgia Senator Nunn used his influence to get us military help, we started to cut out many of the DC-3 flights. Working with DEA in the Central Florida area we got a call that an F-15 fighter plane of the U.S. Air Force was escorting a DC-3 in from the Gulf and forcing it to land in Orlando. The plane landed with the F-15 next to it. The three guys on the DC-3 were scared stiff.

One suspect, during questioning, said they were bringing in a load of Quaaludes from Mexico and flying about 500 feet above the Gulf of Mexico. He said he had no idea where the F-15 came from, but suddenly the pilot dropped down next to them.

As the suspects on the DC-3 stared at the pilot, he dropped his rockets into firing position. They feared being blown out of the sky and no one ever knowing what happened to them. The suspect said he grabbed a handful of Quaaludes and started eating them like popcorn to settle his nerves. The Air Force pilot gave hand signals to follow him and he took them into the Orlando airport. Though facing arrest, he said he was glad to get back on the ground.

Another DC-3 was spotted on its way to land on an abandoned air strip near Apalachicola, Florida. This time the F-15 pilot who provided 'escort' couldn't land there but contacted us. We made arrangements for a welcoming party to greet that plane.

Marijuana Cargo Seized

A four-engined airplane, and 000 pounds of marijuana alued at $3,200,000 were seized nd two men arrested by ieriff's deputies, Marine atrol, FDCLE and customs officers in a surprise raid at the arrabelle airport Thursday orning.

Acting on information that eDC-3 plane that had just land-

Lauderdale.

Those arrested were booked at the Franklin County Jail, and the plane, an old prop type, was flown to Tallahassee for storage.

Officers revealed few details of the case but said the plane is believed to have been flown in from Colombia. Its destination is not known.

county, state and Customs, have been kept increasingly busy trying to stop the flow of marijuana into the state. Recently a 70-foot shrimp boat with several tons of marijuana was seized at Tarpon Springs. No arrests were made.

"We're probably getting only 10 per cent of the marijuana coming into the state by various means", an officer who declined

> Plane held cargo with value estimated at
> $3,200,000.

U.S. Customs had their air wing at Homestead Air Force Base on the edge of Miami near Key West. We got to know these guys really well and worked with them on a regular basis. One of our FMP Investigators and I were there on the day a Cuban pilot flew a Russian MIG in from Cuba and landed at the Air Force base before anyone realized our air space had been invaded. Apparently the Cuban pilot believed he could get lots of money for a Russian MIG and decided he would rather live in the land of the free with a pocketful of U.S. Dollars than in Castro's Cuba. The pilot made out, but I can't say the same for the Base Commander and others who failed to see an enemy aircraft come in to the USA unobserved.

I had an opportunity to talk to some of our Air Force pilots at TAFB in Panama City, Florida, about the role they were playing in the drug traffic entering Florida by air. They said it was fairly easy to spot when they saw an aircraft cruising into Florida at 100 to 500 feet above the water. One pilot told me that before the Air Force got the word from Sen. Nunn, he intercepted a DC-3 over the Gulf and dropped his rockets down. The occupants of the DC-3 frantically started pushing bales of marijuana out of the aircraft. He estimated several thousand pounds of marijuana went into the Gulf of Mexico. After they dumped their load the Air Force pilot peeled off and let them go. He said, "I figured the guys in the DC-3 would get themselves killed when they showed up with no marijuana for the money invested, especially when they said a fighter plane made them do it."

Rags to Riches (1973)

A short time after I had the investigators in place in my drug unit with the Marine Patrol, Captain Gordon McCall, district commander with an office in Panama City, sent a uniformed officer to Tallahassee with a cardboard box full of small green plants. He brought them into my office and advised he had found them growing wild on the bank of the Intercoastal Waterway (ICW) in Gulf County. The Captain wanted me to look at them and see if they were marijuana plants.

They were small marijuana plants. They apparently had grown where a load of marijuana had been off-loaded on the bank of the ICW. The officer had two or three different sizes which led me to believe this was a regular drop off site for vessels passing through the ICW from the Gulf. We inspected the site, and as suspected, there were several different sizes of marijuana plants indicating several different off-loads.

We set up surveillance in a State Forestry Tower in view of the ICW and invited FDLE to work with us. We began noticing a lot of traffic at a big barn within a mile of the off-load site. On the 23rd of December we determined the barn was definitely connected with the off-load site and we had enough probable cause to raid the barn.

Largest marijuana seizure in U.S. history at that time, 1973, in Overstreet, Florida. LaVelle far right talking to DNR Director Harmon Shields

Inside we found 26 tons of marijuana bales. This was the largest seizure of marijuana ever made in the United States up to that time. We arrested the owner of the farm, Sparky Raffield, a commercial fisherman from Bay County.

I advised him of his rights and told him he probably should call a lawyer. He said "Man you caught me, why should I call a lawyer? I told him he could spend several years in prison. He replied, "I'm just caught. That's the price you have to pay sometimes. I don't need a lawyer to tell me that."

The following day was Christmas Eve and I visited Sparky in the Gulf County Jail. I advised him of his rights again and again he declined. He agreed to give me a statement, but refused to give me any details on any others who were involved. He had off-

349

loaded the marijuana from a large shrimp boat and hauled it to his barn with his tractor. It was to be picked up later by someone else and hauled to other locations. He said he would tell me anything I wanted to know, but he wouldn't squeal on his friends. He did just that. No amount of questioning could change his mind about giving the identity of his friends.

I had known Sparky ever since I started work at the Bay County Sheriff's Office in 1957. He had several children and a wife and a good reputation as captain of a party boat and commercial fishing. After finishing with a formal statement, I asked if he was sorry he had gotten involved in smuggling now that he faced prison time.

He sat there, silent, for a moment or two then smiled and said, "LaVelle you have known me for a long, long time and you know I have never had anything but an old shrimp boat, a wife, and a rented house full of hungry youn'uns. Look at me now. I have this nice farm, a tractor, a new truck, new barn, cows, chickens, and my kids have cars of their own. You asked me if I would do it again? Yes, sir, I dang sure would. For the past two or three years I have been 'n--rich' and I am not sorry one bit. Hauling marijuana on a shrimp boat pays a lot more than hauling mullet or shrimp and is much easier."

Sparky explained in detail how they went about bringing in loads of marijuana from Columbia. He furnished details, but would not give up his contacts or the money people. He described the operations as follows:

A contact person went to certain money people in the community and showed them how they could get a high rate of return within 30 days if they fronted the money to bring a load of drugs into the country. The only risk was if the load was busted or hijacked before they got it to the buyers. At that time law enforcement people knew we were lucky if we caught 10 percent of the marijuana and other drugs being shipped into the United States. The finance people stood a 90 percent chance of being winners. According to Sparky, very few declined taking a chance. Many poor commercial fishermen became millionaires almost overnight.

I asked Sparky how he could find the exact spot he was supposed to make his pick-up on the Columbia coast. He said, "No problem, they gave me a LORAN reading. If there's a beer can on the spot and the reading is correct I can drop an anchor on top of it. I asked a friend, who owned a shrimp boat if this was true and he said, "With Sparky that was true." Sparky was an expert on navigation.

Sparky wouldn't tell me how many loads he had brought in, but did give me an example of how he almost got caught one time. He said he had sent two people to pick up a load from Columbia on his shrimp boat. They were to bring the load back into the ICW from the Gulf at Port St. Joe.

As they were getting into the channel to go under the bridge on U.S Highway 98 the propeller on the shrimp boat fell off. They immediately threw out the anchor and dived overboard and swam to the shore. They left the boat alone with several tons of marijuana on board. The two guys went down the highway and called Sparky from a phone booth and told him what happened. He told them to go back to the boat and stay there until he could bring another boat out and tow them in.

They were afraid to go back because two Marine Patrol officers had been in the area and passed by the shrimp boat two or three times. Sparky picked up a smaller boat the following day and went to the location and tied on to the loaded boat and pulled it all the way down the ICW to the site where an off-load crew was waiting to unload it. He said a patrol boat passed by a couple times while he was towing the shrimp boat and he just waved at them and they continued on. The two guys that had brought the load left and he never saw them again.

Sparky pled guilty in the 26-ton seizure case, went to prison and never testified against his friends. He said enough that I felt sure I knew some of his money people, but there was no way we could prove it without Sparky's testimony. Some of these people were well-known business people in the Bay County area and some held very important political positions with the State and Federal government.

Sparky didn't stay in prison very long. He was suddenly let out on early release. I am sure someone in power wanted Sparky out of prison before he decided to cut a deal with law enforcement or before he got over being loyal to his friends and started talking.

Sparky came home a different person. He found the Lord while in prison. A lot of people seem to find the Lord when they are in jail and that's called "jail house religion." It usually lasts until they get out of jail. It was different with Sparky, it stuck.

After prison, Sparky got a trolling boat and took people out on half or full day fishing trips or sightseeing trips. He tied up at Smith's Yacht Basin next to Beck Avenue. Gene Ford, a good friend of mine, said that when he wasn't on the water, he sat in the stern of the boat, facing the sidewalk along Beck Avenue, picked his guitar and sang Christian songs. If anyone stopped for a moment, he told them about fishing trips, what fish were biting, his rates for a half or full day fishing, answered all their questions and after he really had their attention, he told them about Jesus.

I had to go check it out for myself. As I got out of my car on Beck Avenue, strains of music filled the air. It was Sparky thumping on an old guitar and singing *I'll Fly Away*. I sat and talked to him for a few minutes and even bought a half day trip for my family on his boat. The family was somewhat concerned, knowing I had sent Sparky to prison, but I assured them I trusted Sparky much more than I did some judges and politicians I had met over the years. We went and caught lots of fish and had a great time watching the porpoises.

Florida Barge Canal (1978)

I was working on a case and staying at a motel in St. Petersburg, when two Florida Marine Patrol Officers contacted me. They advised they were checking out a report of a large yacht that had entered the Florida Barge Canal from the Gulf of Mexico just before dark. It apparently docked some place in the canal because the boat never came out. This canal was between Inglis and Crystal River, Florida.

The two officers reported they were picking up two Coast Guard Officers in Inglis and hoped to enter the barge canal discreetly and check out the large vessel without being seen. I immediately left St. Petersburg and headed for the barge canal.

The officers launched their 24-foot patrol boat from a boat landing in Inglis and planned to travel along the coast line and enter the barge canal with no lights. Their intentions were good, but they ran into a heavy fog restricting their visibility to only a few feet. They were off the shore line and could not see the canal.

They circled around and soon determined they were hopelessly lost out in the Gulf and couldn't find the canal until the fog lifted.

One of the officers noticed that three porpoise had been moving alongside their small craft and each time they changed direction, so did the porpoise. The officer reported to me later that someone in the boat suggested they follow the porpoise and see where they took them.

They gradually turned the boat and followed the porpoise swimming in front of the boat. The officer said, "Major, I didn't put this in my report because all the guys would make fun of us. But so help me, those porpoise took us straight to the mouth of the barge canal and up to this vessel where bales of marijuana were being off-loaded onto trucks and trailers on the bank."

No doubt God was on the side of the good guys that night. The officer said that there was no way they would have found the entrance to the barge canal until the fog lifted, which would have been two or three hours later.

The officers notified other officers standing by in patrol cars. They moved in by way of a small two-lane dirt road that ran from Highway 98 about a half-mile down to the canal where the vessel was tied up.

The off-load crew could not get their vehicles out so they took off through the woods on foot. For the remainder of the night officers of the FHP, FMP, local police and sheriff's deputies combed the woods and Highway 98 for the suspects. There were about eighteen vehicles seized along with a large Blue-Bird motor home, being used as the command post. The yacht, out of Jamaica, had about 26 tons of marijuana on board.

The Jamaican in charge was a guy who went by the name of Keith Jordan. We learned he was well known in Jamaica after questioning the arrested crew and receiving intelligence from the Jamaican government. People in Jamaica feared him and some even worshipped him as Jesus Christ. Some of the Jamaican government officials we talked to later were fearful of Jordan finding out they were helping Americans.

Several hours after the raid, an FHP Officer picked up Jordan on the highway hitchhiking. He tried to convince the officer he was just passing through on his way to Miami, but the trooper didn't buy his story. He was cuffed and deposited in the Citrus County Jail along with twenty others.

Religious cult pot suspects freed on bond

Sentinel Star Bureau

INVERNESS — Eight religious cultists charged with possession of marijuana and conspiracy were freed from the Citrus County Jail Monday after an Islamorado bonding agency posted reduced bonds of $100,000 each.

The seven men being held in the county jail were freed after the Shaffer Bonding Agency posted the bonds. A woman, Mary Anne Morrison, 24, of Miami, who was being held at the Sumter County Jail in Bushnell, also was released.

The eight were being held in lieu of $500,000 bond each but the 2nd District Court of Appeal in Lakeland Friday ordered a hearing for the eight defendants by 5 p.m. Monday to determine if the state could provide "probable cause" for the high bonds.

But 5th Circuit Judge William F. Edwards signed an order Monday lowering the bonds.

Citrus County Circuit Court clerks said the "probable cause" hearing was not held.

Released were: William F. Reid, 26, Ray J. Smith, 30, Michael J. Booth, 30, Steven R. Burns, 30, Robert W. Lawler, 25, Bradford E. Rush, 32, Carl D. Swanson, 33, and Morrison.

The eight were among 18 arrested after a Feb. 2 raid on a 60-foot yacht from which 13 tons of marijuana was being unloaded at the mouth of the Cross-Florida Barge Canal.

The Zion Coptic religious cult claimed that smoking marijuana was a part of their religion.

Lawyers quickly arrived in Crystal River and demanded the sheriff feed the group a special diet because they were a religious group called the Zion Coptics. The sheriff informed the lawyers the prisoners had to eat what the other inmates ate.

After conferring with their clients the lawyers again approached the sheriff and offered to pay for all the food for the jail if the sheriff would prepare the special food their clients wanted. The sheriff told me later he could not pass that up and agreed. Large trucks started bringing in all kinds of food from Miami for the Coptic group as well as what the sheriff requested for the other prisoners.

The judge set $100,000 bond on Jordan and a couple others; $50,000 was set on the rest of the suspects. By this time they had been in jail for two or three weeks and the sheriff told me he was getting attached to this weird bunch. They were saving the county a lot of money by paying the jail food bills.

As soon as the preliminary hearings were over and bond was set, a private jet came into the area from Miami and some people brought cash money to put up bail for all the persons arrested. Not only did they make bond they put up bond for many of their American cell mates who were in jail for various criminal charges.

A big stretch limo pulled in front of the jail. Jordan marched out and a beautiful blonde lady driver rushed around and opened the side door for him. He got in and she quickly drove away. So far as we know Jordan was back in Jamaica within a few hours after making bond.

Utilizing state, federal and county officers, we set up an escort for the seized vehicles, trucks and marijuana. Everything was transported to the county fairgrounds in Tallahassee and placed under guard.

Drug raids resulted in the seizure of not only drugs but equipment such as boats, trucks and motorhomes.

FDLE assisted in processing the marijuana and other evidence seized as well as taking a small sample from each bale of marijuana so we could destroy this huge truck load of dope.

In an effort to learn more about Jordan and his operation in Jamaica, we got permission from Mr. Shields, my boss, to fly to Jamaica on the FMP twin engine airplane. Besides the pilot and me, we took along investigators from IRS, US Customs, FDLE and DEA.

The U.S. State Department had to get permission to fly over Cuba and this took a few days. Finally we took off and while flying over Cuba we were intercepted by a couple of Russian MIGs. That caused a few tense moments watching the heavily armed MIGs flying next to us and eyeballing us. We wondered if they had gotten the word that we had permission to fly over Cuba. They finally peeled off and left us as we cleared Cuba.

Constables in Jamaica

Arriving in Kingston, Jamaica we were met by a group of constables on a large government van and escorted to the Sheraton Hotel where we checked in for the night. Having been warned not to drink their water, we each had a bottle of beer after dinner and sat around the pool discussing our next move.

Several times individuals approached us and tried to bribe us into taking them back into the U.S. I was amazed at how desperate some of these people were to get out of Jamaica. All the ones who approached me were women. They offered money, sex, maid service for my family for as long as I wished. Some just begged and pleaded for us to sneak them onto our aircraft and get them out of Jamaica.

Leaving the hotel the following morning, we were picked up by five heavily armed constables driving a large van. They gave us a grand tour through town. There were a lot of people and vehicles around, but no street signs, stop signs or traffic lights. As our driver neared an intersection, he just blew the horn, barely slowed down and roared through.

We noted several trucks near the airport and waterfront that had Zion Coptic decals on the doors. This was the beginning of our grand tour of Jordan's empire. We went far up in the mountains and much of the travel was on old river beds that had dried up. They had been converted into trails for tourists.

As we left the city, the constable in charge of our detail told us they had made a marijuana bust the previous night. He said they had arrested an employee from a local mattress company trying to slip a mattress on board a ship that was stuffed with marijuana instead of cotton. We asked how many were arrested and he said everyone connected with the company. He stated that, by their law, anyone who worked in a corporation or owned stock in the corporation was subject to arrest. I thought we were tough on dopers.

As we neared Jordan's headquarters, it was obvious the constables were getting nervous. They kept telling us to be very careful as the Coptics had guards everywhere. There was a chain link fence, about six feet high with three strands of barb wire on the top, totally enclosing the Zion Coptic property belonging to Jordan.

Zion Coptic leader, Keith Jordan's guarded compound in Jamaica

The IRS investigator started taking pictures of the fenced-in area and the constable in charge started yelling, "Put down the camera. Put down the camera!" He did not, and the trip suddenly ended with the van making a hasty trip back to the city.

On the way back to the city, the constable pointed out several persons in prison uniforms working on the roads. He proudly pointed them out and said those were the ones they arrested last night.

I asked if it was legal to work a prisoner before he was tried and convicted. He said, "They were tried this morning, convicted and sentenced. They are now wards of the government." These people dealt their justice out with unbelievable speed.

The following morning we went to the government building at the request of the IRS investigator for a record search on the Zion Coptic group. They reluctantly agreed. Again we found doors closed and no information available. We decided to head back to the USA, much to the delight of the constables.

U.S. officials on the Jamaican trip

Depositions were held in Miami for the 21 defendants. Each defendant had an attorney defending him. Since I held all the evidence and photographs and did many of the interviews, I stayed on the witness stand for 8 hours. We did break one hour for lunch. They had 21 lawyers and we had one Assistant U.S. Attorney, who happened to be a young lady and very sharp. She was learned in Federal law and quick to jump on the other lawyers when they strayed from agreed ground rules.

The first three were tried and found guilty and the other 18 (including Jordan) never showed up for trial and forfeited their bonds. However, two of the 18, about a year or so later, were killed in a plane crash near the Suwannee River, bringing in a load of drugs on a twin engine plane.

The vehicles and motor home that we seized became the property of the State of Florida. Forfeiture hearings were held on all the property and no one showed up to contest.

God sent a whale to swallow Jonah and ultimately got him on the right track. Did He send three porpoise to lead these Marine Patrol officers straight to the smugglers?

Marijuana Burning

One of my investigators located a large warehouse in Tallahassee where marijuana was being stored just off I-10 awaiting transport to other parts of the nation. As a result of our raid, we seized over 41 tons of marijuana, another record- breaking seizure.

Tallahassee warehouse with 41 tons of marijuana.
LaVelle speaking to federal agents.

In the meantime, former LCSO detective Jim White had finished law school and was a legal advisor to Governor Bob Graham. Jim helped get a destruction order from a judge to burn the marijuana at the county landfill. I didn't go initially, but Jim was enthused about the seizure and accompanied the officers to witness the destruction.

Needless to say, there was a great fire and a number of officers were present from the city, county and state. What they didn't take into account was the possible effect on the officers breathing too much of the smoke from the burning marijuana.

359

Jim White, center, with LaVelle and an FMP officer at a marijuana
burning in Tallahassee. This photo was taken about 5 years after
Jim's undercover work. He went on to law school and became a
prosecuting attorney, law school professor and legal adviser to
Governor Graham

Several of the men were getting high. The marijuana was
spread out and needed to be pushed up into a pile. There was a
bulldozer sitting nearby, but no driver. I was told that Jim
volunteered to drive it.

He got the dozer started and did pretty well pushing a load up
to the fire, but didn't know how to stop. He went through that fire
and managed to come out on the other side unhurt.

At this point, one of my investigators called and suggested I
come out to the landfill. When I got there I made them get further
back from the smoke.

 Common sense trumps education sometimes.

Sandy Creek Case (1977-78)
An officer from the Bay County FMP Office brought some plants
found on a small creek adjoining the Intercoastal Waterway to
Tallahassee for identification. It was marijuana.

We immediately opened an investigation on Sandy Creek.
We found several bales of marijuana floating and a skiff sunk near

360

the edge of the canal. It appeared that a large load of marijuana had been off-loaded and probably interrupted for some reason.

Further investigation determined that two young sisters had been reported missing by their mother and it was believed that they were in the company of two white males. The two males Hood and Sims were well known to local law enforcement. I had had prior dealings with them from my years spent with the Bay County Sheriff's Office and as Chief of Police in the City of Springfield. (See story about Challenge to a Duel by Drunk Junior High Student.)

A few days later two scuba divers from Perry, Florida found four bodies weighted down with builders blocks in a deep spring outside Perry. The bodies were identified as the two young girls and the two white males reported missing in Bay County.

After finding the marijuana debris, we tried to get other agencies involved in the investigation. Because of the evidence at the scene, it was obvious this was a very big load of marijuana and a lot of people had to have been involved in the off-loading and hauling the drugs away. DEA and Customs Patrol did assist, but the local Bay County Sheriff's Office did not offer any assistance. FDLE did not show any interest. After the bodies were found and identified suddenly we had many agencies offering assistance and support with the exception of the BCSO. They never did show any interest.

To make matters even more complicated, a few days after the botched off-load of marijuana, we received a report of a missing yacht, the PIRATES LADY. This yacht was last heard of when it docked in Apalachicola, Florida, about the same time and date of the Sandy Creek incident. This was where the Intercoastal Waterway emptied into the Gulf of Mexico. From evidence gathered at the off-load site, we had tentatively identified the drug vessel as the GUNSMOKE.

FMP Investigator Patterson in Bradenton, Florida, made contact with a confidential source. This person had furnished reliable information in the past, according to Patterson. The source advised the investigator that the Gunsmoke had indeed begun to make a prearranged off-load of marijuana in the Intercoastal Waterway and Sandy Creek.

He said the people who were killed happened up on the off-load site and an argument took place between one of the victims and the two guards posted on the dirt road that came off Highway 22 to the off-load site. The victim was shot by one of the guards and the other three were tied up and placed in an off-load worker's van.

In the meantime, a tug boat came down the ICW and his spot light shined across the Gunsmoke. Fearing they had been spotted and hearing that an intruder had been killed the off-loading was quickly discontinued and the trucks and other vehicles fled the area.

The Gunsmoke fled up the ICW and pulled into Port St. Joe, Florida. They tied up near the Pirates Lady and went aboard and found two people working on some equipment. They took possession of the Pirates Lady and the two men on board and headed out into the Gulf of Mexico. The intentions were to scuttle the Gunsmoke and use the Pirates Lady.

After looking over all the state-of-the-art equipment on the Pirates Lady they knew this vessel would be impossible to keep without being detected. With this in mind they scuttled the Pirates Lady after killing the two occupants. They continued on down toward Bradenton and called friends who came out in the Gulf and met them. They scuttled the Gunsmoke and went into a marina near Bradenton.

363

By this time we, the Florida Marine Patrol, found more help than we ever imagined. The agencies that got involved after the bodies were found and the Pirates Lady went missing included FDLE, FBI, DEA, US CUSTOMS, COAST GUARD, as well as several local and state agencies on the Gulf Coast. But we still needed help additional assistance to locate the vessels.

We asked for help from the U.S. Navy and struck out. We did get assistance from the Air Force after U.S. Senator Nunn from Georgia met with the drug task force in Miami. We explained our situation and asked for his help in getting the military to assist. He told us he felt that he might be able to assist us in that matter as he happened to be on the military appropriations committee.

Sunken vessel may hold clues to many crimes

By MICHAEL WHITELEY
Times-Union Business Writer

A Congressional subcommittee probing drug smuggling, murder and piracy on the high seas will ask the White House and the U.S. attorney general for help in raising the sunken shrimper Gunsmoke from its watery grave off the coast near St. Petersburg.

The Gunsmoke, a 55-foot steel-hulled shrimper, was linked last year to an aborted Panama City pot-smuggling operation and the execution of four people whose bodies

were feared hijacked along the Gulf Coast of Louisiana, Alabama and Florida during 1976 and 1977. The FBI was assigned to the case and has made no arrests to date.

Four days before the Pirate's Lady disappearance, the marijuana laden Gunsmoke dropped anchor off the shore of Sandy Creek, near Panama City. There workers began to off load about 40 tons of marijuana. The operation was aborted when two ex convicts and their female compan ions drove up to the loading site and quarreled with guards in the smug

An all-out search was made by military aircraft, Coast Guard, Florida Marine Patrol air craft and patrol boats. There was no sign of either the Gunsmoke or the Pirates Lady in the Gulf of Mexico. That left us with the thought that both vessels could very well have been scuttled to avoid detection.

My boss, Harmon Shields, Executive Director of the Florida Department of Natural Resources, made contact with NOAA (NATIONAL OCEANIC AND ATMOSPHERIC ADMINISTRATION). They agreed to meet our 51-foot state patrol boat off the coast of central Florida and begin a bottom search in the Gulf. There were two NOAA patrol boats about 65 feet long with a crew of sailors and divers. They explained they were on their way to an assignment on the other coast and could only assist us for a day or two

The NOAA Commander explained how the search was going to be conducted. The two NOAA boats would run parallel to each other and stay a great distance apart. They would let a steel cable down with buoys attached to hold the cable at a depth just off the bottom of the Gulf. When they hooked something the buoy on top of the water would go up and down like a fishing cork. They would stop both vessels and their divers would board a life boat and go to the location of the hang up and go down to investigate what caught the cable.

Within the first few miles the divers went down several times and found old wrecks and miscellaneous junk on the bottom. About 17 miles off the St Petersburg beach, they hit pay dirt. They found the Gunsmoke laying on the bottom in about 80 feet of water. NOAA dropped buoys and marked the location.

Gunsmoke located in 80 feet of water by NOAA
17 miles off St. Petersburg

They stood by until our divers went down and verified the vessel was indeed the Gunsmoke. The Commander wished us luck saying he would like to finish the drag looking for the Pirates Lady, but he was committed to another location on the other coast.

365

We were concerned about a school of sharks around the wreckage. We assigned our dive team to go down in pairs armed with powerful spear guns. One diver was to search for evidence and the other was to guard for sharks and assist his partner in the event he got tangled in nets, cable or needed any other assistance. They could only stay down a certain amount of time before being relieved by two other divers.

The first team reported that there were cables loose all round the deck and inside the vessel. They also reported that the vessel appeared to have many bales of marijuana still on board. The cables caused problems and tangled one of our divers up on one occasion. The other diver came to his rescue and prevented what could have been a catastrophe.

The divers were instructed to look for bodies and anything that could link this boat to Sandy Creek or the four murder victims. To get inside the vessel the divers had to cut some wires and cables that were holding the bales of marijuana down. As they cut and released the bales of marijuana, they made a fast trip to the surface. Before long there were bales of marijuana floating all around our 51-foot patrol boat.

The divers reported there were many grouper and other fish as well as sharks around the Gunsmoke. They told us about one especially large grouper that followed them around like a yard dog. As they examined things on the vessel and inside the cabin and hull, they could look around and there was that big grouper looking over their shoulder or beneath them watching everything they did.

LaVelle with Asst. U.S. Attorney Don Modesitt preparing to dive on the Gunsmoke.

Customs Patrol and DEA were with us continually and a great help. We even had Assistant U.S. Attorney Don Modesitt from

Tallahassee arrive and help monitor the diving detail. The divers kept kidding Modesitt about going down with them to have a close up look at the Gunsmoke. To my amazement he did go down and did just fine.

To be totally sure we had all the evidence, we decided to try to get the Gunsmoke raised in order to do a thorough search. There was only one hole in the hull of the vessel that could easily be patched.

DEA tried to get the government to assist in bringing it up and they declined. Customs Patrol refused also. Mr. Shields went through the governor's office and was turned down. We contacted a private firm that did that type work and they agreed to bring it up if they could have the vessel when we finished processing it. We agreed.

This was a very high profile news case that frequently made headlines. So everyone, especially on the Gulf Coast, was aware of what we were doing.

The second day the contractor worked on bringing up the Gunsmoke, he called me and advised some of his crew were confronted on the beach after work and their lives threatened if

The marijuana shipment investigation, later connected to murder and hijacking, became known as "Operation Gunsmoke"

they continued to work. Also some of his equipment was damaged. We immediately moved our patrol boat back to the site and stood guard.

This didn't stop these unknown persons from threatening his crew. We had a good idea that those doing the threatening were big time smugglers of drugs out of Columbia and Mexico. The contractor notified us that he had lost a lot of his equipment and would no longer attempt to bring up the Gunsmoke.

U.S. Attorney Don Modesitt impaneled a Federal Grand Jury and we started bringing in suspects to testify. One of the suspects agreed to testify in exchange for immunity before the Federal Grand Jury. We sent an officer to pick him up and bring him to Tallahassee. When the officer arrived in St. Pete, the man who agreed to testify was found on the beach, dead. An autopsy showed he died from an overdose of heroin. According to friends and other witnesses, this man had never been a heroin user.

One of the chief suspects, identified as the person who arranged for the load and played a big role in organizing the entire off-load at Sandy Creek, was found to be a confidential source for an FBI agent in Tallahassee. An FDLE agent and one of our FMP investigators contacted the FBI agent about finding this man. He said he had no idea where he could be. We later found out that after the investigators left him, the FBI agent allegedly contacted the source, warned him we were looking for him and he left town that night.

Mr. Modesitt issued a warrant for this person and he was quickly picked up crossing the Texas border into Mexico. FDLE Agents brought him back to Tallahassee to face the Federal Grand Jury. There were approximately 20-25 people indicted in the smuggling operation. The U.S. Attorney turned over the information to the State Attorney, Leo Jones of Panama City, Bay County, Florida.

Soon after Mr. Jones got his hands on the information, unbelievable deals were made. Co-conspirators and several people, who were principles in the smuggling operation, walked.

One man, David Goodwin, who was on the off-load crew, owned the van the two guards used to transport the murder victims. After shooting Sims, one of the victims who rode up on the off-load site that fateful night, the guards for the smuggling operation loaded Sims and the other three victims into Goodwin's van and drove to Taylor County. One of the guards went into town and brought back builders blocks to weigh down the bodies after they shot the other three and dropped them into a deep spring. But it was David Goodwin who was charged with murder.

To the best of my knowledge the money people and organizers of the drug operation never went to prison. The two people who killed the four people were sent to prison where one died soon after arrival and the other paroled out after serving a short sentence. (I heard this one was even elected Mayor of a small city in Mississippi since the murder.)

The Goodwin boy, who happened to be a former college student of Sally Jo's, was tried by Mr. Jones for murder and sentenced to life. He is the only one still in prison. If I ever witnessed a miscarriage of justice, this was one of the worst. For what this man did, all 25 people were as much involved or far more, but none went to jail except to two mentioned above. Two of the money people were from Texas and flew their own airplane to Tallahassee for the hearings. They landed in Panama City and gave Mr. Jones a ride from Panama City to Tallahassee and back. They never served a day in prison.

This case has to go down as one of my greatest disappointments in our legal system during the 32 years of my law enforcement career. All the officers I talked to were very disappointed and wished Don Modesitt, the Assistant U.S. Attorney, could have handled the case.

Didn't Get the Word
Depending on the part of the state we were working and the ongoing circumstances, the local sheriff's office and police were often invited to join in on raids and off-loadings of drugs in their respective counties and cities.

Prior to an interception of a large drug shipment or a raid on a storage house we had a meeting of supervisors from the various agencies. We went over the intelligence information and the role to be played by each department. There were always a large number of new faces from the various agencies. Because of this, we had a problem knowing who the good guys and the bad guys were on a detail.

Special Agent Ginley of DEA came up with the idea that each federal and state agency take turns and buy a large quantity of caps identical in color. A cap was issued to each member of the task force just prior to a raid. Each detail we worked, we changed the color of the caps.

**Working a joint operation,
LaVelle, center**

On one particular raid near Jacksonville, we had a mole (or undercover person) working with the bad guys and furnishing us information. We gave him a cap and advised the supervisors that we had a person working inside the operation. This information was to be passed to the other officers. The mole would be wearing one of our caps and when the raid went down he was going to run. We emphasized that he was to escape and no one was to try to apprehend him.

The raid went as planned. It was looking good for our side until the undercover guy took off. A local policeman, who was a last minute add-on, did not know about the cap deal. He jumped up and yelled, "Halt!" The guy continued to run so this police officer started shooting at him with an M1 carbine.

The carbine had a banana clip that held lots of rounds of ammo and it must have been full. As the policeman was firing and kicking up dirt, our undercover guy was lifting his cap about every two jumps while zigzagging and running full speed toward the woods. That cop had to be one of the world's worst marksmen. He fired almost the entire clip from his weapon and never touched the guy before a supervisor got to him and stopped his firing. We never saw that informant again.

As I learned in the Marine Corps, no matter how well you plan a project, there's always that ten percent that doesn't get the word.

Bay County Sheriff

After working drug smuggling statewide for seven years, I was promoted to regional director with the Florida Marine Patrol and assigned to an office in Bay County in 1978. With the encouragement and help of fellow law enforcement officers, friends and family, I decided to run for Sheriff of Bay County. I was fortunate to be elected to two terms and served from 1981-1989.

LAVELLE
PITTS FOR SHERIFF

**THE RIGHT MAN
at
THE RIGHT TIME**

During my eight years in office I was privileged to initiate numerous law enforcement programs for the county.

- A SPECIAL DRUG & ORGANIZED CRIME UNIT which increased drug arrests by 303% since 1980 until 1987, seized over $1,842,160 in property and cash, and drugs valued at $13,134,700.
- Instrumental in bringing the BLUE LIGHTENING DRUG TASK FORCE to Northwest Florida and served on the State Board of Directors. Obtained an offshore patrol boat from U.S. Customs for interdiction of drugs.
- Initiated MUTUAL AID COMPACTS with surrounding counties and municipalities.
- Helped form the TRI-STATE LAW ENFORCEMENT ASSOCIATION to exchange information with authorities in Alabama, Georgia and Florida.
- Specially trained 8-man SWAT TEAM.

BCSO Swat Team exercise at Bay Bank on Harrison Avenue

- A K-9 POLICE DOG UNIT for riot control, protection of officers, pursuing escapees, finding lost citizens and detection of drugs.

373

• A DIVE TEAM UNIT formed to respond to water-oriented emergencies, such as recovering evidence, drowning victims, or retrieving stolen property.

• Every sworn officer was certified as MEDICAL FIRST RESPONDER or in emergency first aid.

• The MOTORCYCLE UNIT was established to provide safety escorts for public activities and funerals as well as fast response in heavy traffic emergency situations.

• The BEACH & WATER SAFETY PROGRAM consisted of two marine patrol units, mobile water conditions & flag program, and 4-wheel drive beach patrols.

• Over 1,350 men and women learned the obligations of owning and the safe use of a gun in Sheriff's Office sponsored HAND GUN CLASSES.

• A SEARCH & RESCUE TEAM comprised of specially trained and equipped BCSO units to put in service in case of a major emergency such as hurricane or plane crash.

• A CRIME PREVENTION UNIT with over 50,000 Bay Countians participating 1981-87.

Another crime watch neighborhood is added to Bay County.

**Photo taken with our neighbors at the corner of Hamilton Ave.
and 2nd Court. L-R: E.L. "Everlasting" Vance, LaVelle, Sally Jo,
Ella Mae Vance.**

- The NEIGHBORHOOD CRIME WATCH program, 1981-87 over 10,000 participants.
- The CRIME STOPPERS program which led to solving over 53 crimes ranging from narcotics to murder (through 1987).
- OPERATION CHILD PRINT provided parent with an "insurance policy" for identifying missing or runaway children.

Photo taken at Cove Elementary School

- OPERATION CHILD FINDER augmented the child fingerprint program by providing TV stations with videos of youngsters.

375

- The SCHOOL RESOURCE OFFICER program furnished a full-time officer in each high school and a rotating officer in the middle schools.
- LAW ENFORCEMENT EXPLORER POST provided youngsters interested in law enforcement careers with practical experience in the field.
- SENIOR CITIZEN IDENTIFICATION CARDS signed by the sheriff to provide positive I.D. an vital information for senior citizens.
- A VICTIM ADVOCATE officer to work with victims of crime in obtaining medical, financial or legal assistance.

Bay County Sheriff's Office and Jail as it appeared in the 1980s
Photo Credit: *Centennial Stories, Celebrating the History of Panama City, 1909-2009*, Marlene Womack

Hostage Volunteer (1981)

During my first year as Bay County Sheriff, I received a call at home from my dispatcher, Anita Newsome. She advised that there was a hostage situation at City Drugs on Harrison Avenue. She had the subject, Tom Haskins, on the phone who advised that he and his girlfriend were holding twelve hostages at gun point. Anita said police had surrounded the store.

Haskins called to advise that he would release the hostages if the sheriff agreed to come in as their hostage. She asked me what I suggested. Haskins could hear our conversation. I told her to tell him I would come in as his hostage, but he had to release the hostages he was holding first. He agreed. I left the house, drove downtown and parked my vehicle. Several officers met me and advised the hostages had been released and Capt. Joe Coram, my chief investigator, had gone inside to try to talk to Haskins and he was now a hostage.

I gave my service revolver to an officer and went to the front door where Haskins, who was armed with a revolver, met me.

When I walked in the store, I was pushed up against the wall. Haskins said, "Sheriff, you know the drill. Up against the wall and spread 'em." I looked around and saw Joe sitting on the floor with his back against the wall.

Joe kind of looked at me with a sad look. I did as Haskins ordered. Haskins searched me for a weapon. I was a little upset that Joe had gone in and was now a hostage too. It turned out later to have been a good decision.

I thought back over the years when I had first met Tom Haskins. He worked as a confidential source for the drug squad for several months until he was caught doing his own business on the side. I had always had a good relationship with Haskins until he went bad. He was arrested and after he got out of jail, he left town and I had not seen or heard from him for several years until he contacted me a couple of days prior to this hostage situation. He had called me at the sheriff's office and advised he was back in town with his girlfriend. They were both hooked on drugs, broke and really needed medical help. I advised him to go to Bay Medical Center and tell them his problem. I heard nothing else until the phone call from my dispatcher. Haskins next ordered us to help push a large counter up against the front door so no one could rush in unexpectedly. I told him I had a bad back and couldn't help him. He turned to Coram and ordered him to help. Coram said the counter was too big and too heavy to move. Haskins stuck the pistol up to Coram's head and said, "I told you to move it." Coram did.

After securing the front door, Coram and I were escorted to the pharmaceutical department and ordered to sit on the floor.

Suspect Tom Haskins

...is escorted in handcuffs from City Drug Store by Bay County sheriff's investigators Monday after he and Frankie Darlene "Dolly" Baggett were arrested on charges of robbery and kidnapping. The pair are charged with robbing the store and holding about a dozen employees hostage. They were arrested when Sheriff LaVelle Pitts and Chief Investigator Joe Coram disarmed Haskins in an office in the drug store. The photograph was taken by News Herald Publisher Scott Tucker from the roof of Kettle Aquatics across Harrison Avenue from the drug store.

The airwaves told the story

Haskins being escorted from City Drugs at the close of the hostage incident.

Coram sat down and leaned back against the wall. I walked over to the desk and sat down, telling Haskins that because of my back injury I could not sit on the floor. About that time, the phone rang and Haskins said, "Okay. You just sit there and answer the phone."

I answered the phone and the person on the other end asked who was speaking. I told him the sheriff. He said his wife was an employee. He had heard the news over the television and was worried. I told him it was okay his wife had been released and was outside. He asked if the suspect was with me and had a gun. I said, "Yes standing right in front of me." The man immediately hung up. Tom and his girlfriend, Dolly, were busy trying to find some drugs to ease their addiction pain. The phone rang several times—people wanting to check on prescription orders. I advised the store was temporarily closed and to call back later.

Haskins then told me to call Channel 7 and 13 and invite a reporter to come down and witness what was going on. I called both stations and told them what Haskins had said, but

378

emphasized that they did not have to come down. But newsmen that they were, they were eager to come for the news story.

Larche Hardy from Channel 13 and Bill Hudson from Channel 7 arrived and were let in (after Coram moved the counter again). They were immediately spread eagled on the floor and thoroughly searched along with their equipment. Haskins advised them to film anything and everything going on. They did and after a few minutes Hardy started gathering his equipment up and Haskins asked him what he thought he was doing? Hardy said, "I have no more batteries and have to go get more."

I pointed to an electric outlet and said, "Larche, just plug it in."

Larche could have done without my suggestion, but Haskins was hardly favorable to his leaving. Besides, I thought maybe with four of us, we might have a better opportunity to grab the gun. If all else failed, then the film could be used as evidence.

Haskins and Dolly started to get really irate and demanding. Haskins told me, "Call the governor and get him down here." He also demanded an airplane and $50,000 before he let anyone out of the building. I explained that would take time and there was no way the Governor of Florida would come down.

Dolly then took the gun and said, "Let's kill one of them and throw them out the front door to show them we're serious." I assured her that the people outside and inside were very confident they were serious.

All this time I was very conscious of the SWAT team snipers on the building across the street. I had seen them climbing up as I was

Bay County Sheriff Lavelle Pitts

...talks with Panama City Police Chief Leroy French, Investigator Joe Coram discussed two robbery and kid (right) and police Lt. James Purvis after he and Chief napping suspects

A relieved Sheriff Pitts, thankful for his department and other law enforcement support throughout the hostage situation.

entering the drug store. I was concerned that if someone shot through the front glass and missed, one or all of us could be shot by Haskins or Dolly.

Haskins and Dolly had found some morphine now and were giving each other shots. Haskins got his first and started trying to give Dolly a shot. She insisted he put it into an artery. She even dropped her pants and let him shoot some into her buttocks.

She said, "If you don't want to see what I've got, then look the other way."

I told her that it didn't matter what we saw, we possibly wouldn't live to tell anyone. I tried to keep a cheerful conversation going because the two were getting dangerously high. First one and then the other handled the gun. The hammer was pulled back and the finger of their gun hand tightened and loosened on the trigger. Being familiar with weapons, I knew that a revolver cocked would go off with very little pressure. I was especially concerned when Dolly had the gun. She seemed to really want to shoot one of us and was acting more irrational than Haskins.

After Dolly got several shots of morphine and didn't get as high as she expected, she told Haskins to put the needle in the artery on her neck. Haskins took his belt off and looped it around Dolly's neck and pulled it tight so the artery stood out. He was having a hard time holding the gun and using the syringe with one hand and keeping pressure with the belt. He finally turned to me behind the desk and asked if I would give my word not to jump him if he laid the gun down to give Dolly a shot.

I told him he had my word and I leaned back and put my feet up on the desk. He laid the gun on the far edge of the desk and started inserting the needle into Dolly's neck. I was telling him he was going to kill Dolly and he kept looking up at me and saying he knew what he was doing. He seemed to have forgotten Capt. Coram. Suddenly Coram leaped from the floor over the corner of the desk and grabbed the gun. The hostage situation ended with no one hurt.

the Sheriff's Star

JULY-AUGUST 1983

Captain Coram Congratulated

I was privileged to nominate Capt. Coram for Officer of the Year in the State of Florida. He won over a score of other deserving officers throughout the state.

I found out later that the FBI got the film of the hostage situation and used it as a training film in Quantico, Virginia. It was used as an example of a bad way to handle a hostage situation because the sheriff (or leader) should not put himself in harm's way, leaving no one in charge.

I provided the FBI with the ill-advised example of trading myself for hostages, but I believe there are some FBI agents who would have done the same.

Do Angels Wear Camouflage?

While serving as Sheriff of Bay County, I received a phone call late one night that an aircraft had crashed in a thickly wooded area north of the airport near Burnt Mill Creek. My dispatcher advised it was a private aircraft and the pilot was Rev. Charlie Fowler.

Driving the 25 to 30 miles to the area the plane was believed to have gone down, I thought about the preacher. He was a popular evangelist in the north Florida area and in several other states. I knew him and had visited in his church on the beach. He and his family were very talented in music and ministry.

I arrived just west of Burnt Mill Creek on Highway 388, and found that along with patrol cars, several other cars lined the highway. The family was present and many of their church members and gathered to give them support.

It was a dark night and there weren't many roads or trails leading off the highway into the wooded area. A search would be difficult until daylight. I sent three four-wheel drive vehicles into the wooded area but to no avail. According to the Tyndall Air Force Base control tower, he could have gone down any place in an approximately ten mile area.

The family and friends huddled together and prayed.

I asked for assistance from TAFB and was told they could not respond to civilian aircraft. I decided to go to the top. I called General Horner, who was a colleague I had worked with on several projects in the past. (He later became Air Force Commander for the U.S. in the Gulf War.) He assured me that a helicopter would land at our site at first light.

Charlie Fowler crash site, 1986. LaVelle is on the far right.
Fowler was underneath the man who has his arm in the air.

The General was as good as his word and a chopper lit down on Highway 388, next to our patrol car at the crack of dawn. It was a large chopper and had medical people on board, including a flight surgeon. The pilot advised he had instructions to search the area I deemed necessary.

We briefly went over the details of what we knew. The pilot said he could take two of our people with him on the search. I called one of our officers over, who was also a paramedic and the two of us boarded the chopper. We had only been in the air four or five minutes when the pilot spotted the crash site. He pointed out the area. It looked really bad.

The preacher had come in for a crash landing in a large field of planted pines that were 10 to 30 feet high. As he came down, his plane started cutting off the pines like a giant lawn mower until he came to rest with the big pines, roots, wires and engine all up in the cock pit with him.

The pilot landed the helicopter and the medical people took over quickly. They checked on Fowler and called out that he was still alive. I gave orders for the deputies to keep all onlookers out of the woods until further notice. Two deputies brought a four-wheel drive vehicle to the crash site and set up as guards to keep the public out so the medical people could work.

We later let a vehicle bring in representatives from the two television stations, the sheriff's office public information officer and a News Herald photographer. They were allowed to take pictures and film as long as they stayed back and did not interrupt the rescue efforts of the medical crew. There was a hunter dressed in camouflage kneeling next to Fowler with his hands under Fowler's head. This hunter looked like the comedian, Dom DeLuise and I wondered how he had gotten so close to the airplane since the officers had sealed off the crash area. I assumed this was one of his church members who had been searching earlier.

Our paramedic walked over to the hunter and advised he was going to have to step back so they could work at cutting the wires off the preacher's body. The hunter gently laid the preacher's head back on the ground and got up and backed up about five or six steps behind the medical people and deputy. I didn't think too much about this at the time. I remember I felt kind of sorry for the guy because he looked so sad.

They got the wires loose enough to drag the preacher away from the cockpit of the plane and laid him on the grass. The doctor had to work on stopping the bleeding that had started after the wires wrapped around his body were cut away. The medical people told me that the wires from the cockpit had acted as a tourniquet and kept the preacher from bleeding to death during the several hours he laid on the ground over night.

As the doctor cut the wires, some of the cuts spouted blood from arteries. The doctor stopped that bleeding and started cutting the wires again. The doctor advised that they needed to stabilize him enough to get him into the chopper and to the hospital. The doctor worked from the lower legs to the preacher's upper body. As he got to the chest area I heard him say, "Sir you will have to move back so I can continue my work."

The hunter was kneeling next to Fowler's head again. He immediately moved back behind the group in a small cleared area and stood there silently as workers prepared and placed the preacher on a stretcher and then onto the aircraft.

I asked Mike Broadway and one other officer to remain and guard the crushed remains of the aircraft until the arrival of the FAA investigators.

Little did I know that this request would become a life-changing experience for Mike and many others when he relates his story.

I went back in to the crash site after dark with my flashlight. I was going to try and find Rev. Fowler's Bible. I knew that all preachers carry Bibles and I wanted to find his. I turned over every leaf, every bit of wreckage, but I couldn't find it anywhere. I was at the nose of the plane when I heard footsteps. I looked up and there was that hunter. He pointed at me and asked, "What are you doing?"

"I'm looking for Rev. Fowler's Bible."

The hunter said, "Don't worry about Rev. Fowler's Bible, it's right where he would have been killed."

I looked to see if my partner was nearby. How had this hunter gotten past him? When I turned back, the hunter had vanished. I looked around, ran back and forth and then back to the unit where my partner was. I couldn't find the hunter anywhere and my partner hadn't seen anybody.

Deputy Broadway told me later he believed the hunter was an angel because there was no other way he could explain it. I was surprised he came up with something like that, but this incident had made a change in him that was hard to miss.

Broadway made such a big deal of it that I started thinking about the hunter I had seen. I called our Public Information Officer and asked him to gather photos he had taken along with copies of photos and raw footage of the crash scene taken by the News Herald, Channel 7 and 13 and bring them to me. When I received them, I laid the photos out on the long conference table in my office. I checked every photograph and looked at all the film. There was no sign of the guy in camouflage.

In the space behind the medical people where I knew the hunter had been standing, there was nothing but grass and bushes. I looked at the long distance shots of the entire area. All the people working there could be clearly seen and identified, but not the hunter.

I called my paramedic deputy in and asked if he remembered asking someone to move away from the preacher so he could help the doctor. He said he did remember someone dressed in camouflage that he asked to move. He also remembered the doctor asking the same guy to move after they got the preacher out of the wreckage. I let him look at the photographs and he had a kind of a strange look on his face. He couldn't see him in any of the pictures or tapes, although everyone else that was there was on film.

Mike Broadway's supervisor came to me and advised, "We need to do something about Mike. He keeps telling people about an angel. I think he's losing his mind." I didn't explain what I had seen or what was "not showing up" in the photographs and TV tape. I just told him to leave Mike alone.

I have thought about that incident many times since then. Angels are usually depicted with halos and robed in white. But could this stranger in camouflage, who didn't show up on film, have been Rev. Fowler's guardian angel? I believe he was.

Note of interest:

Before Mike shared his story about the hunter with Charlie at the hospital, Charlie told his wife about a hunter that was with him in the plane during his semi-conscious state on the night of the crash.

385

Because of this incident, Mike Broadway became a strong Christian believer and has gone into ministry work–forever changed by the heavenly presence at the scene of the crash.

"Be not forgetful to entertain strangers: for thereby some have entertained angels unaware." (Hebrews 13:2)

Lynn Haven Poker Game

Sheriff Doc Daffin had a firm belief that the sheriff should always have a listed phone number. If a citizen had a problem and wanted to talk to the sheriff, they should feel free to do so. Based on this belief, I have always had a listed phone number in the phone book.

(There are times I have wished otherwise and I'm sure Sally Jo has. She answered a call in the early morning hours when I was out on a call. A drunk called from a phone booth to say he was about to commit suicide. Being concerned about him, she spent the next hour trying to talk to this guy until he was silent. A deputy was sent to check the phone booth. She had talked him to sleep.)

Sheriff Pitts in office at BCSO, 1988

One night I received a call about 2:00am. It was an upset woman who said her husband was playing poker every week and had lost almost everything they had. The game was being played in a house owned by an official in the City of Lynn Haven. The game was regularly attended by city officials, some high profile businessmen.

She asked if we were letting it run because of the people involved in the game. I assured her this was not the case and asked for the address. I also explained we had to have more than this to obtain a search warrant. I couldn't just walk in a house without being invited. She threatened to walk in herself with a shotgun.

I got dressed and drove to Lynn Haven. On my way, I called the station and asked if we had an investigator working. Frank McKeithen answered and advised he was 10-8. (Almost every time I got called out at night, McKeithen seemed to be working, yet he was in his office working during the day also.)

I met Frank just outside Lynn Haven and briefed him on the information. We decided to break up the game, knowing we couldn't get in without a warrant. We stopped about a block away and walked down the street to the house located a short distance behind McDonald's.

Unknown to us, they had a lookout. He was near the place we parked, hidden in a large ditch beside the street. The guy was asleep, and as luck would have it, this guy's first name was Frank.

We eased up on the porch. There were a number of cars parked out front and all the window shades were pulled down. We heard loud talking and laughing going on inside. Frank knocked on the door and someone asked, "Who is it?" Frank advised "Frank." Someone unlocked the door and said, "Come in."

We walked in and saw a group of men sitting around a table covered with money and holding cards. Frank told them to sit tight and keep their hands on the table. He looked at me and said, "Sheriff, I don't have anything to write on." I went back to the car to get a pad.

I cut across the yards of a couple homes, got a pad from the front seat of my car and slammed the door shut. The noise of the door woke up Frank, the lookout. He jumped up from the ditch

387

and started running across the lawns to the poker house. It startled me when he ran, so I ran after him.

As he jumped up on the porch, he started yelling, "Everybody get out! The sheriff's here! He's right behind me!" About this time, he spotted Frank McKeithen, lost his voice, and leaned against the wall.

In law enforcement, some breaks come from unexpected sources.

Frank, the investigator, started taking names and counting money. Frank, the lookout, started looking sickly. Finally, Frank, the lookout, asked if he could go home. I told him he could. As he was leaving, McKeithen told him how much we appreciated his help.

The woman who reported the high stakes game was correct about the big name players. Some had already left before we arrived, but the checks they left behind identified them. Hopefully breaking up the game helped keep the woman in milk money, but come election time checks from some of those high stakes players benefitted my opponents.

Solving a Murder before a Victim is Found

My mother loved to fish. Every chance she got, she hooked her 14-foot Kennedy Craft to her old car and headed to Wewahitchka (Wewa). She had one big problem, however, she couldn't back the boat down the ramp to launch it. When she arrive in Wewa, she drove around Wewa until she spotted Chief of Police Preacher Glass on his patrol car and waved at him.

He followed her to the boat landing, launched her boat in the river and told her he would be back late that afternoon to pull her boat out and put it back on the trailer. He did this several times and I was grateful for what he did for my mom.

While campaigning to become Sheriff in Bay County, I saw Chief Glass who recommended I consider hiring a certain officer who had been helpful to him and would make a good deputy for me if I was elected. The man was Frank McKeithen

When I took office I interviewed Frank, his capabilities were obvious and I put him to work in the criminal investigation section under the command of Captain Joe Coram.

Frank loved his job and seemed to work all the time.

In the event of a serious crime, I had a standing rule that I be called out regardless of the time day or night. I required an investigator be on duty 24 hours a day. Duty was assigned on a rotation. When I signed on the radio and asked if an investigator was 10-8, almost always McKeithen came on the air and said, "Sheriff, I'm 10-8."

I asked Coram why Frank was always on duty. Coram said this guy just loved the job and somehow managed to be in or around the office during the day also.

One day, I received a call that a young lady had mysteriously disappeared from an insurance office in Lynn Haven. Everyone had left the office for lunch and left her in the office to answer the phone until they returned. When they returned she was missing and the office was in disarray.

The business was located just south of Lynn Haven facing Highway 77 with a large wooded area in back of the office. A little dirt road and trails ran through much of the woods. I had the entire area closed with officers standing guard at all exits from the woods leading to Highway 77. Any one coming out of the area was detained for questioning. Twenty or thirty officers and volunteers spread out, forming a scrimmage line within sight of each other to try to locate the missing lady.

One of the vehicles detained was a truck out of Tallahassee. An officer brought the driver to me. The guy said he was delivering some type equipment and had pulled off the road to eat his lunch. I looked around for an investigator. All seemed to be busy questioning someone or in the woods looking for the girl when Frank pulled in the parking lot.

I asked Frank to take this person to his office and question him. After he left, I walked out a short distance into the woods where the deputies were searching the bushes and a tie-dye swamp that was very thick. I stood about 50 or 75 feet from the

389

back door of the office and saw something on a bamboo vine down near the ground. I walked out for a closer look and there was the missing girl, almost naked. One of her stockings was caught on the vine. Other than that she was completely concealed with the tall grass and bushes.

I sent my crime scene people to the body and someone called me from the insurance office and said McKeithen was on the phone. I walked back to the office, picked up the phone and said, "Frank, we have a body."

Frank said, "I have the killer and a confession."

Frank had gotten a confession from a killer before we knew for sure we had a crime or even found the victim.

Frank is one of many fine officers I had the privilege to work with. He went on to be Sheriff in Gulf County and at the time of this writing is Sheriff of Bay County.

UNDER GOD'S PROTECTION

Looking back over a lifetime of events, I am amazed at God's intervention in my life. I did nothing to deserve his protection and have to credit a praying mother. Mama lost four of her children at a young age. I think this gave her extra incentive to pray for Ruth and me. To the best of my knowledge, Mama never went to bed at night without praying for us. She prayed for our salvation and our protection. Anyone who happened to live within shouting distance of our home when Mama prayed can vouch for this. She was serious and loud. I am convinced that my mother's prayers gave me a covering over the years.

Close Calls

One of my first close calls took place at a wash hole in Ten Mile Creek known as "chalk hole." This was a favorite swimming hole for all the kids. Lavohn Price and I were playing in the shallow water, because neither of us could swim. There were no adults present and we shouldn't have been in the water.

I waded a little deeper and deeper until the water was up to my chin. Suddenly I stepped in a hole and went out of sight. I don't know how long I was down when a hand grabbed me and pulled me from the water. It was one of the older teenage girls and a distant cousin of mine. She dragged me out on the bank and I spit and sputtered for awhile until I got my breath back. No doubt I would have died had this girl not been watching me when I went down. I don't even remember her name.

When I was six years of age, Lavohn and I were wading in a bayou in Panama City. I again stepped in a hole and went out of sight. This time I recall thinking I was going to die. I struggled and somehow ended up getting my feet on solid ground and making it to shore.

Another time Lavohn and I were running our horses down a dirt road. My large plow horse stepped in a hole and fell tossing me over her head. The horse weighed about 2,000 pounds and she ran over me when she got up. There was a perfect hoof print on my back. It took my breath for a while but no bones were broken. While serving in the USMC and stationed at Quantico, Virginia, I drove my old car to Panama City a couple of times on a 72-hour pass. If I had been caught going that far from the base, I would have been in trouble. The trip was over 900 miles one way and I drove straight through, only stopping for gas and coffee it took eighteen and a half hours of steady driving. I got very sleepy. Many times I woke up with two wheels off the highway. I drove 70 and 80 most of the way. There were very few police on the highway back then. With God's protection, I never had a wreck or got caught speeding.

On the firing range at Parris Island, my platoon was going through hand grenade training. We were lined up behind a wall with a drill instructor next to each of us. We were to pull the pin, throw the grenade, and fall behind the wall at the same time. The Marine to my right pulled the pin and instead of throwing the grenade, he dropped it, fell to his knees, covered his ears and closed his eyes. The drill instructor grabbed the grenade just in front of me and tossed it over the wall as it exploded. The kid on his knees was pulled off the line and we never saw him again.

In law enforcement, I was following an escaped convict through the woods trying to keep him in sight until we could get the girl he was holding hostage. Every few minutes, if I got a little close, he turned and started firing a pistol at me and the officer with me. We hit the ground and heard the bullets go through the leaves or ricochet off trees around us. Some of those bullets were very close and we couldn't return fire because he held the girl close to him. (See the Nine Shot Six Shooter story.)

When I led the raid on a night club and their guard fired at me, I saw the flash and felt the sting of powder on my face as I dove for him. (See Pussy Cat Go-Go Club story.)

During the hostage situation at City Drugs, the perpetrators were shooting up on all kinds of drugs while waving a cocked pistol around and threatening to shoot. (See Hostage Volunteer story.)

As Chief of Police in Springfield, Florida, I went to a house where a husband was drunk and had beat up his wife and threw her and her two kids out in the cold. He was armed with a .38 special pistol. When I arrived, the mother and children were out in the front yard in their nightclothes. All were crying, cold and scared. She asked if I could get her husband to let them back in the house. I sent Officer Gallagher to the back door and I entered through front door with my pistol in my hand. I faced a drunk, angry man with a .38 cal. pistol pointed at me. We stood for a moment with our weapons pointed at each other. He threatened to shoot me for coming into his house.

JJ Gallagher & LaVelle, Springfield PD

My backup, Gallagher, came through the back door with his weapon out. I started talking to the guy and trying to get him to lay his pistol down and let his family come back inside. I explained that if he shot I was sure to get one shot off and Officer Gallagher could certainly kill him.

He said he had nothing to live for. I pointed outside to his children and wife and told him he had three good reasons to live. I told Gallagher to hold his fire unless the man fired first.

The wife and two kids started crying and begged us to not hurt him. After about fifteen minutes of talking and hearing his family beg, he put the gun down and raised his hands. He spent the night in jail and his family had the house all to themselves. The following day I was told by one of the city commissioners that the man had a bad reputation and had shot two or three people.

LaVelle learning to fly

I used my G.I. Bill to take flying lessons at the local airport. On one occasion, the trainer was teaching me the land and take-off drill. We were flying a two passenger Piper Cub. At the east end of the airport, a power line had to be cleared before landing on the runway. I was afraid of hitting the power lines with my wheels and kept coming in too high.

The instructor kept saying, "No, no that's too high. Take off and try again."

After the fifth time my instructor was getting flustered and told me to try it again. I was flustered too. During my sixth landing I pushed the plane's nose down and got so close to the power lines that my wheels touched the lines. The plane shuddered and dipped toward the ground. I was just barely able to pull the nose back up for a safe landing.

I was scared stiff because when we hit the line we were traveling at about 70 mph. When the plane was safe on the landing strip, I looked at my instructor, who was kind of green around the gills, and asked if that was close enough. He answered in a solemn voice, "Yeah that was close enough." That ended my lessons with that instructor. Again it was a miracle we were not killed.

On a cold and blistery winter night, I found myself facing a big .38 revolver and the man holding it said, "I think I'll just kill me a cop." (See Domestic call, Panama City Beach.)

These are just a few of the close calls I can remember over my lifetime. Looking back now, God's protection and grace is obvious. But I was to face an even greater test.

My Greatest Test and Testimony

On October 22, 1987, I was the sheriff and chief law enforcement officer of Bay County. My office for the past six years had been ranked the number one law enforcement agency in crime fighting and cases cleared by arrest in the thirty-six largest counties in the State of Florida.

I had a thirty-one year career in law enforcement and received numerous awards and recognition for my work in fighting the importation of drugs into the State.

I walked into the courthouse that morning and my world came crashing down around me. I was arrested on four felony charges, booked into my own jail, fingerprinted, photographed and heard the steel doors slam shut behind me.

Within the next hour I was bonded out and fired by Governor Martinez and ordered to vacate the Office of Sheriff.

I have been told that to have a testimony you must first have a test, so this is my testimony.

Through a tangle of events and politics, sexual harassment accusations were lodged against me. Then criminal accusations were filed with Governor Graham's office in 1986. This brought FDLE into the investigation which progressed for weeks and then months. Complaints arose against my department such as grand theft, forgery of documents, auto theft, misuse of county equipment, aggravated assault, attempted rape, even accessory to an alleged murder. These are the major items FDLE focused their investigation on.

This ignited a continual barrage of negative press. It's hard to remember a day when there wasn't a damaging news story in the local paper, and most of the time on the front page. The pressure continued to mount.

In the above anecdotes I have shared about my childhood, high school, Marine Corps, college, law enforcement experiences and close calls. I have experienced numerous highs and lows with God basically relegated to "God of the moment." I only called on him in moments of great need or danger.

But this time it had become apparent that this was a case I wasn't going to be able to solve by myself or with a quick prayer. One night as I lay in bed trying to sleep, my mind went back to that afternoon on the banks of Wrights Creek. I got up, went in the bathroom and knelt to pray and rededicated my life to the Lord. Sometime during that prayer and unexplainable peace covered me. God was right where I left him waiting for me to return. I felt like that ship engulfed in a great storm in the hymn *The Lighthouse*– "When I'm tossed it (the lighthouse) sends out a light that I might see...if it wasn't for that lighthouse, where would this ship be?"

Unknown to me at the time, Sally Jo had also recommitted her life to the Lord. We had always gone to church and Sunday school, but we began daily Bible study and prayer, earnestly seeking guidance and direction from God's Word.

Things started to change. Not so much that the circumstances got better (they actually got worse), but for me in particular I had a great peace about the whole situation. People, like the Full Gospel Businessmen came into our lives, encouraging us with prayer and scripture. Many of these people we never knew before, but we shared one thing in common–love for the Lord.

When an especially bad headline hit the front page of the newspaper, I received a call from a lady who said the Lord prompted her to give me the scripture Isaiah 41:10-13. This scripture says in part to "fear not for I am with thee," and became a source of strength for me to handle each day's responsibilities.

At the end of four months, FDLE released a statement that they had no grounds or evidence of any criminal wrongdoing. Governor Graham ordered the investigation closed.

Relief was short-lived. When new Governor Martinez took office, he ordered the investigation reopened and appointed State Attorney Russell from St. Petersburg to personally come to Bay

County along with his staff to continue the investigation.

When Russell arrived in town (May, 1987), we attended a special church service in which a visiting minister from California was preaching. He knew nothing of our troubles but after the service prayed these words over me, "Though the enemy raised this situation up and meant it to destroy you, meant it to take you down, you are going to see it work for your good...with a fresh peace."

Meanwhile the investigation continued to intensify. A grand jury was impaneled by Mr. Russell.

On October 9, 1987, we were invited by friends, Gene and Priss Ford, to attend a church meeting at Christian International in Walton County. We did not know the minister and he did not know us, but the ministry was dedicated to helping people hear the voice of God. After his sermon the minister, Bill Hamon, pointed me out and said "The Lord says He has put you in a crucial place, but I am going to come against the council that is counseling against my wisdom. The Lord says take your stand, be righteous, be holy, I am going to fight your battles. God says I am working in you and I am going to protect you. I saw a prying rod like an old crowbar; I saw the devil trying to pry you out of your position. I saw the Lord come down, pour cement around and resettle you back."

Naturally, we were comforted by this word and assumed the worst was over. But as the scripture in Isaiah 55:8 proclaims, "My thoughts are not your thoughts, neither are your ways my ways."

On October 22, 1987, I was indicted on four charges of perjury, arrested and removed from office without pay. That night we attended church services at Christian International and again the minister pointed me out and said, "The Lord says son, you can't fight your own battle, but I can. You can't defend your own cause, but I can. The Lord says son, watch how I do it."

For the next seven months my family and I lived on faith. We didn't know how we would make it from one month to the next. I could not draw unemployment because I was an elected official. I couldn't get another job because of hearings and depositions. Supporters formed a group called Citizens for Justice and through fish fry fundraisers and others giving food or money at the end of each month we were able to put food on the table and pay our bills.

We prayed about an attorney and one was recommended to us by another sheriff in south Florida. My wife and I went to see him and were in agreement that he was the right one for the case. His fee was $50,000 which we didn't have, but he still took case.

When it came time for the trial, the State offered a deal. I could plead Nolo Contendere to one misdemeanor of my choice, sign an agreement not to run for sheriff again, and they would withhold adjudication and release me. If I turned down their offer, I could get twenty years in jail, lose my retirement, face the embarrassment of publicity in the news media, and destroy my family. In addition our lawyer said he would accept the $18,000, we had paid him from selling some property, as payment in full if we accepted the deal.

I talked to my wife and we both agreed—our answer was no. My lawyer couldn't believe the good deal offered or that we turned it down. My wife said, "You think we're crazy don't you?"

He said, "Yes lady, I think you're crazy, anything can happen in a trial."

But we felt the Lord's assurance when we saw the headlines prior to the trial starting that spoke of ripples.

Pitts' perjury trial starts Monday

Verdict will send ripples throughout Bay County

GREG MAY
Staff Writer

The perjury trial of suspended Bay County sheriff LaVelle Pitts is scheduled to begin this week, determining whether Pitts will face imprisonment or can return to office in triumph.

Whatever the outcome, the verdict will send ripples throughout the county, with implications for this year's sheriff's election as well as for a federal lawsuit that could threaten county coffers.

Jury selection begins Monday morning in the Bay County Courthouse. The six jurors chosen to try the case will be the ones to decide what has been debated at grocery store counters, across dinner tables and over drinks since Pitts' suspension from office Oct. 23.

Did Pitts, a 30-year law enforcement veteran and staunch advocate of "morality" laws, lie when he denied having sexual relations with female Sheriff's Department employees?

Pitts, still addressed as "sheriff" by some, repeatedly has denied charges of sexual misconduct since the first accusations surfaced two years ago.

But when Pitts stated his denials in a closed hearing before Bay County grand jurors in

LaVelle Pitts was suspended from office on Oct. 23

October, they didn't believe him.

Their presentment, issued with the indictment, concluded that Pitts sexually assaulted one female sheriff's employee and attempted to do so with another.

They also accused Pitts of engaging in sexual intercourse with several female employees, and said he found ways to punish the women when they ceased having intimate relations with him.

But Pitts was charged with none of these claimed offenses; the statute of limitations, which sets time limits to prosecute a crime, had expired in every instance.

Pitts was instead charged with lying four times — once for each answer he gave to questions concerning sexual misconduct with his female employees.

One of the perjury charges claims Pitts lied about having sexual intercourse with his employees; another accused him of lying about attempts to have sexual intercourse with employees; and two others related to his denial of having sexual relations with employees in his office or in a department automobile.

WHOM TO BELIEVE?

Pitts has said he is confident he will be exonerated in court because the charges are based on one person's word against his.

He has labeled the accusations an political attacks aimed at removing him from office. Pitts has claimed "a certain group of people" wanted to remove him from office because of his successful 1982 campaign to establish a county "morality" ordinance.

That ordinance, approved by voters in a referendum, attempted to eliminate topless

dancing and risque contests, such as "Hot Legs," in lounges.

"It's one person saying I did something and me saying I didn't do something, and they (the grand jurors) are taking their word for it," Pitts said after he was charged.

The identity of the accuser, or accusers, has been shrouded publicly.

In final pretrial hearings April 21, Pitts' attorney Mike Gillick had asked presiding Judge Don Sirmons to provide the defense with a "statement of particulars" outlining specific details on each count.

Such a statement would list the names of the women Pitts was accused of having sex with and would state when the acts occurred.

But Sirmons denied the motion, apparently agreeing with prosecutor Bernie McCabe that such information was available through deposition hearings in witness interviews.

McCabe, a Sixth Judicial District assistant state attorney appointed to prosecute the case, said the defense should be able to piece together the specifics based on pretrial discovery.

INTERWOVEN CASES

Several of those who were sub-

➤ See **Pitts, 9A**

The term "ripples" stood out because on the day of the indictment another prophetic word was spoken over me stating, "…the news media would begin to pick up on this thing at a time in the future, but they wouldn't pick up on it as a human interest story but there would be fear that would begin to ripple, I saw it as a ripple…"

The trial began and was purported to be the biggest held in the county up to that time. The courtroom was filled to capacity, the parking lot stayed full and people hung around in the halls and grounds outside.

The trial was projected to last weeks, but only lasted one. After the prosecution rested and it was time for the defense, my lawyer called and said, "Something woke me up early this morning and it was like a voice told me to put the sheriff on first. I know that sounds crazy, but for some reason I think that it's the right thing to do."

We both were fully aware that this is just not done. The defendant, if he takes the stand at all, always goes last so he has the benefit of hearing what all the witnesses have to say beforehand. But I had a pretty good idea of Who was behind his early morning revelation. He asked if I was willing, and I told him I was ready.

399

The judge said, "Call your first witness." When my attorney said "I call LaVelle Pitts," I looked at the State Attorney and saw utter disbelief on his face as I started for the witness chair. It was obvious he was caught by surprise and was not prepared. When I sat down, the scripture from Isaiah 54:17 came to me–"no weapon forged against you will prevail, and you will refute every tongue that accuses you."

It's normal to be nervous when you take the witness stand, but this day I was completely relaxed and the prosecutor was the one who was nervous. After the defense rested, it was time for closing arguments. I had been in and out of courtrooms for thirty years but never heard a more compelling closing than the one presented by my attorney. Afterward, his law partner said he had never heard him give a greater closing. My wife said, "I believe he must have been anointed."

Seven and a half hours later at 11:05 pm, the jury returned. The courtroom was packed, the parking lot filled, news media was there with live feeds.

The jury foreman handed the verdict to the Clerk of the Court and she read, "As to count one, we find the defendant not guilty, as to count two, we find the defendant not guilty, as to count three we find the defendant not guilty, as to count four we find the defendant not guilty."

Excitement erupted in the courtroom. Channel 7 news director, Joe Moore, was the first news person to interview me. "Sheriff, to what do you attribute your victory in this case?" I answered, "Prayer."

Pitts: Acquittal part of God's plan

Modern-day prophets gave sheriff faith

GREG MAY
Staff Writer

Speaking before a church congregation Sunday night, Bay County Sheriff LaVelle Pitts said his recent acquittal of four perjury charges was part of God's plan and had been foretold by prophets.

Pitts and his wife Sally Jo told about 250 people in the St. Andrew Assembly of God that modern-day prophets had assured them God would grant victory in the case and not allow their family to be destroyed.

"I was not bitter. I was not down," said Pitts, who likened his experience to that of the biblical figure, Job. "I had that feeling of peace — I really did."

He said that in the end, the trial has led to good things for his family and Bay County. "God was touching people and we didn't realize it," he said. "Never in 30 years (of law enforcement experience) have I seen Christian people band together as I have in this particular case. One thing's for sure — you can give God the glory."

In speeches that together lasted more than 1½ hours, the Pittses said they had been unwavering in their refusal to accept a plea bargain instead of going to trial.

They said that at various religious services occurring before the trial, people gifted and then tried.

"Even our closest friends, some had doubts," he said.

He said friends had advised him to accept a "sweetheart"

"I said, 'We're going to win, We're going to win,'" Pitts said. "I told so many people ... 'God's never lost a case yet.'"

Pitts dabbed his eyes several

Pitts and his wife spoke at the request of the church pastor, the Rev. Crawford Railey, who said the couple have regularly been meeting in the sanctuary

Sheriff LaVelle Pitts and wife Sally Jo said prophecy gave them faith for Pitts' perjury trial.

LaVelle and Sally Jo after acquittal

Our attorney, who knew about the prayers spoken over this situation, now asked for a copy. The psychologist hired to help with jury selection wrote to us after the trial and said in part, "Congratulations on your victory and your vision. Many people, myself included, tried to let you know the road ahead and were afraid for you. You had the faith to "walk through the valley of the shadow of death" and stay with your beliefs. That is a rarity these days and a wonderful model you have presented to us all."

The governor reinstated me in office, May 19, 1988. I received my back pay, making it possible to pay the balance owed my attorney.

However, a civil trial was still pending. The criminal trial was at my personal expense, but the civil case on the same issues involved the county and sheriff's association. Attorneys negotiated settlement rather than going to trial which they reasoned would have been more costly to taxpayers.

I was soundly defeated in the 1988 sheriff's race, but through it all learned some valuable lessons. Remember the California preacher saying this situation would work for good?

Shortly after being reinstated in office, my wife and I were asked to share our testimony at a local church. Unknown to us a man in the audience had planned to commit suicide that night. He later told us that after he heard what we went through, his problems didn't seem so bad after all. This man later became a preacher and strong prayer warrior.

Since leaving the sheriff's office, my wife and I have had the privilege to host dinners at our home in which guests from our community share their personal testimonies of God's work in their lives. Amazingly, one of my former deputies, who had joined the lawsuit against me, met with me and we both forgave one another. This man gave his testimony in our home—proof of God's power, not only to heal physically but emotionally. This ordeal did indeed work for good.

Through difficult trials, I learned to stand by faith in victory and humility in defeat.

A Prayer for My Family

I pray that God will richly bless and protect each of you and your families all the days of your lives and that you will be in heaven with me one day.

God only promises us one day at a time and he doesn't promise we'll complete this day. It is certain that we are going to either hell or heaven and we'll live for eternity in one place or the other. Romans 10:9 says, "If you confess with your mouth the Lord Jesus and believe in your heart that God raised Him from the dead, you will be saved."

A simple, heartfelt prayer like this one from my pastor, Craig Conner, can assure one's place in heaven.

DEAR GOD, I KNOW THAT I AM A SINNER. I ASK YOU FOR YOUR FORGIVENESS. I BELIEVE JESUS IS YOUR SON AND HE DIED FOR MY SINS. I WANT TO BE YOUR CHILD AND ALLOW JESUS TO BE LORD OF MY LIFE. I TURN FROM MY SINS AND WILL NOW FOLLOW YOU. IN THE NAME OF JESUS I PRAY. AMEN

Just think, with one short sincere prayer, you can know you'll spend eternity in heaven. I'll look for you there.

I love you, Dad.

And for anyone else who might read this prayer, I encourage you to adopt it as your own.

Sincerely, LaVelle